Yours 'Til
Hell Freezes

....

A Memoir of
Kevin Barry

Yours 'Til
Hell Freezes

———————

A Memoir of

Kevin Barry

SÍOFRA O'DONOVAN

CURRACH
BOOKS

First published in 2020 by
Currach Books

 CURRACHBOOKS

Block 3b, Bracken Business Park, Bracken Road Sandyford
Dublin 18, D18 K277
www.currachbooks.com

ISBN: 978-178218-926-8

Set in Adobe Garamond Pro 11/15
Cover design by Alba Esteban | Currach Books
Book design by Maria Soto | Currach Books
Printed by ScandBook, Fallun

For my father Donal
who thought of this book
and for my grandfather who laid the foundations

And in memory of Kevin Barry, Kitby Barry, Mary Dowling,
Ellen McCardle and all my ancestors

CONTENTS

FOREWORD

This is a well-written book, full of vivid and fascinating detail. Síofra O'Donovan is eminently qualified to be the author, both professionally and for family reasons. Possibly the most iconic of Irish republican martyrs, Kevin Barry was her grand-uncle and an older brother to her maternal grandmother, Monty Barry. Jim O'Donovan, Monty's husband and Síofra's grandfather, was himself steeped in the culture of militant republicanism and his life journey became in its own way highly dramatic and controversial. Donal O'Donovan, son of Jim and father of Síofra, wrote a previous biography entitled *Kevin Barry and his Time*, published in 1989 by Glendale Press. Síofra has also had access to private papers and documents relating to her grand-uncle.

Some readers might expect that there wouldn't be a lot to write about the young UCD medical student, 'just a lad of eighteen summers', who was hanged at Mountjoy Prison on 1 November 1920. They would be wrong. As background to Kevin's short but deeply interesting and highly dramatic sojourn on this earth, there is a family history based in Carlow and Dublin that connects with many aspects of Irish life and reflects the impact of the Great Famine, the Land League agitation and other major events. The book also contains many insights into Kevin's remarkable personality: his outgoing and sociable nature, skilled use of language and, above all, his burning commitment to the struggle for Irish independence. Personally speaking, it was interesting that he was strongly influenced by the saga of the Manchester Martyrs – Allen, Larkin and O'Brien – since I have a family connection with Michael Larkin. The book also has an extraordinary account of Kevin's final days and hours which makes for a graphic and at times gripping read.

In addition to her close family connection with the subject of this book, Síofra O'Donovan is a novelist and travel writer who also teaches writing in schools as well as in mental health and prison facilities: small wonder that this is such a highly readable piece of work. She has done her grand-uncle proud with this volume.

Deaglán de Bréadún

NOTE: Deaglán de Bréadún is a columnist with the Belfast-based *Irish News* and a regular broadcaster in English and Irish. His books include *The Far Side of Revenge: Making Peace in Northern Ireland* and *Power Play: The Rise of Modern Sinn Féin*, as well as three books in the Irish language.

PREFACE

The memory of a hero is a thing that moves, over time, into the realm of myth. We don't know the truth of who the hero was, nor why they sing ballads about them. We only know those artful delineations made by myth itself.

A lad of eighteen summers, high upon the gallows tree.

When you are the descendant of a hero, you live in their shadow. I tried to run from the overwhelming charisma of this boy-hero-great-uncle Kevin Barry, whose story was sung by Paul Robeson, Leonard Cohen and every traditional Irish band you can think of. Yet my grandmother, Kevin Barry's sister, would not allow the song to be sung in the house. It was maudlin, she said.

But Kevin wasn't maudlin. An oval portrait of him hung in my father's study – a copy of a painting by somebody in the H Company of the IRA. The face and shoulders of Kevin Barry had a slightly airbrushed look, set against a monochrome and patriotic green background. Kevin had a quiff of hair like Tintin and was wearing a trench coat with the collar upturned. He beamed eagerly around my father's study, like a friendly family ghost. Beside this portrait was another one of my grandfather, Jim O'Donovan, in a rectangular frame, painted by Leo Whelan. A true die-hard, my grandfather's convictions had him locked up long after the War of Independence. His face, in the portrait and in real life, was sterner and more chiselled. When I was brought to see him in his nursing home, he never looked at me. I looked at him, in his wheelchair, at his hand with missing fingers – blown off when he was demonstrating a hand grenade he'd just invented. I found the stubs of his missing fingers fascinating. For some reason, we called him 'Beep-beep', although I have no idea why. I heard more recently that he occasionally demanded bottles of whiskey from my alcoholic father and other visitors. He needed an anaesthetic for the past and for the tragedy of his wife Monty, who then lay prostrate on her bed down the corridor in the same nursing home, riddled into paralysis by several strokes. A woman of acerbic wit and sharp intelligence was living her final years in a terrible limbo.

My grandmother Monty was the first dead person I ever saw. I stole a glimpse of her in the open casket at her funeral in the nursing home chapel. I never forgot her still, waxy face and the smell of candles and incense hovering around her. My father quickly took me out to the cold corridor with my cousins and we were told to wait there until the funeral service was over. I heard the drone of praying, and the priest muttering gloomily from the altar. She, Kevin Barry's second-youngest sister, was gone. My grandfather was gone too by 1979. They were all slipping away, leaving my father angry and intolerant of our inability to grasp who these people were. He wanted me to carry the chattels of our family history, but I did not want to do it. He would sit in his green armchair and tell me stories of how Kevin Barry cycled over the Wicklow hills to drink in the hotels in Glendalough and Aughrim, how my grandfather locked himself in a room at night in the family home in Shankill, County Dublin, speaking German to his secret friends in Nazi Germany. How my great aunt Kitby, Kevin Barry's older sister, sailed to America with Countess Markiewicz, on De Valera's orders, to fundraise for the Republic. But my father always came back to Kevin. Kevin spinning around on his bike in his Belvedere cap, drinking, dancing, pulling Belgian girls, out on the streets in ambushes, down alleyways carrying arms. And in the end, hanging on the gallows, just like in the song. The stories seeped into me. I resisted, but there was nothing I could do, because they were part of me.

I have recently felt that the source of my father's alcoholism lay in the difficulties he had with his father. When he was recovering from a peritonitis operation in 1940, his father brought him *David Copperfield*, which he defiantly refused to read. They say that Mahatma Gandhi was a hard man to live with, and that his son Harilal spent his life rebelling against the Mahatma's stern morality. Harilal was an alcoholic gambler who imported British clothes, and even converted to Islam after his father's assassination by a far-right Hindu. The O'Donovan home was not headed by a saintly guru of abstinence and *ahimsa* (non-violence). Jim embodied principles that were entirely opposed to this, and yet they fought for the same thing. Jim, an expert in chemical weaponry, was so fuelled by his desire for a united Ireland and complete freedom from British rule that he let little, including the safety of his own family, get in the way.

My father became an alcoholic in the shadow of his father's unrelenting idealism, and perhaps that of his uncle Kevin Barry, under whose shadow he also lived. But in relation to his father, my father lived with the same neglect as Harilal did, his inner landscape marred by a father married to principles. His childhood memories were of dark-hatted men in a green Morris Ten with 'Dark Rosaleen' attached to its bonnet. His parents' strange nocturnal visitors were, he came to suspect, to do with the IRA. When my father was twelve years old the German spy, Herman Goertz, was put up in my father's room in the family home. Goertz moved on to the garage or the orchard by day, hiding behind the eucalyptus tree. My father, in this visiting spy, found another father – one who had heroically parachuted out of the sky, who hid his codes under the eaves of the stable and was fed dinners by my grandmother Monty. As far as my father was concerned, he was a hero, dropped from a Heinkel 111 bomber near Ballivor, County Meath, where an amused farmer asked, 'Do you not know Ballivor?', when the spy inquired as to where on earth he was. When Goertz was leaving my father's orchard to find another safe house, he gave my father his Third Reich knife and revolver. He kept them until they were stolen from our home during a burglary in the 1980s. My father had no understanding of Goertz's political ideology nor that his father had invited the spy to Ireland to work with the IRA, although he had some suspicions. What he knew was that he had found a surrogate father in the orchard. Herman Goertz took his own life in 1947 when he was instructed to leave Ireland. My grandfather had kept his cyanide capsule safely all those years.

Although I grew up with these gripping tales of espionage and family militarism, it was Kevin Barry who made the greatest impact on me. The rest of it was just too frightening and strange, such as the thought of my grandfather Jim drinking tea with Hitler (which he didn't, of course), or speaking to him on his radio from the family home (which he didn't do either). I took refuge in our family hero, the boy who beamed at me from the oval portrait in my father's study. I wrote essays about Kevin Barry for history class, described the ambush on the Monk's Bakery in detail, faithfully recording the account written in Sean Cronin's 1965 pamphlet on Kevin Barry. I could see his face as he was driven with the British soldiers to Bridewell prison. Irate, but amused. I wrote about the arrest on 20 September 1920 and about the short time he spent in Mountjoy prison before his execution on 1 November. He was hanged the day before my birthday and, although we lived decades apart, I felt that his death was a shadow that followed me everywhere. And so, in my father's footsteps, I write this book about Kevin Barry in honour of them both. I draw from my father's book throughout this one, because I could not have done this without him and my original intention was simply to republish his book. When he passed away one cold January night in 2009, I promised that I would bring the story of Kevin Barry back into the world.

My father Donal ODonovan, 1989

Chapter One

THE GHOSTS OF THE PAST

I have a strange array of ancestors. One hanged decades ago in a war, and one whom I only remember in a wheelchair with three stubs for the fingers on his right hand, blown off by a hand grenade of his own making. My great uncle and my grandfather. Two of many ancestors, of course, but these two dominated the end of my early childhood. All the stories in the family on my father's side seemed to revolve around them.

When my father, after a long career in journalism and a shorter, more unhappy one in the Bank of Ireland, finished a successful book about Irish-American businessmen in the 1980s called *Dreamers of Dreams*, he was looking for a new project – he was never one for a lull in action, most especially now that he was sober, after decades of drinking. From his green armchair, he asked me what he should write next, while he pulled things out from under his fingernails with his Swiss army knife tweezers. I thought, at eleven years old, that it could not be more obvious – he had to write the story of Kevin Barry.

And so it began. I went with my father to Tombeagh, the ancestral farmhouse on the River Douglas, 'just north of the Doreen, with medium sized flying fields covering about eighty-six across of pasture'.[1] He liked that kind of exactitude and he loved that place even thought he had no bull's notion of how to farm. No. 8 Fleet Street in Dublin was the Barry family's town residence where my grandmother Monty was mostly reared and where Kevin Barry had been born. But Tombeagh, in Hacketstown, County Carlow, was the ancestral home, and is known by locals as 'the house of the martyr'. (So I was told by the present inhabitant of Aghavannagh House, the old barracks that Kevin Barry tried to burn down in the summer of 1920.)

---

1   Donal O'Donovan, *Kevin Barry and His Time*, Dublin: Glendale Press, 1989. p. 17

The Barrys were known as 'strong farmers' around Carlow. They practised dairy farming until the 1980s when, under EU directives, dairy farming was dismantled and subsidised. Since then, Kevin Barry junior has not been able to have a full dairy farm as the Barrys had for decades. There are only a few cows on the farm now and Kevin Barry junior jokes that his son Michael is not born for cattle herding. 'When the cattle see him coming, they run a mile. He doesn't tolerate them either. Yet he likes the sowing, himself, and the tractor and the combine. He fell into a combine when he was a child.' [2]

The house at Tombeagh is a sturdy whitewashed farmhouse with two stories. The outhouses that were there in Kevin Barry's time are still standing. There is even an old plough, rusting in the barn to the right of the old house. The lintel of the door to the house is still very low, and the enormous fireplace in the kitchen is as it was then too. There are narrow little corridors and mysterious, poky rooms that always fascinated me as a child. Somewhere in the house is a concealed attic room where men on the run in the War of Independence were hidden – apart from De Valera, who was too 'long' to fit in the room.

At the time that Kevin Barry lived in Tombeagh there were hens in the back yard and the Barrys sold eggs. There was a well on the first turn in the lane that flowed overground down a ditch. The water from it was only used to cool the milk, not to cook, as it was a farm well. Every farm had one in those days.

Over iced cakes and hot tea, my father and I met old aunts, uncles, distant cousins and veterans of war on our Carlow expeditions. My father spent many hours with his cousin Kevin Barry, his first cousin, son of Kevin Barry's brother Michael Barry. The Barrys still live in the ancestral Barry house at Tombeagh. While he was researching his book most intensively around Carlow, my father stayed in a small caravan in a field above Tombeagh, in the townland of Drumguin, where his grandmother, Mary Dowling, was from. At other times, my father brought me with him while he picked his cousin Kevin's brains about the political spectres of the past while, in the back rooms, I was told stories of the headless horseman on the drive and of the ghost of Kevin Barry's sister Kitby,

---

2   Interview with Kevin Barry junior at Tombeagh, June 2018.

who, Kevin told me, stood on occasion at the top of the stairs. She had declared from her deathbed in Rathgar: 'I will never leave Tombeagh'.[3] Kevin Barry would come home from the pub late at night and scuttle past the cold patch at the top of the stairs to the bedroom. The formidable and domineering Kitby Barry never left the family – just as Kevin never did. She was the force behind her brother's short military career, a woman who refused to stand and sing 'God Save the King' in the Grafton Picture House during the Great War.[4]

Ancestors

The Barrys have been at Tombeagh since the 1700s. Edward O'Toole, Kevin Barry's schoolteacher in Rathvilly National School, wrote about the Barrys in his memoirs, identifying them as an Anglo-Norman family.[5] The first to come to Ireland was Gerald Barry (1146–1223), who is considered to be the common ancestor of the Barrys in Ireland. [6]

Geraldus de Barri (Geraldus Cambrensis), the first recorded Barry to arrive on Irish soil, came to Ireland as a tutor to the sulky young King John in 1185. He thought of Ireland as a land of idle louts and said, 'The men were as bad as their masters, devoted to Venus and Bacchus.'[7] In his *Topographica Hiberniae*, he observed of the Irish their strange flowing beards and odd clothes and that they were far too in love with leisure, yet he appreciated their 'commendable diligence [only] on musical instruments, on which they are incomparably more skilled than any nation I have seen'.

Geraldus, then, was the progenitor of one of the most infamous Irish martyrs of the independence movement. Tutor to the Anglo-Norman Plantagenet king who began the colonisation of Ireland, he was certainly

---

3   Interview with Kevin Barry junior, June 2018.

4   Kathleen Barry Maloney (KBM), Witness Statement (WS) 731, p. 15, Bureau of Military History (BMH).

5   Edward O'Toole, *Whist for your life, that's treason – Recollections of a Long Life,* Dublin: Ashfield Press, 2003, p. 140.

6   MacCaffrey, James. 'Giraldus Cambrensis', in *The Catholic Encyclopedia*, Vol .6 , New York: Robert Appleton Company, 1909.

7   The Project Gutenberg e-book of Ireland under the Tudors, Volume I (of II), *Ireland under the Tudors*, by Richard Bagwell

Mary Dowling and Tom Barry, Kevin Barry's Parents.

an unlikely ancestor. Taking a leap forward we find, through oral family history, that the Barrys were booted by Cromwell out of Cork, where they had first settled in Ireland. They had already settled in Tombeagh by the 1700s and, in 1750, a 'Black Tom' Barry is recorded as living there. Edward O'Toole cites other Barrys in the area surrounding Tombeagh, from the 1700s – the Barrys of the Cross, the Barrys of the Brook and the Tailor Barrys, who still live in the area today.[8]

Triona Maher was one of the people my father visited frequently when he was researching his book about Kevin Barry. She was my father's first cousin, the daughter of Shel Barry and Bapty Maher, a bastion of family history and the guardian of many private documents and letters. Her family tree that went back to the 1700s to 'Black Tom', who married a widow in 1750. Kevin Barry junior speaks today about the Barrys who 'came up here from Youghal in Cork, a Norman family that took 15 acres, trying to get away from Cromwell. Three or four families of Barrys came up from Cork, and landlords granted them lease of the land here. They took possession of it under the Land Acts in the 1880s. The farm grew over the years as they acquired the Upper Lands, up the road from Tombeagh.'[9]

....

8   O'Toole, p. 141.
9   Interview with Kevin Barry junior, 2018

Black Tom's eldest son Tom had four children with a widow called Finn from Ladystown, and one of those children was called Kevin, which is where the name first enters the family. That Kevin went to America on a boat and died on the way home and is still seen by the Barrys of Tombeagh as a ghost 'in the dusk of a summer evening'.[10] The son of this ghost Kevin had a brother called Michael who became the father of Judith and Tom Barry. They inherited the house and land at Tombeagh that lies on the River Douglas over sloping pasture fields, and the enterprising siblings would push their frontiers into the dairy industry in Dublin.

Rebels in the Barry Family Tree

For the grandchildren of 'Black Tom' the 1700s was a time of putting down roots and becoming strong farmers. The end of that century brought the most significant organised rebellion against British rule. This is when the first rebel appears in the family tree – John Hutchinson, a Quaker yeoman from Dualla, County Tipperary, who was disowned by the Society of Friends on 16 March 1787, when he married a Catholic girl, Kate Meagher. His godfather, Sir John Lontaigne, bought him a farm in Ballyhacket, near Rathvilly in County Carlow, thus saving him from destitution.[11] The casting out of Hutchinson had been a severe one, and he was lucky he had his godfather to bail him out.

Disownment of John Hutchinson

Whereas John Hutchinson of Roscrea Son of Benjamin Hutchinson was Educated amongst us the people Called quakers & Some times attended our religious Meetings but for want of being Obedient to the divine Reproof of Instruction in his own mind, hath Committed the Sin of Fornication which he did not Deny when Charged therewith, therefore we are Concerned to testify Against him the said John Hutchinson & Deny him to be of our Society nevertheless we desire that by a Sincere Repentance

---

10   O'Donovan, p. 10.
11   Information from Dorothy Dowling to author, 2020.

and Amendment of life he may yet Experience the Fear of the Lord to be before his Eyes whom to know is life Eternal. Signed in by order & on behalf of our Monthly Meeting for MtMelick [sic] held there the 16th day of the 3rd Month 1787 by John Clendennan Clerk [12]

Carlow and Wicklow were focal points and battlegrounds of the 1798 Rebellion, and one of its rebels, Michael Dwyer, became a legend. He may have been related to the Barrys,[13] but my father only mentions that Dwyer was the uncle of Ann Devlin, servant of Robert Emmett, and didn't claim that there was any blood connection between the Dwyers and the Barrys.[14]

Dwyer had joined the Society of the United Irishmen and fought under General Joseph Holt at Vinegar Hill in Wexford, in Arklow and in Hacketstown. When the Rebellion failed, Dwyer, with a group of United Irishmen, 'took to the hills for five years and was pursued so relentlessly that the Military Road was built in 1801 to make access easier for the redcoats'.[15] Dwyer, who led a guerrilla campaign against the British military and yeomen in the Wicklow mountains from 1798 to 1803, hid in the Wicklow mountains from the redcoats, who mounted an expensive campaign to catch him. On the Military Road from Glencree to the Glen of Imaal (Dwyer's birthplace), five military barracks were constructed, each to hold a field officer and a hundred men. A bounty of £1,000 was offered for Dwyer's head.[16] One of the barracks built was that at Aghavannagh, which, in the summer of 1920, by order of the Active Service Unit of the IRA, Kevin Barry and the C Company in Carlow attempted to burn down, 120 years or so after it was built. That they did not do so may have been thanks to the resident housekeeper, who was a hard bargainer.

....

12 By kind permission of Michael Moriarty and Dorothy Dowling, Dowling Family Estate.
13 According to a family tree that belongs to the Kevin Barry estate the Barrys are related to Michael Dwyer through the McArdle line.
14 O'Donovan, p. 66.
15 Ibid.
16 Ibid., p. 67.

Kevin was nurtured on tales of the Battle of Hacketstown, the pursuit of Michael Dwyer in the Wicklow Mountains (1798), the hounding to death of Parnell, and the vivid recollections of Kate Kinsella.[17] To a young boy, stories of the wild Irish rebels in the mountains who resisted the redcoats for five years must have been thrilling. Vince Hearne, the musician, describes this song as being 'really exciting for a small boy':

> At length brave Michael Dwyer, you and your trusty men,
> Are hunted o'er the mountain and tracked into the glen,
> Sleep not, but watch and listen with ready blade and ball,
> For the soldiers know your hiding place tonight in wild Imaal.
> The stealthy soldiers followed, and at the break of day,
> Discovered in a cabin, where the outlaw rebels lay,
> They gathered round the cabin and they formed into a ring
> And they cried out Michael Dwyer, surrender to the king.

When the story was related by a great storyteller like my father, a child experienced all the drama of the battle: bravery, challenge, courage, comradeship, defiance, noise, shouting, shooting and, finally, victory and escape. Kevin could not have known that he would go on to be a legend of the same calibre. Today the Glen of Imaal is a military firing range in an isolated part of County Wicklow. The cottage referred to in the incident in 1798 is still there.[18]

In the family home at Tombeagh there is even a piece of the vestments of Father Murphy, the priest who led the Rebellion at Vinegar Hill. Nobody knows how it got there.

There were many songs sung at Tombeagh. Apart from rebel songs, Kevin Barry loved to sing 'Come Back Paddy Reilly to Ballyjamesduff', a romantic song by Percy French, the deeper meaning of which was a lament about the loss of Irish people to emigration. Pat Gorman, Kevin's close friend in Hacketstown, told my father that he remembered Kevin singing this song on many occasions.[19]

....

17 Ibid., p. 33.
18 Vince Hearne, Interview http://www.from-ireland.net/song/michael-dwyer-1/
19 Interview with Pat Gorman by Donal O'Donovan, 1988. Cassette. All rights reserved. Private papers of Donal O'Donovan.

But that sort of love is a moonshiny stuff,
And never will addle me brain,
For the bells will be ringin' in Ballyjamesduff
For me and me Rosie Kilrain!
And through all their glamour, their gas and their guff
A whisper comes over the sea,
Come back, Paddy Reilly to Ballyjamesduff
Come home, Paddy Reilly, to me.

Another song that Kevin loved to sing was 'Tullynahaw'. As Pat Gorman put it to my father, Kevin had 'a crowd of songs and to baste in Tullynahaw'.[20]

Giving a taste of ordher [sic] and law
To man and to baste [beast] in Tullynahaw.[21]

This was ostensibly a cattle-driving song written by Percy French in 1910, set to the air of an older Irish song. It's also about a tricky encounter between an old couple with their cattle and two RIC policeman, Flynn and Kilray.

Well, when they brought back the cow says the Widda 'Ochone!
How I wish them police would leave people alone.
For if I could have proved the oul' reptile was drowned
I'd ha'got compinsation – aye – nine or ten pound'.[22]

Kevin seems to have loved Percy French songs and it's not hard to imagine him singing loudly at a gathering in Tombeagh, surrounded by friends and family. 'He [Kevin] was the heart of the party. His brother Mick used to sing "Róisín Dubh".'[23]

....

20   Interview with Peg Scully and Pat Gorman by Donal O'Donovan 1988. Private papers of Donal O'Donovan.
21   'Tullynahaw', by Percy French.
22   Ibid.
23   Information from Pat Gorman to Jim O'Donovan, my grandfather, in 1953. Material for his book about Kevin Barry, unpublished. Private papers of Donal O'Donovan.

Kevin's older brother Michael was more reserved, and a song like 'Róisín Dubh', ostensibly a romantic lament, was more in tune with his demeanour. Also known as 'Dark Rosaleen', the song dated from the sixteenth century – it was a political song camouflaged as a lament. Nationalism, throughout the nineteenth century in Ireland, cast the lamenting woman, Dark Rosaleen or Caitlín Ní hUalacháin, as the symbol for their lost country.

The Great Famine

The first Kevin Barry to appear on the Barry family tree was the son of Black Tom's eldest son Tom Barry in the 1700s, the Kevin Barry who went to America on a boat, and died on the way home. Since he was the grandson of Black Tom, he may have sailed around 1820, which is too early for it to have been a 'famine ship'. The Great Famine (1845–51) saw Ireland lose about a million people to starvation and two and a half million to emigration. The potato blight is blamed for the Great Famine, 'An tOcras Mór', but the reasons were far more complex. The majority of impoverished cotter farmers relied for sustenance on the potato, a vegetable that grew abundantly in the damp Irish soil. The failure of several potato crops due to the blight, and over-dependence on that vegetable, along with the British government's economic policy of laissez-faire capitalism, were some contributing factors that led to the Great Hunger, as it is called in Irish oral history.[24] Most tenant farmers could not afford to buy market food, which was abundantly available for cash. Rents were crippling the tenants and subsequent evictions swelled the grim famine death toll. 'There never was,' said the Duke of Wellington, a native of County Meath, 'a country in which poverty existed to the extent it exists in Ireland.' [25]

William Forster, who would later become Chief Secretary for Ireland under Gladstone in 1880, came to Ireland in 1846–47 on behalf of the Friends' Relief fund for the famine in Connemara, when the British

24 Cecil Woodham-Smith, *The Great Hunger: Ireland 1845–1849*, London: Penguin, 1962, p. 69.
25 Ibid., p. 20.

had cut the Imperial funds for the famine. They threw the onus for famine relief on the landlords, many of whom were 'absentee' landlords and who avoided 'poor relief' by using the 'Gregory clause', a heartless loophole that deemed any tenant with a plot of over a quarter acre was not 'destitute' and therefore not eligible for 'relief'. It is calculated that only one third of landlords actually contributed at all towards famine relief. [26] Forster described the people he saw in Ireland as 'walking skeletons – the men gaunt and haggard, stamped with the livid mark of hunger; the children crying with pain; the women in some of the cabins too weak to stand.'[27]

Despite this charity, for the severe measures brought in by his Coercion Act in 1881, Forster came to be known in Ireland as 'Buckshot' by the nationalist press during the Land agitations.

The Barrys surely did not come through the famine unscathed, although we have no records or stories of anything to do with them during that time, other than that first Kevin Barry who sailed to America and died on the way back. But he did not live through the famine, as he may have travelled around the year 1820. In any case the famine had a profound effect on Ireland's demographics and its economic and social life. The 'overthrow of the potato' changed the shape and the scale of farming in Ireland, with tillage giving way to dairy farming. Farms were expanding, due to emigration and death. Farmers acquired the land of neighbours who had emigrated or died.[28] Post-famine, the father of an Irish farming family took full control of how his children married. His greatest fear was the subdivision of his land, and there would be no neat little parcels of land gifted as dowries. He clung to his farm until death, so that the eldest son could not marry until he had inherited his father's farm, delaying marriage. This is why Kevin Barry's grandparents, James Dowling (1821–1907) and Ellen McCardle (1838–1920), had an age

26 *Atlas of the Great Irish Famine,* John Crowley, William Smith, Mike Murphy (eds), Cork: Cork University Press, 2012, pp.10–11.

27 Chisholm, Hugh (1911), 'Forster, William Edward', In Chisholm, Hugh (ed.), *Encyclopædia Britannica.* 20 (11th ed.), Cambridge: Cambridge University Press. pp. 675–77.

28 K. H. Connell, *Irish Peasant Society,* Dublin: The Irish Academic Press, 1996, p. 85.

gap of seventeen years, and Kevin's parents Tom Barry (1851–1908) and Mary Dowling (1872–1953) had a gap of twenty-two.[29]

Nationalism versus a political solution, 'Home Rule' in late Nineteenth-Century Ireland

Poetry and song gave wind to the sails of the nationalist movement, but the means to making Ireland a sovereign nation depended on two different approaches. The IRB was founded in 1858 in Paris by James Stephens, wounded in the 1848 rebellion. 'Fenians were arrested, imprisoned and dispersed but the I.R.B continue, if not to grow, at least to live.'[30] The IRB, known as the Fenians from the 1860s, continued as a secret oath-bound fraternal society with the aim of establishing an independent democratic republic in Ireland and to accomplish this 'through armed revolt'.

The Fenian Rising in 1867, planned by the IRB, saw its leaders, John Devoy and James Stephens, arrested even before it occurred. Afterwards, when a group of Fenians ambushed an unguarded prison van carrying two of the thousands of imprisoned Fenians in Hyde Road, Manchester, an unarmed policeman, Sergeant Brett, was shot dead. Three Fenians – William Philip Allen, Michael O'Brien and Michael Larkin, were hanged for it in Salford before 10,000 spectators on 23 November 1867.[31]

Salford is the borough of Manchester where the playwright Ewan McColl wrote 'Dirty Old Town' about grim love in the northern industrial area, immortalised in the version sung by Shane McGowan of the Pogues. A different song rose out of Salford's industrial fog, after the hanging of the three Fenians. 'God Save Ireland' became the anthem for the nationalist movement– a song that would stoke the fires of Ireland's independence movement. Like the ballad of Kevin Barry, 'God Save Ireland' became a tool for propaganda, the three men exacting a particular kind of revenge from their respective graves as they, like Kevin, were elevated to the status of martyr.

....

29   Information from Dorothy Dowling 2020.
30   Terence de Vere White, Kevin O'Higgins, London: Methuen, 1948, p. 25.
31   O'Donovan, p. 33.

God save Ireland, said the heroes
God save Ireland, said them all
Whether on the scaffold high,
Or the battlefield we die,
Oh what matter when for Erin dear we fall?
High up on the gallows tree swung the noble-hearted three
By the vengeful tyrants stricken in their bloom.

They came to be known as the Manchester Martyrs and their commemoration at the Mansion House in Dublin in 1915 became the very event that cemented the thirteen-year-old Kevin Barry's Republican convictions. 'He [Kevin] wanted to join the Fianna Éireann right there and then.'[32]

The other road to freedom was Home Rule, a slower, constitutional approach that would not ruffle British feathers so easily. To the constitutional nationalists, who were the majority, 'the I.R.B was repugnant. It was in order to keep out revolutionary influence that John Redmond [leader of the Irish National Party], had attempted to fill the command of the Volunteers with his followers.'[33]

War on the Land

The Barrys began the process of purchasing their farmholding from Henry Tudor Parnell in 1874, well before the second Land Act in 1881. Tombeagh's eighty-six acres of pasture was once part of the Clonmore estate, originally owned by the Duke of Ormonde, who sold it to the Earls of Wicklow, who then sold it to John Henry Parnell, who 'needed the 12,000 acres to give as his patrimony to his youngest son Henry Tudor Parnell'.[34] 'Prior to that, the notice to quit was in the agreement of any tenure. A Protestant who wanted Tombeagh could take it at any given moment and they could move on the point of eviction.'[35]

---

32 Information from Pat Dowling to Jim O'Donovan, 1953.
33 De Vere White, p. 15.
34 O'Donovan, p. 17.
35 Information from Triona Maher to Donal O'Donovan, 1988. Donal O'Donovan private papers.

Henry Tudor Parnell, brother of Charles Stewart Parnell, was the Barry's landlord for fifteen years, and in the Barry family home there is a receipt from him for half a year's rent, £19 8s 8d, paid in cash by Michael Barry.[36] On 22 December 1875 Michael Barry made his final payment for the land and died the following year, leaving an outhouse and an allowance of £20 per year to his sister Ellen Barry,[37] and the house and farmland to his son Thomas Barry. In October 1879, Henry Tudor Parnell's brother Charles Stewart Parnell was elected president of the Irish National Land League, spearheading an aggressive campaign for land reform, conjoining the zeal of Fenianism with his position as MP, and encouraging the boycotting of landlords. At a Land League meeting at Westport in 1879 Charles Stewart Parnell called on the farmers and peasants to 'show the landlords that you intend to hold a firm grip of your homesteads and land'.[38]

Using his brilliant skills of oratory, Parnell obstructed parliament by giving speeches that lasted for hours.[39] Over 100,000 families were in rent arrears, and by 1880 evictions had almost doubled, from 1, 238 to 2, 110. Lord Lucan, hero of the Crimean Wars, was a landlord in the west of Ireland who was notoriously cruel to his tenants, and Lord Leitrim (3rd Earl of Leitrim) was so detested by his tenants (both Catholic and Protestant) in Donegal that he met his end near his home in an ambush in Milford in 1878. There is palpable rage in the song that would implant him in the folk memory of Ireland:

> 'Go on my boys' says Rory. 'Make ready present and fire'
> At his old brain they took fair aim and they hurled him in the mire
> To revenge the joke, his head they broke, and his carcass there
>   did maul
> Stuck him in a pool, his head to cool, below in Donegal

36   Private papers in the Kevin Barry estate.
37   O'Donovan, p. 17.
38   R. Barry O'Brien, *Life of Charles Stewart Parnell*, London: Smith, Elder & Co., 1898, pp. 11, 28.
39   Paul Bew, 'Parnell, Charles Stewart (1846–1891)', in *Oxford Dictionary of National Biography* (online ed.), Oxford: Oxford University Press.

The policemen like beagles gathered round this dirty beast
And the devils all, both great and small, they had a sumptuous feast
He was dissected like a bullock down at Manorvaughan Hall
And the devils ate him, rump and stump, that night in Donegal.

Not all landlords were despots. There is a story in the Barry family about Kevin Barry's great great [maternal] grandfather, Laurence Dowling. His landlord was most probably Colonel Henry Bruen, MP for Carlow from 1812 to 1837.[40] One day in 1820, when Bruen was hunting in the fields that he leased to Dowling, his horse collapsed. Laurence Dowling offered to care for the horse until it healed. A year later, the horse had healed under his care. In return, Bruen offered to train Dowling as a veterinarian. This brought him up in the world, to the degree that, by 1821, he would be in a position to marry the now eligible Margaret Hutchinson – daughter of the illustrious and rebellious John Hutchinson who lived at Ballyhacket House.[41]

Henry Tudor Parnell was a decent landlord. As the brother of the more famous Charles Stewart, it is not surprising. The Barry family became the established owners of their land during those years of turbulent agitation, and when Tom Barry inherited the eighty-six acres around Tombeagh, that farm became his own. By 1879, he was already in a position to send his sister Judith to Dublin to reconnoitre the city with a view to expanding his dairy business in a rapidly growing city. [42]

William Forster, who had so charitably come to give aid to the starving Irish in 1847 when the British government had thrown the towel in, became Chief Secretary of Ireland in 1880, under Gladstone. On 24 January 1881, he proposed the Coercion Bill to keep the Irish tenants in order – under this new legislation trial by jury was suspended. Over 950 people were imprisoned by the Liberal party that they had been sure were allies. As far as Edward O'Toole, Kevin Barry's future

---

40   Bruen of Oakpark Papers, see also No. 23 MSS 48,331–48,341 NLI, Collections 170 and 23.
41   Information from Dorothy Dowling, 2020.
42   O'Donovan, p. 18.

schoolteacher, was concerned, this was 'the first act of war on the part of the English cabinet against the Irish land movement ... leaving Ireland a volcano of human passions on one side, a bastille of Government vengeance on the other.'[43]

The Second Land Act in 1881 was a desperate attempt to manage the growing Fenian violence in Ireland and England and it was enacted to ensure that Ireland did not join the ranks of the nationalist movements that were raging across Europe. The act brought into being the Three Fs: fixity of tenure, fair rents and free sale. Yet, by 20 October 1881, Parnell had been imprisoned in Kilmainham Gaol for 'inciting tenants not to pay rent'.[44] His response from prison was to issue a 'no rent manifesto', and the riposte from the British government was to deem the Land League illegal.

Edward O'Toole refers to how 'Buckshot Forster' (as he was called by the Nationalist press), was authorised by Gladstone to 'deliver Ireland over to a bitters of despotism for which Europe had scarcely a parallel, leaving Ireland a volcano of human passions on one side, a bastille of Government vengeance on the other'.[45] O'Toole had been a nationalist since the 1860s, and may have had an influence on the young Kevin Barry, who had lost his father by the time O'Toole became his teacher in 1908.

Stories at Tombeagh

In the turmoil of land reclamation and rebellion, there was always a song to release the angst of struggle and to keep the spirit of the pursuit of freedom in sharp focus. It's not, however, as if everyone was at home singing rebel songs in rural (nor urban) Ireland in the lull between rebellions. Kevin loved to sing Percy French songs, but, apart from singing, there was storytelling, still a rich tradition in Ireland, and often narrated by seanchaí. This tradition was still very much alive in Ireland at the time. My father gave me a tattered volume of folk tales written down by Seumus MacManus, one of the last great seanchaí. This book, well thumbed and

43   O'Toole, p. 42.
44   Joseph Lee, *The Modernisation of Irish Society 1848–1918*, Dublin: Gill & Macmillan, 2008, p. 87.
45   O'Toole, p. 45.

unravelling along its spine, is inscribed in the frontispiece in pencil, in Kitby Barry's handwriting:

Kathy and Sheela Barry, Tombeagh, Hacketstown, Co. Carlow[46]

The book, whose title and publication date have disappeared due to the condition of the book, contains old Irish folk tales like Billy Beg and the Bull, Murroghoo-More and the Murroghoo-Beg, Shan Ban and Ned Flynn, The Black Bull and the Old Hag of the Forest – full of old Irish pastoral storytelling motifs of shapeshifting animals, giants, crafty old magic-wielding witches, ungrateful daughters who got thrashings from their mothers with 'a good stout sally rod' – saved, of course, by a king's son. The book may be a copy of *In Chimney Corners: Merry Tales of Irish Folk-lore*, published in 1904 by McClure, Phillips & Co. in New York, but the book is so worn it is impossible to tell.

Kitby, Shel and their mother, sitting with Nana Dowling, would read these stories in the evenings to each other and to the younger children, so it is entirely possible that Kevin would have heard them by the fire at night in Tombeagh. McManus tells us:

> These tales were made not for reading, but for telling. They were made and told for the passing of long nights, for the shortening of weary journeys, for entertaining of traveller-guests, for brightening of cabin hearths. Be not content with reading them …[47]

In those days, Tombeagh was dimly lit with gas lamps. Kevin Barry's maternal grandmother, Nana Dowling, had been living in Tombeagh since 1908, when Tom Barry died. Her own husband, James Dowling, had died the year before and Kitby and Shel thought it was better for Nana Dowling to be installed at Tombeagh, rather than stay at her own empty home in Drumguin, the neighboring townland. Nana Dowling would always have been there when Kevin came down from Dublin in the summers, after he started secondary school in 1913.

---

46 Private papers of Donal O'Donovan.
47 This is from the introduction to the book that my father gave me. MacManus, Old Folk Tales, p. x.

Nana Dowling, in her later years, would rarely have come down from her upstairs room. There are many stories surrounding her, but there are a lot of stories at Tombeagh that intrigued me as a child. There was the one about 'a headless horseman [that] used to come down the lane',[48] and the one about the ghost of that first Kevin Barry who died at sea, coming home from New York seen, as my father told me, at Tombeagh, 'in the dusk of a summer evening'. Kevin Barry junior was told about a curious funeral, as a child: 'My mother's father went up the road for a walk and saw a funeral at the bend in the road … he saw the horses and traps … there was no funeral that day … it was a ghost funeral.'

My father and my aunt Sheila told me the story of Nana Dowling meeting an old woman at the bridge when she was out with her pony and trap, going to the village. The woman came out from behind the bridge, and asked Nana to get her a pound of bacon on credit from the butcher. She told her her name. Nana Dowling told this to the butcher, who asked her for a description of this woman, and, on hearing it, he declared that she had been dead for ten years.[49]

Triona Maher, who lent so much of her time to my father when he was researching his book, recalled being in Tombeagh when she was sixteen or seventeen years old. Nana Dowling would wander around the house every night, with 'candle grease all over her face', asking the whereabouts of her son Jimmy. Jimmy, Nana Dowling's youngest son, was given £10 when his father died in 1907 and another £140 spread over four years. His older brother, Mike Dowling, was to 'allow him to keep and feed from the produce of said farm two head of cattle, under three years old', and in return Jimmy was to work at Drumguin.[50] Nana was very protective of Jimmy and tended to fret about him.

It did seem, however, that Nana Dowling may have had a touch of dementia in her later years. Triona Maher told my father, 'The priest used to come out and Granny would tell him all kinds of things that my mother Shel did to her and the priest would go along with it, saying "ah

48   Interview with Kevin Barry junior, May 2018.
49   Corroborated by Susan Stafford, daughter of Sheila Hannah and a great-niece of Kevin Barry.
50   Assignment of Kevin Barry's private papers.

she's a terrible girl".'[51] She told my father about an incident when, one evening, they thought that the renowned thief Kenny the Robber was prowling around the house at Tombeagh. Nana had come to the door holding a poker after it burst open, but it was just the grey mare rubbing against the door.

Nana Dowling died in the same year as Kevin Barry, but about six months before him, on 4 March 1920. She is buried in Tinneclash in the Dowling family plot, beside the Barry family plot. Triona Maher told my father in 1988 how her mother, Shel Barry, was in Tombeagh just after Nana Dowling died and how she could hear the swish of Nana's petticoat on the linoleum floor in the bedroom where she'd slept. She heard it for two nights after she died. 'Shel and everyone in the house thought Nana was coming back. But then she went to check and found the old grey mare was scratching herself on the wall outside.'[52]

The stories from Tombeagh have never ceased to fascinate me. It is a house so rich in history that it is fortunate it is still inhabited. This is where Kevin Barry spent so many years of his young life. The last time he left this house, in early September 1920, is somehow evoked in the words of Seumus McManus the seanchaí in the introduction to his tattered old book of folk tales. He ominously foreshadows Kevin Barry's fate:

> In the old folk tales our boys went off, their mothers cried and when we are on our knees at night, saying the Rosary, we always pray for the girls and boys who are in the strange land. Some of them do not find their fortune. They never come. Their mothers in Ireland still cry. The door is open and the hearth bright. If this book happen into the hands of any of these their tears will moisten its merriest page ... for ... they shall remember ...[53]

---

51   Interview with Triona Maher, Donal O'Donovan, 1988. Private papers of Donal O'Donovan.

52   Ibid.

53   MacManus, Old Folk Tales, p. xii.

Chapter Two

THE BLACK SHILLELAGH

A black walking stick lived in the umbrella stand of my childhood home. Among the colourful tent-like umbrellas, this walking stick did not make a great impression. It was made from gnarled wood stained with a dark varnish, and it looked out of place in the 1970s umbrella stand that had a giant rose painted on it. I would play games with it, swishing it into the darkness of the hallway as if I were wielding a sword, or pretending it was a witch's broom. I had no idea that this was a shillelagh made from blackthorn. These were a kind of cudgel used in Bataireacht, traditional Irish stick fighting, which went on to become far more violent and politicised than hurling.

Decades later, long even after my father passed away, I discovered that Kevin Barry had made this shillelagh himself. It didn't belong to some stooped old man somewhere, as I had always imagined. It disappeared from the family chattels when we moved house, but I doubt I even noticed it was gone. It showed up in the National Museum catalogue when I was researching the Kevin Barry collection – there it was, the walking stick that had vanished from our hallway. Donated by Donal O'Donovan in 1983, titled 'Kevin Barry's walking stick' in the catalogue.

Kevin Barry's Birthplace

Mary Dowling (1872–1953) of Drumguin, the neighbouring lowland to Tombeagh, had about a hundred acres in its estate. Mary Dowling, the daughter of James Dowling and Ellen McCardle, married Tom Barry (1851–1908) in 1895. She was just twenty-four years old and Tom Barry was forty-four. The couple moved to Dublin where Tom had already purchased a town house at 8 Fleet Street, Dublin, and a dairy yard in

Pimlico. They had seven children. Triona Maher maintains that Mary Barry 'had a terrible life, Nana [Mrs Barry], she was bewildered by everything that happened to her'.[54]

When I was about ten years old, my father brought me to the *Irish Times* offices, where he had been features editor, to meet the editor, Douglas Gageby, who leaned so heavily on my father's Cross pen when I asked him for his autograph, that he squished the nib. Afterwards, my father marched me down D'Olier Street, across Westmoreland Street to Fleet Street. He wanted to show me the blue-and-white circular plaque to Kevin Barry, fixed on the wall of the ESB building, which has now vanished into the throng of Temple Bar pubs and clubs. He stood there with me beside him, his neck craned upwards, with an air of expectation that I should show reverence. Afterwards we had chips and tea and sticky buns in Bewley's Cafe. I could not imagine that there had been a house there at 8 Fleet Street, full of a family of Barrys in the early twentieth century. All I knew was that Kevin Barry was not that much older than I was, that he was hanged, and that a lot of people sang about him in pubs.

Kevin was born at 8 Fleet Street on 20 January 1902. Mrs Barry had had a few miscarriages by then, so the cook and pillar of the household, Kate Kinsella, helped to rush the baby to St Andrew's Church on Westland Row to have him christened. Kevin was Mary and Tom Barry's fourth child. There is a photograph of him at two years of age, dressed in boots, stockings and a petticoat covered by a white pinafore, with a straw hat on his blonde, fringed hair, 'his two feet planted firmly on the ground at the ten to two position, his eyes belying his age, [with] a steady gaze'.[55]

Kevin Barry's prayer book is still in the house at Tombeagh, with his Fleet Street

Kevin Barry at 2 years

54 Triona Maher to Donal O'Donovan, 1988.
55 O'Donovan, p. 16.

Kevin Barry's prayer book in Tombeagh, County Carlow, with his Fleet Street address inscribed. By kind permission of the Kevin Barry estate. Photo by Síofra O'Donovan

address inscribed in flowery handwriting, dated 30 January 1910. When he made his first communion, his father had been dead for two years. Although Tom Barry's dying wish was that Fleet Street would be sold and the family would move back to Carlow, that never happened. Kevin Barry's aunt, Judith Barry, Tom Barry's sister, had forged ahead since 1879 to establish the Barrys' dairy business in Dublin. She was the one who had chosen the Fleet Street town house in the first place because it had a dairy yard at the back. Tom Barry bought the house and yard from Mrs Case (who ran a dairy at No. 56) and a prospering urban dairy business began to grow, enhancing the eighty-six-acre family holding at Tombeagh. 'Aunt Judith had set up 56 Fleet Street, where she and Tom started the Dairy business in Dublin. The [Dublin] corporation had wanted to build a power station there so in 1892 they moved to no. 8 Fleet Street, later bought from the Barrys by a Mrs Healy.'[56]

Triona Maher described to my father how 'Tom [Barry] bought cows fresh calved and milked them till they went dry. Milch cows were usually bought in the Dublin Market, but Thomas Barry was not above driving a herd of cows in front of him. He sometimes bought at Baltinglass

....
56   Triona Maher to Donal O'Donovan, 1988.

Fair and drove the cows up the road through Blessington and Tallaght to wherever summer grazing might be, a two- or three-day walk of forty miles.' Her mother, Shel Barry, Kevin Barry's sister, also drove the cattle by road to Dublin. 'Forty-two miles or so. They'd buy the cattle in the fair at Baltinglass. They kept a number of cows at Tombeagh for feeding. They couldn't take cows on the train, the milk wouldn't have stood the journey.'[57]

Dublin was a vibrant metropolis at this time, and its growing middle classes in the suburbs of Sandymount, Ballsbridge, Rathmines and Rathgar were changing the demographic of the city which, although it still lay between the Royal and Grand Canals, was relatively small compared to what it is today. It was the second city of the British Empire, yet it was also the hub of the emerging nationalist movement, no matter how the bourgeoisie 'fumble [d] in a greasy till', they could not deny the flavour of change as the Great War rumbled through the trenches of Europe. There was a majority of Catholics and Protestants in Dublin, but there were also strong communities of Jews and Quakers. The Jews mostly populated the area around the South Circular Road, where Kevin Barry's uncle Pat Dowling lived, and where he would frequently stay as his political activism grew, to protect the family in Fleet Street.

Dublin at that time still had enough rural land for the Barrys to graze their cattle around Inchicore, Bushy Park and Terenure.[58] 'Tom Barry would have taken a land lease for 11 months in the conacre practice. Cows, of course would not have milk unless they had calves. The calves were sent to Tombeagh until they were old enough to be sold. In the [Pimlico] Dairy yard, there were men to milk the cows. He [Tom Barry] might have kept 30 cows at a time.'[59]

One of the greatest treats for the Barry children was a Sunday drive in the pony and trap out into the country to see how the cows were doing. They drove to the Long Mile Road, passing the Halfway House public house. The Barrys had expanded into 58 and 59 Pimlico, where Tom

57   Ibid.
58   O'Donovan, p. 20.
59   Triona Maher to Donal O'Donovan, 1988.

Barry secured leases in the Liberties – 'a long, narrow street that stretched from the Coombe to Ardee Street, up to … Marrowbone Lane.'[60] Four doors down from Tom Barry's premises was the home of labour leader James Connolly and his family. Connolly had founded *The Workers' Republic* from that location.[61]

The Births of Kevin Barry's Siblings

Kathleen Agnes Barry was the first child born at No. 8 in 1896, the year after Tom Barry married Mary Dowling. She came to be known as Kitby, and she was Aunt Judith's favourite, because or perhaps in spite of the fact that she was a force to be reckoned with. My father remembered Mary Barry as 'a gentle person, slightly bewildered by all that was going on around her'.[62] He later described her as 'a woman of great dignity. She, whom we called Nana, was a widow for 45 years and she did not want to depend on anybody for her living. So she lived in Tombeagh and Dublin until the family home in Fleet Street was sold for offices and she moved to a cold-water flat in Molesworth Street. There is a woman in Brisbane who was working in Woolworths off Grafton Street in the late 1940s and early 1950s. She remembers Nana waving hello to the front staff of the Woolworth's every day for years as she walked home from Mass in Clarendon Street.'[63]

After Kathleen (Kitby), Sheila (Shel) was born on 11 October 1899. Michael Barry was the first boy, born with a caul (an extra layer of papery skin, thought of as an omen of good fortune in Irish tradition) in 1901. He grew to be the tallest Barry, was gentle and reserved and had less education than the others as he was expected to manage, the farm at Tombeagh. Eileen, known as Elgin, was the next child – born on 13 November 1903 at 8 Fleet Street. Then came my grandmother, Mary Christina (known as Monty), born in 1905, and then Margaret Dolores, known as Peggy, who was born in 1906. Shel Barry was the second born, after Kitby, and Kevin Barry was the fourth born after his brother Michael.

---

60   Máirín Johnston, *Around the Banks of Pimlico*, Dublin: Attic Press,1985.
61   O'Donovan, p. 20.
62   Ibid.
63   Talk by Donal O'Donovan to the Carlow Historical Society in 2005.

Mrs Barry, centre, with left to right back Shel, Michael, Keivn and Kitby and bottom left to right Monty, Peggy and Elgin. ca. 1912

The Barrys were fee-paying students at the Convent of the Holy Faith in Clarendon Street under the direction of Sister Mary Justine.[64] Kevin Barry was in the same class as the actor Noel Purcell. Shel Barry remembered how severe Sister Justine was when girls giggled: 'Girls, girls, Our Lady never laughed,' she would say. Elgin Barry was, my father noted in the margins of his manuscript of *Kevin Barry and his Time*, 'miserable at the school', but she loved the playground on the roof which stretched out over public and private roofs down to Chatham Street from the Carmelite Church.

The 1901 census records Tom and Mary Barry as living at 8 Fleet Street, Dublin. Their marriage was a short one. In 1908, Sir Christopher Nixon, physician to the Lord Lieutenant and Director of Clery's department store, treated Tom Barry for his heart problem and charged him ten guineas for each visit to Fleet Street (which he expected to be paid on arrival). Tom died on a Saturday in Fleet Street, on 8 February 1908, from fatty degeneration of the heart. He was sixty-five years old. Mrs Mary Barry was widowed at the age of thirty-six, and left with seven children. Kevin Barry was just six years old.[65]

The following Tuesday Tom Barry's remains were taken by train to Baltinglass station. The enormous funeral cortège at Tinneclash followed the coffin to Tom's 9- x 12-foot grave, ordered by Mrs Barry. Fanagan's undertakers charged her £17 and 18s, and refreshments at Tombeagh and Fleet Street came to £5. The women stayed at home on the funeral day preparing the food, making sure there was enough whiskey for the mourners. Today, the gravestone is worn and darkened by time.

Tom Barry's Legacy

Tom Barry left the world with an estate worth £2,714 and 9 shillings. He had not just been a hardworking farmer but also an astute business man, and to keep all his worldly activities in balance, he made sure he was generous to the Catholic Church, donating a stained-glass window to the Augustinian Church on John's Lane and a coloured mosaic to the Church of Adam and

---

64   O'Donovan, p. 23.
65   O'Donovan, p. 25.

Eve at Ticknock, County Wicklow. He gave plaster Sacred Hearts and a Virgin Mary to Jervis Street Hospital.[66] In his will, he left £10 to Reverend William Farrell of St Andrew's Church on Westland Row, to have Masses celebrated for the repose of his soul and the souls of his deceased parents.[67]

Tom Barry had explicitly instructed the trustees of his will to sell 8 Fleet Street and the dairy yard at Pimlico, along with his cattle.

'I desire that my wife and children during their minorities or until marriage as the case may be shall reside on my said farm at Tombeagh and ... shall be worked for maintenance of my said wife unless and until she remarry ... .'[68]

His wish was largely ignored by his sister Judith, who had dedicated her later life to building up the city enterprise. Tom left £300 to his widow and £250 to his sister Judith. Judith quickly overruled the family solicitor, Mr Murphy, who had urged caution in being hasty about keeping the Dublin business going. When she would not listen to him, he caved in. Fleet Street would not be sold. The Barrys, or some of them at least, would stay there. But the only way for this to happen was for Judith Barry to buy the house on the open market – which she did for £100, 'directly going against her brother's wishes. There was no stopping her, but her interest was not selfish – it lay in protecting the widow and her family.'[69] Judith Barry went on to be the force behind the Dublin dairy business for the next four years. She did follow her brother's wishes in selling the dairy yard at Pimlico to John Grennan, of 54 Meath Street, for £90, and by selling the cattle for £1,470, 17 shillings and 10 pence. But Fleet Street would remain the stronghold of the Barry women and children, despite Tom Barry's will. After his departure, the family became a matriarchal one. All the decisions in the Barry household were made by women. This would become an important aspect of Kevin Barry's short life.

'The widow', Mrs Mary Barry, is listed in *Thom's Directory* of 1910 as running a dairy farm. The decision to keep Fleet Street caused the family

---

66   Ibid.
67   O'Donovan, p. 27.
68   O'Donovan, p. 27 (15 January 1908).
69   Ibid.

to be split up. Shel Maher (née Barry), Kevin Barry's older sister (born 1899), told my grandfather Jim O'Donovan that Mary Barry went to Tombeagh at that time with the younger children, including Kevin. But Kitby, Shel and Elgin, along with Aunt Judith, stayed at Fleet Street, and from there they attended Secondary school.

When Aunt Judith died in 1912, sixteen-year-old Kitby, Kevin's eldest sister, stepped in to bolster and support her mother. She became, in her own words, 'my mother's chief advisor in all affairs.'[70] She was one of those 'dominant figures', as Elgin's son Michael O'Rahilly called her. Donal O'Donovan noted that Mrs Barry was 'overshadowed by Kitby. She was just that kind of person. She didn't mind responsibility and she took it. The others didn't stand up to her, and Nana [Mrs Barry] thought a great deal of her. Kitby had been Auntie's [Judith Barry] favourite and Judith probably dominated Nana anyway.'[71]

Shel did not stay long in Dublin. She had to leave school in 1915 and take over managing Tombeagh. According to Shel's daughter Triona Maher, 'Shel was always resentful that she had to go down there [to Tombeagh] when the Housekeeper became unreliable.'[72]

Mrs Barry had installed a housekeeper and Nana Dowling (Kevin Barry's maternal grandmother, Ellen McCardle) in Tombeagh. Her eldest son Michael took over the sizeable farm (around a hundred acres), and married in 1909. Things were getting out of hand at Tombeagh with the unreliable housekeeper, and, most probably, the declining health of Nana Dowling, who may have had her head in the clouds. Shel's competent hand was needed. Over the next few years she became very active in the Carlow branch of Cumann na mBan, the women's branch of the IRA. Her brother Michael, who was managing the dairy farm at Tombeagh, became involved in the C Company of the Carlow Brigade, and in the summers when Kevin came down from Dublin (where he lived from 1915), he would take part in ambushes and raids with his older brother in the C Company.

....

70   KBM, WS 731, BMH.
71   O'Donovan, p. 22.
72   Triona Maher to Donal O'Donovan, 1988.

When Kevin was still young at Tombeagh, he loved 'tormenting the housekeepers with unmerciful treatment, playing tricks on them.'[73] When Kitby came down from Dublin she would indulge the children. 'Kitby had spoiled Peggy and Monty unmercifully, just as Kevin was spoiled [by her] too. They used to make rings around Kitby and got all sorts of things out of her like sweets and money, as she was working in Dublin at the time.'[74]

When Kevin Barry got a bit older, he went on to spoil his little sisters Peggy, and my grandmother, Monty. Peggy told my grandfather Jim that when he took them to Mass, 'he would tell us for God's sake to walk in front of him, so that no one would think we were with him. I remember when Mother would have to leave us all in Tombeagh how kind he was to us "younger ones". He always put a few sweets or an apple under our pillows to find when we woke up.'[75]

Rathvilly School

Edward O'Toole had a great reputation nationwide as a schoolteacher, and for this reason Kevin was enrolled at Rathvilly National School where he taught, and not in Hacketstown School, which was closer to Tombeagh. Kevin had been ousted from the school on Clarendon Street in Dublin after his father died. Rathvilly was a landlord's village dominated by Lord Rathdonnell of Lisnavagh House, three miles from Tombeagh. Kevin and Michael Barry would leave the pony trap in Rathvilly, 'just below the doctor's and they'd go to school from there'.[76] But my father wrote that they went to school by donkey and trap.

'As soon as they reached Rathvilly Moat, they often held a race with Willie Jackson of Knockboy on his way to the Protestant school. By this time, Mrs Barry had begun to send milk by train from Rathvilly to Dublin. Jimmy Barry was a kinsman [who] lived with his brother Micky on the road to Ticknock [who] drove the milk cart for her and

73 Shel Barry to Jim O'Donovan, 1953.
74 Triona Maher to Donal O'Donovan, 1988.
75 Information from Peggy Barry to James O'Donovan, 1953.
76 Interview with Kevin Barry junior, 2018.

sometimes carried the boys from school. Micky Barry was a tailor, so they were known as the "Tailor Barrys".'[77]

Nancy O'Toole, the daughter of Edward O'Toole, had a shop in Rathvilly, the nearest shop to the school. She wrote about Kevin many years later, in the *Irish Press*:

> About the only time I can think of Kevin showing any signs of Devilment was when he drenched my plaits with water one day. I used to carry buckets of water from the well to our home and one day I met Kevin with a Pal as I was going along with two buckets full to the brim. The pair of them dipped their hands into the water and splashed it all over my long pigtails until my hair was soaked. I made up a story to my father about how my hair got so wet to keep Kevin out of trouble.[78]

'Devilment' is something we can see by now was a mark of Kevin's character. Kevin may have had a thrashing from a bully of a teacher at Rathvilly National School, 'who duly smacked his ears for his impudence'. [79] The principal of Rathvilly, Edward O'Toole, who was also a dedicated historian, wrote histories of the parish of Rathvilly. In his memoir,[80] he outlined a brief genealogy of the Barry family. O'Toole was a member of the Royal Society of Antiquaries of Ireland.[81] He studied the standing stones of Carlow in some depth – one of them still stands at Tombeagh, in the south of the farm. O'Toole was certainly very scholarly but, more importantly for Kevin Barry, he had been an active nationalist from 1860. In his memoirs[82] he recalled the early years of the IRB in County Carlow. Its members were mostly young men with little military training but heads full of dreams of independence. They had drill books instead of instructors, which meant that when they were given rifles and

77   Ibid.
78   O'Donovan, p. 32.
79   http://www.turtlebunbury.com/history/history_heroes/hist_hero_kevinbarry.html
80   O'Toole, p. 37.
81   O'Donovan, p. 31.
82   O'Toole, p. 37.

revolvers they had no idea how to use them. In December 1879, a dry frosty month of snow, O'Toole and Jack Whitty went to Tullow to shoot starlings with a 'British bull dog pistol'. When O'Toole attempted to load the barrel with ill-fitting cartridges it exploded, leaving his eye damaged and his fingers burst. During his recuperation the liaison officer of the supreme council of the IRB came down to tend to him, sealing his commitment to the IRB. In 1880, the IRB and the Land League split when Charles Stewart Parnell, the leader of the Land League, refused to join the IRB, and there was such bad feeling that Parnell's public meeting in Wexford that summer saw him pelted with eggs, 'and forced to call the meeting off'.[83]

O'Toole recollected how, in 1911, rural science and school gardening was introduced to national schools as a new subject. Nine-year-old Kevin Barry was a keen student.

> To show Kevin's keen, quiet sense of humour, he would sometimes slip in a garden flower in his own bunch of wild flowers and if the teacher showed any hesitation in identifying it, one could see his eyes dancing with enjoyment. On one occasion he brought me in a flower which was quite common near his home, but not so common in Rathvilly, it has a round fishy leaf resembling a coin of the realm. I asked Kevin if he knew the name of the flower and he said he did and that his mother had told him its name was pennyleaf [it is in fact pennywort].[84]

83 Ibid, p. 38.
84 O'Toole, p. 137.

Chapter Three

'AN UNCOMPROMISING REPUBLICAN'

My father loved Dublin, its little back streets and its wide streets like Dame Street and Westmoreland Street. He taught me the names – Andrew Street, Aungier Street, O'Connell Street, Fishamble Street, where Handel had his first performance of the *Messiah*. Every street had a secret story. Some had lost their names when the British left – like Sackville Street, which morphed into O'Connell Street. Daniel O'Connell stands stately at the point where the street intersects with the Quays, immortalised in a bronze statue created by Henry Foley, darkened by time.

When my father brought us to Earlsfort Terrace to concerts in the National Concert Hall, an imposing building with a colonnade, he proudly told us that this was where he had studied legal and political science, where his father Jim studied chemistry, and where Kevin Barry, almost concurrently, studied medicine. Earlsfort Terrace housed University College Dublin until the late 1960s. On these Dublin trips, I was also dragged around the military collections in the National Museum where I was to admire Michael Collins's Volunteer uniform (which I mistook for Kevin Barry's in my memory until recently) encased in a dusty glass cabinet. I remember being shown a brown leather wallet that had documents stuffed into it with a list of raids, injuries and deaths during the War of Independence and Civil War, a 1920 Smith and Wesson revolver that had been captured in a military barracks and the bicycle that Terence Simpson of the 2nd Battalion rode to the 1916 Rising, confiscated by Crown forces.

And, of course, a hand grenade that belonged to my grandfather – perhaps it was the 'Irish Cheddar' that was his 'trademark', made from potassium chelate and paraffin, but certainly not the grenade which, on 10 May 1922, blew his two right hand fingers off while he was 'demonstrating the composition of grenades and their use in action'[85] in Monasterevin.

The doctors wanted to amputate my grandfather's hand but he did not consent, and that hand went on to write the first biography of Kevin Barry, never published. My father was horrified at how bits of grenade shrapnel used to come through the skin on my grandfather's hand.

I was more interested in the ancient bog men in the National Museum, their wrinkled brown bodies and their thick nails and their puckered eyelids. I wondered if I could hear them breathing in that strange, deathly quiet case. I liked the big Neolithic stone mills for grinding grain and the cat god Basta painted on a cat's mummy case in the Egyptian room. But I was always steered away from the Neolithic and Egyptian rooms to the rooms with cabinets full of guns, uniforms and grenades.

Dublin 1911

Dublin in 1911 was about to heave itself into a tidal wave of monumental change. The 1913 Lockout rose up out of the Dublin slums in a city that had a flourishing bourgeoisie and an underbelly of squalor throughout its notorious tenements. In the Henrietta Street tenements 835 people lived in just fifteen houses. Around a third of families lived in one-roomed accommodation. The infant mortality rate was 14 per cent, an appalling percentage even for Europe at the time. Kevin Barry was very vocal about such injustices in his school essays at Belvedere. Granted, he was from a privileged background and attended a prestigious secondary school run by Jesuits, but his sentiments were striking. In an essay entitled 'Industrial Unrest', dealing with the second great industrial strike in Belfast, his left-leaning zeal is quite apparent:

> We are today passing through a crisis which is unparalleled in the history of the world. It is the culmination of four years of starvation, privation and misgovernment – the nemesis which awaits

---

85 David O'Donoghue, *The Devil's Deal, The IRA, Nazi Germany and the Double Life of Jim O'Donovan*, Dublin: New Island Books, 2010, p. 25.

war profiteers, place hunters and grasping capitalists. It is probably the beginning of the end of aristocracy … [86]

The four-week walk-out involved 40,000 shipyard and other engineering workers, Catholic and Protestant, who were demanding a shorter working week and better conditions. Kevin put the causes of the strike down to hunger caused by 'bad wages or misgovernment', and compares the strike with the 1913 Lockout in Dublin, which was 'a forcible demonstration of the power of Labour … and the power of agitation in the person of … James Larkin and his able lieutenant, COMMANDANT JAMES CONNOLLY'.

James Connolly lived at 54 Pimlico with six other families, a total of thirty people. Pimlico was in the heart of the Liberties in Dublin, which belonged to the Earl of Meath. People lived in appalling conditions.

Originally built by King John Plantagenet in 1204, Dublin Castle was the bastion of British power in Ireland, the heart of the British administration in Dublin. The Earl of Aberdeen was the Lord Lieutenant and Augustine Birrell was the Chief Secretary. The balance of power was shifting away from the Anglo-Irish landlords in Irish society as Dublin's rapidly emerging bourgeoisie rose up through the professional and administrative ranks of society. The sympathies of the new middle class did not always lie with the Fenians, but with the more moderate system of Home Rule. It would have been hard to see, in Dublin in 1911, how independence would ever be gained, despite the shifting demographics. In October 1911 a monument to Charles Stewart Parnell was unveiled by the leader of the Irish National Party, John Redmond. The inscription (from one of Parnell's speeches) reads:

> No man has a right to fix the
> boundary to the march of a nation.
> no man has a right
> to say to his country
> thus far shalt thou
> go and no further.

[86] 'Exercise copy book', held by UCD Archives. © Public domain. Digital content: © University College Dublin, published by UCD Library, University College Dublin <http://digital.ucd.ie/view/ucdlib:3911 P93/7

Although Dublin's infrastructure was developing, horses and bicycles were still widely used. However, the motor car was creeping its way on to the Dublin streets and a network of tram lines was put in place. Parnell, his arm raised towards Henry Street, looks as if he is directing traffic there.

Kevin Barry returns to Dublin

In 1915 Kevin Barry returned to Dublin from Tombeagh, aged thirteen, to attend the O'Connell Schools on the North Circular Road, run by the Christian Brothers. The O'Connell Schools were prestigious at this time, maintaining an educational standard that put them above Clongowes Wood College.[87]

This is where Frank Flood and Kevin Barry met, and their fates, as accomplices in the cause, were entwined. Kevin had only a short stint at the O'Connell Schools, from 30 April to 18 June 1915. His father's occupation was recorded as 'dairyman'. The fathers of his classmates were publicans, coachmen, builders and grocers.[88] My father found, at the museum in the O'Connell Schools, two of Kevin's set squares and two bayonets taken by Frank Flood and Kevin Barry in the successful raid they took part in on the King's Inns, on 1 June 1920. They would be the only students of the ten volunteers hanged by the British at Mountjoy Jail. On 14 March 1921 Flood was hanged for treason as a first lieutenant in an active service unit.

'There is nothing to show why Kevin left O'Connell Schools except the belief among members of the family that Kathy [Kitby], now 19 years old and earning, decided that he should be given the opportunity afforded by a more expensive school. Aunt Judith, herself "a bit of a lady" within the family circle and ever anxious for business success, would have heartily approved of Kathy's ambition.'[89]

What is interesting is that it had become Kitby's decision to see that Kevin's education improved and it was she too who made the decision, in 1915, to send him to St Mary's College, Rathmines, run by the Congregation of the

---

87   Desmond Keenan, *Ireland, 1850–1920*, Bloomington: Xlibris Corporation, 2005, p. 327.
88   O'Donovan, p. 33.
89   Ibid.

Holy Ghost. In less than a year, the Easter Rising would be over. He was enrolled in the preparatory grade in September 1915 but he changed schools again in 1916 when the school was closed down.

While Kevin was at St Mary's he got his hands on tickets for the Manchester Martyrs' commemorative concert in the Mansion House. Many of the students' parents were activists, and this is how he came across the news about the event. The martyrs Allen, Larkin and O'Brien were deified by the song that followed their execution, 'God Save Ireland', and within five years of attending the commemoration, Kevin Barry would also be a martyr, immortalised in a 'maudlin' ballad.

Kevin bought a ticket for Kitby and they went together to the concert in November 1915. It was an exciting event where they met their friend Bobby Bonfield, a dental student from the Moyne Road in Ranelagh, who would go on to be a volunteer in the 4th Battalion. Kitby would later meet Bobby during the Civil War, in the siege of the Hammam Hotel where she was fighting with Cumann na mBan. Eoin MacNeill, president of the Irish Volunteers, 'made a fiery speech'[90] at the concert.

At this time Kevin and Kitby were the only committed Republicans in the family: 'We felt then that we had found our proper atmosphere, although outside of Bobby Bonfield and the McNeill Boys there was no single person in the packed Mansion House that we knew. From that on, we were always discovering people among our friends who had the same ideas ... I was 18 years old.'[91] Kevin was just thirteen.

Kitby's son, Patrick Barry Moloney, recollected in the *Belvederian* in 1945 that after the event 'there and then, he [Kevin Barry] wanted to join the Fianna Éireann: but he was so young at 13 that his family thought it unwise.'[92] Fianna Éireann had been founded in 1903 and reorganised, at the suggestion of Hobson in Belfast, by Countess Markiewicz, second in command of St Stephen's Green Garrison in 1916. Elgin Barry strongly believed that Kevin had already joined the Fianna then.

....

90   KBM, WS 731, BMH.

91   Ibid.

92   *The Belvederian*, 1945.

A Matriarchal Family

Kevin, fatherless, was surrounded by staunch women. Kate Kinsella, who had rushed him to St Andrew's Church to be christened, had been the cook at 8 Fleet Street. Since 1879. She was from the Liberties in Dublin and she was greatly loved by the children, to whom she taught rebel songs. She had many stories, like that of when her mother carried a baby outside the jail when Daniel O'Connell was released after he was imprisoned for conspiracy in 1844. Kate had resisted 'physical force movements' emphatically for many years, yet she had been a friend of Tim Kelly, one of the Invincibles who killed Lord Frederick Cavendish, the Chief Secretary for Ireland, in the Phoenix Park Murders in 1882, and her own father had been a close friend of 'Skin the Goat' James Fitzharris, who drove a cab of Invincibles to carry out the murders.[93] It was 'one of the most audacious acts of nationalist violence for years'[94] and would turn Sir Michael O'Dwyer, (a Jesuit-educated Irishman who would go on to become Lieutenant Governor of the Punjab, and was instrumental in the Amritsar Massacre in 1919) to thoughts of shame for being an Irishman.

Kate Kinsella was truly against violence as a means of gaining independence, until 1916 when 'the firing started on Easter Monday'. Kate was on Sackville Street that day, and saw everything. Kitby described how Kate 'went out into the street … dashed past me, lit two candles on her little altar. I said "What are those candles for, Kate?" She said, "for the boys in the Castle", and from that until her last breath she was an uncompromising republican.'[95]

Kate may have been illiterate, but she was 'a wizard at mental arithmetic. We would read out sums for her from our books and she would do our sums in her head.'[96] As the conflict against Britain deepened, she became more and more committed to the cause, and by the time of the Civil War she was acting as the Brigade's treasurer while Kitby was away.

93   O'Donovan, p. 24.
94   Anita Anand, *The Patient Assassin, A True Tale of Massacre, Revenge and the Raj*, New York: Simon and Schuster, 2019, p. 21.
95   KBM, WS 731, BMH.
96   Information from Elgin Barry to Donal O'Donovan, 1988.

'Her ample bosom also contained GHQ and brigade dispatches.'[97] She died in 1937, aged eighty-four, and was buried beside Aunt Judith Barry in Glasnevin Cemetery.

The 1916 Rising

'England's problem [The Great War] was Ireland's opportunity.'[98]

The enlarged and reconstructed General Post Office on Sackville Street was reopened for business in March 1916.[99] Within a month, it would be the focal point of a revolution that apparently came out of the blue. Under Thomas Clarke's guidance the IRB members of the Irish Volunteers planned the 1916 Rising, and it was largely masterminded by James Connolly, involving his Irish Citizen Army, the women's branch of the IRA, Cumann na mBan, and the Irish Volunteers, led by Patrick Pearse, 'the son of an English monument maker, who had married an Irish woman'.[100] Well known in the Gaelic movement, Pearse's speech in August 1915 at the graveside of O'Donovan Rossa, Irish Fenian and member of the IRB, made public the revolutionary zeal that Pearse embodied. It was 'an incitement to revolt. It was the speech of a mystic, a man to whom the resurrection of a free Gaelic Ireland was a task of the deepest, religious significance, a man who had dedicated himself to the idea of martyrdom'.[101] He had ended with:

> We pledge to Ireland our life, and we pledge to English rule in Ireland our hate. This is a place of peace, sacred to the dead, where men should speak with all charity and with all restraint; but I hold it a Christian thing, as O'Donovan Rossa did, to hate evil, to hate untruth, to hate oppression, and hating them, to strive to overthrow them.

---

97   O'Donovan, p. 24.
98   Interview with Michael O'Rahilly, 2019.
99   Keenan, p. 390.
100   Terence De Vere White, *Kevin O'Higgins*, London: Methuen, 1948 p. 16
101   Ibid, p. 17.

The Volunteers, at this time, had little support from the Irish people and were on occasion attacked by mobs for being pro-German. Nevertheless, the IRB, who had been planning a rebellion since 1915, infiltrated the Volunteers. The Rising was met with 'some derision and widespread anger', and when Eoin MacNeill, commander-in-chief of the Volunteers, heard that the Germans had been enlisted to help, he called off the Rising as he did not trust his lieutenants, now known to him as IRB men. The German merchant ship the *SS Libau*, carrying 20,000 rifles and ammunition, was scuttled when the ship was intercepted by three British destroyers. Captain Spindler and his crew were interned for the rest of the Great War. Roger Casement, who had masterminded the international arms shipment, was captured and never even got to meet the *Libau* and Captain Spindler. He was hanged as a traitor in London in August 1916.

When MacNeill got wind that the Germans were involved in the planned rising, he cancelled the Volunteers' meeting on Easter Sunday. But to the initiated, the rising would proceed and at 'ten o clock on Sunday night, Thomas MacDonagh, Commandant of the Dublin Brigade of the Volunteers, gave an order for mobilisation. The insurrection was going to take place without the chief of staff. [102] The real leaders were the lofty Pearse, who was commander-in-chief, and James Connolly, that brilliant strategist who envisioned a republic for Ireland that was socialist, but who had no mystical desire, like Pearse, to 'shed his own blood … he complained of Pearse's obsession with this'.[103] He was convinced, however, that armed demonstration 'was essential to capture the attention of the world, and he was prepared, although a pacifist by inclination', to take up arms.[104]

On the morning of the Rising, the rebels were addressed by the commanding officer, Commandant Edward Daly, and given fighting positions in the Church Street area, where Kevin and the H Company's ambush on Monk's Bakery would take place in September 1920. MacNeill's Volunteers, having withdrawn the day before on his orders, left about 1,200 men to front the insurrection. Key locations in Dublin were seized

102 De Vere White, p. 18
103 Ibid.
104 Ibid., p. 19

on Easter Monday and the Proclamation of the Republic was declared from the General Post Office by Pearse. [105]

This sent shock waves through Dublin's elite. Social engagements were interrupted and, inconveniently, called off. On Easter Monday, the Earl of Fingal was to take Captain Kelly, the recruiting officer, and his wife to the races. The Right Honourable Sir Horace Curzon Plunkett, a committed Home Ruler, rang the Kildare Street Club, where it was confirmed that there was indeed a rebellion under way in Dublin, so the Kellys, already on their way to the races, turned back and entered Dublin Castle through the back door, which, surprisingly, was not yet surrounded.[106]

Within three days, 6,000 British soldiers had arrived to manage the revolt. They were attacked as they marched into Dublin, and most of them had no clear idea of where they were or what they had come for.[107] By the end of Easter week about 16,000 British troops and 1,000 RIC policemen had been mobilised. At 8.30 on Friday 28 April, after Pearse's speech in the GPO, there was an exodus from the Post Office on to the fire-swept street. Among the rebels was Michael Joseph O'Rahilly, whose son, Mac O'Rahilly, would marry Elgin Barry, Kevin Barry's sister. Michael Joseph O'Rahilly was killed in a charge on a British machine-gun post on Moore Street, while covering the retreat from the GPO during the fighting. He was the only man to be killed in action in the Rising. 'Kevin O'Carroll was only sixteen when he went "out" with Pearse in 1916. He was beside The O'Rahilly when the latter was killed on Moore Street; Kevin himself was badly wounded in the stomach.'[108]

Kevin Barry's uncle Pat Dowling, who lived on the South Circular Road, witnessed the looting of Lawrence's toy shop on O'Connell Street. He saw rifles fired from sandbags at Trinity College, and soldiers at the Shelbourne Hotel. That day he also saw women 'shaking their fists at the rebels and shouting: "If yez want to fight, why don't yez get out

105 Ibid.
106 Keenan, p. 392.
107 De Vere White, p. 19.
108 C. S. Andrews, *Dublin Made Me*, Cork: Mercier Press, 1979, p. 115.

to Flanders!"'[109] The latter incident was clear evidence of the divide in Ireland over conscription.

After Patrick Pearse agreed to surrender on Saturday, 29 April, around 3,500 rebels were imprisoned and others were taken to internment camps in Britain. Fewer than 500 men had died in the skirmishes that broke out, but many civilians were killed by British artillery, as there had been no attempt to distinguish them from the rebels. The Rising leaders were executed following courts martial. 'Connolly had to be propped in a chair as he was too severely wounded to stand while the soldiers shot him.'[110] General Maxwell, in charge of the British Forces, employed brute force to quash the rebels, yet 'the insurrection, though it has failed, will leave a wonderful effect on the country,' said Thomas Clarke. 'We will die, but it will be a different Ireland after us.'[111] It brought the full tide of physical force republicanism back into Irish politics in a country that had found some satisfaction with the prospect of Home Rule.

My father kept up a correspondence with his uncle Mac O'Rahilly, whom Elgin Barry married in 1935. Among my father's papers are letters between him and Mac in which the latter discusses the reasons for the failure of the Rising. In 1978 Mac wrote that his father, Michael Joseph O'Rahilly, had first opposed the Rising because he did not want to take 'the Oath of Secrecy that one had to take in the Irish Republican Brotherhood'.[112] This was later corroborated by his son, Michael O'Rahilly. [113] Mac O'Rahilly wrote vehemently that 1916 could not be justified. He was convinced that the Rising was 'inspired by the British' and he had three reasons for believing this:

> I don't mean Asquith or Birrell but a Secret Service group akin to the CIA or the FBI. The first evidence is the admitted fact that the British garrison in the GPO had no ammunition. The second

109 O'Donovan, p. 62.
110 De Vere White, p. 19.
111 Ibid.
112 Private letters between Donal O'Donovan and Mac O'Rahilly, 1978.
113 Interview with Michael O'Rahilly, 2019.

– when Roger Casement was interviewed by Hall he was told that the Irish Volunteers were a 'festering sore' in the body politic and the sooner they were cut out the better. The third – The Aud was allowed to get into Tralee Bay when it could have been intercepted off the coast of Norway.[114]

In the final breath of the letter he declared that it was conscription more than anything else that united the country against Britain and that it was this that turned the country against Britain, not the Rising.

> Had they not executed the 1916 men, it would have fizzled out. Then Kevin was executed. The British had become accustomed to executing people. His court martial was a mere political will to execute Kevin and to make an example of him. This was, of course, to go against them.[115]

The execution of the leaders of the Rising was a punishment for what Churchill would soon call the 'baboonery' of the Irish 'rebels'. The signatories of the proclamation were now, with the exception of Eamon De Valera, shot or hanged. Around 1,800 Volunteers and Sinn Féiners were deported to England where they were confined 'in prison camps, and now had excellent opportunities of reorganising and making plans, selecting leaders, making contacts, which would never had occurred under ordinary circumstances'.[116] Instead of stamping it out, internment served to bolster the rebellious spirit. Maxwell's purge did, however, have the intended effect on the streets as there was little to show in daily life, post 1916, that there was a change in public opinion. The 1918 elections gave Sinn Féin seventy-three seats out of 106. Within three weeks of the result, twenty-nine of the Sinn Féin members met and declared a Republic. The proceedings were conducted in Irish, and lasted twenty minutes.[117]

----

114 Letter from Mac O'Rahilly to Donal O'Donovan, 1978, Private estate of Donal O'Donovan.
115 Interview with Michael O'Rahilly, 2019.
116 De Vere White, p. 20.
117 Letter from Mac O'Rahilly to Donal O'Donovan, 1978, Private estate of Donal O'Donovan.

In his last report to the British PM before his resignation after the 1916 Rising, Augustine Birrell, the disgraced Chief Secretary for Ireland, wrote: 'It is not an Irish Rebellion. It would be a pity if *ex post facto* it became one, and was added to the long and melancholy list of Irish rebellions.'[118]

A Republican family

Kitby said that from 1916 onwards, the way was clear. 'As a family we were in full sympathy with the Republican movement and gave every help, such as contributing to the collections, selling flags, keeping things for people … '. [119]

The barrage of pressure for conscription in the Great War ushered some of the Irish public to another form of resistance. Having a duty to 'serve their country' brought with it a new wave of dissent. Kitby described how, when she was watching a movie in the Grafton Picture House, she refused to stand to sing 'God Save the King'. Even though she regarded France as a traditional ally, and saw 'shoals of young men volunteering for the British Army', this did not mean that she in any way supported the war effort. She was 'somewhat shaken by Redmond's [John Redmond, leader of the Home Rule Party] offering us to the British at the outbreak of the war'.[120] Kitby had followed the Home Rule movement in newspapers and meetings since she was about twelve and attended the great Home Rule meeting in O'Connell Street in 1912, at which Patrick Pearse spoke. 'My first knowledge of any Irish movement other than the Home Rule movement came with the announcement of the arrest of Ernest Blythe for anti-recruiting activities.' [121]

118 Donal O'Donovan, p.43.
119 KBM, WS 731, BMH.
120 Ibid.
121 Ibid.

Chapter Four

'A FAIRLY SOLID FELLOW'

Nobody would suspect a Belvedere boy of throwing himself into the impending war against the British. Not even his best friend in Belvedere, Gerry McAleer, was aware that Kevin joined the C Company of the 1st Dublin Battalion in 1917. Being a Belvedere student was essential, in Kitby's eyes, to Kevin's future career. When St Mary's School closed after 1916, Kitby quickly organised for him to be enrolled at Belvedere, which was run by the Jesuits. Mrs Barry paid four guineas a term for Kevin to attend.

Belvedere was regarded as one of the best schools in the country. In 1841 the Jesuits purchased Belvedere House on Great Denmark Street, in the heart of Dublin, about half a mile from the GPO. Built in 1870 by Michael Stapleton for the 2nd Earl of Belvedere, George Augustus Rochfort (1738–1814), it still has exquisite stucco work, crafted by the great stuccadore Michael Stapleton. James Joyce was a past pupil, as was the poet Joseph Mary Plunkett, who was executed in 1916. Cathal Brugha, who died in 1922 in the siege of the Hammam Hotel during the Civil War, was also a Belvedere graduate.

Boy Soldiers

Kevin was older than many of the boys who been conscripted during the Great War. The legal age for conscription was eighteen, but some of the youngest conscripts had faked their age to fight for their countries, the truth revealed only after their deaths. Sidney Lewis was just twelve and George Maher was thirteen when found crying during heavy shelling in the trenches.[122] Kevin was certainly young when he joined the

122 *Teenage Tommies*, BBC Two, first broadcast 11 November 2014.

Volunteers and, as we know from his uncle Pat Dowling, when he was fourteen he desperately wanted to join Fianna Éireann after the thrill of the Manchester Martyrs' commemoration concert in 1915, but his mother was having none of it.

It was perhaps only his eldest sister Kitby who knew that he joined the C Company of the 1st Battalion of the Dublin Brigade in 1917, at the age of fifteen. Kevin's contemporaries in the IRA were often as young as he was. Vincent Byrne of the E Company in the 2nd Battalion had joined when he was fourteen and a half. He went on to work in the active service unit known as the 'Squad' from 1919–21, carrying out assassinations of key members of the British elite when he was still just a teenager.[123] One of his officers was Mick McDonnell, who gave the order to Kevin Barry to burn down Aghavannagh Barracks in 1920.

Conscription in Ireland

On the wall of the courtyard in Belvedere there is a black marble war memorial that lists boys who lost their lives in the Boer War, The Great War, the 1916 Rising, the War of Independence and the Cypriot War. The list is longest for those who fought and died in the Great War, so we may assume that many of the Belvedere boys, whether by choice or duty, were loyal to the Crown.

1915 had seen a stalemate in the Great War on the Western Front and a fresh hunt for recruits. The Lord Lieutenant in Ireland, Lord Aberdeen, was replaced in February 1915 by Sir Ivor Churchill Guest, 1st Viscount Wimborne, a first cousin of Winston Churchill. The commander-in-chief of the British Army in Ireland, stated at a meeting with Lord Wimborne at the Vice-Regal Lodge, that 1,100 recruits were needed from Ireland every week. It was decided that there would be a new Department of Recruiting, directed by Lord Wimborne, but within seven weeks only 1,106 had signed up, despite there being an estimated 400,000 men of military and recruitable age in Ireland.[124]

---

123 Vincent Byrne, WS 423, BMH, p.1.
124 Keenan, p. 388.

On 8 June 1915, the Irish Parliamentary Party opposed compulsory conscription because 'it is unnecessary and because any attempt to enforce it would break up the unity of the people of these islands.'[125] The North Meath executive of the United Irish League, a nationalist party, opposed conscription: 'It is the duty of Irish members [enlisted in army] to come back and help Ireland to get Home Rule.'[126] The total number of recruits in Ireland from 2 August 1914 to 8 January 1916 was 86,277.[127] The Compulsory Service Act, passed in the House of Commons on January 1916, gave an exemption to Ireland, much to the annoyance of the Unionists. The *Irish Times*, an ardent supporter of conscription in Ireland, encouraged Irish doctors to insist on a reversal of this decision and to seek conscription.[128]

In 1916, the Military Service Act in Britain brought in conscription for all single men aged between eighteen and forty-one. In May 1916, this was amended to include married men. Opposition to conscription in Ireland remained vehement, especially after the 1916 Rising. In 1918, when Lloyd George extended conscription to Ireland due to the dire need for manpower, Sinn Féin pledged to oppose it, thus garnering support for their party in a country that was getting ready to begin its own war with Britain. C. S. Andrews, who was at UCD with Kevin Barry and who was also a volunteer in the H Company of the 1st Battalion, wrote that there was 'wild rage at the British Prime Minister's announcement that the British intended to apply conscription to Ireland. The anti-conscription pledge [denied] the right of the ruling government to enforce compulsory service in this country; we pledge ourselves solemnly one to another to resist conscription by the most effective means at our disposal.'[129]

Nevertheless, over 200,000 Irishmen fought in the Great War and 49,400 died. Churchill was well aware of the role of the 10th Irish Division in Gallipoli, yet he did his damndest to make heroics out of Gallipoli. The scale of the Irish sacrifice and the subsequent lack of

125 David Durnin, *The Irish Medical Profession and the First World War*, Basel: Springer Nature Switzerland AG, 2019, p. 32.
126 Ibid.
127 Keenan, p. 389. *Weekly Irish Times*, 5 February 1916.
128 Durnin, p. 32.
129 Andrews, p. 118.

acknowledgement of this by the War Office annoyed both Redmondite nationalists and southern unionists alike. The idea, later to be enshrined in the Republican song 'The Foggy Dew', that it might be better to 'die 'neath an Irish sky than at Suvla', began to form in the minds of young men. The loss of life at Gallipoli undoubtedly helped create the atmosphere in which Ireland's separatist and republican leaders felt morally justified in launching their insurrection in Dublin in 1916.[130]

Non-mainland conscription was not confined to the Irish. India also had to support the war effort. 'As many as 74,187 Indian soldiers died during World War I. Their stories, and their heroism were largely omitted from British popular histories of the war, or relegated to the footnotes. India contributed a number of divisions and brigades to the European, Mediterranean, Mesopotamian, North African and East African theatres of war. In men, animals, rations, supplies and money given to the British its assistance exceeded that of any other nation.'[131] The Indian troops were 'killed in droves before the war was into its second year. Indian Infantrymen stopped the German advance at Ypres in 1914 while the British were recruiting and training their own forces … .'[132] The thin, bespectacled lawyer Mahatma Gandhi, wearing coarse homespun, returned to India in 1915 from South Africa. In time, he and Jawaharlal Nehru would look to Ireland as a model for its movement for independence. The hunger strike of Terence MacSwiney and his legacy, *The Principles of Freedom*, would become a handbook for Gandhi and Nehru.

The poet and National Volunteer Francis Ledwidge joined the British Army and was ready to die at the Third Battle of Ypres in 1917. But when the signatories of the Proclamation for Independence were executed in 1916 while he was on military leave, his sentiments soured. Among the executed was his good friend and mentor Thomas MacDonagh. Ledwidge wrote, 'If someone were to tell me now that the Germans were coming in over our back wall, I wouldn't lift a finger to stop them. They could come!'[133]

---

130 Paul Bew, *Churchill and Ireland*, Oxford: Oxford University Press, 2016, p. 86.
131 Shashi Tharoor, *Inglorious Empire*, Minneapolis: Scribe US, 2018, p. 74.
132 Ibid., p. 75.
133 http://www.irishcultureandcustoms.com/Poetry/FLedwidge.html)

A growing question now, for many, was how to thwart the British while they were still at war. Dying for one's country had taken on a new meaning. Kate Kinsella, the cook at 8 Fleet Street, would use her 'ample bosom' to store and ferry dispatches and funds. Francis Ledwidge would do nothing to stop the Germans. The Barrys were becoming more and more embroiled in Republicanism. Kevin had joined the Volunteers by 1917 and Michael Barry was already involved in the Carlow Brigade. Shel Barry was committed to the Carlow branch of Cumann na mBan. As for Kitby Barry, it is possible that she was envious of her brothers and her sister Shel, who were all in Volunteer activity by 1917 (the younger Barry girls were not yet involved), but she was devoted to managing her mother's affairs both in the house and at the farm. After Kevin's death, in late 1920, she joined the University branch of Cumann na mBan. Yet, as early as 1915, she was a committed Republican.

Belvedere

Just as he had been when James Joyce was at Belvedere, 'plump bald' Sergeant Major Wright was conducting drill class at the school when Kevin Barry was there. Wright was also drill master at Loreto Convent on St Stephen's Green, where Kevin's sisters went to school. Joyce has left us an account of his experiences at Belvedere through Stephen Dedalus in *A Portrait of the Artist*.

> On Friday confession will be heard all the afternoon after beads. If any boys have special confessors perhaps it will be better for them not to change. Mass will be on Saturday morning at nine o'clock and general communion for the whole college.

In contrast to the heavy religious atmosphere, or perhaps in its shadow, were the nearby streets Stephen Dedalus wandered through on a December evening:

> After early nightfall the yellow lamps would light up [in] the squalid quarter of the brothels.

Fr Joseph McDonnell was a prefect of the Sodality of Our Lady, founded in 1563 for young schoolboys, and was still spiritual director of Belvedere in Kevin's time there. Kevin belonged to the sodality, and this was significant

Belvedere Rugby Team with Kevin Barry to the far right, in uniform.
1917. Kind permission of Evanna Kennedy, daughter of Gerry McAleer

in the days before his execution, when he was preparing for death. Tom Counihan, his mentor, a member of the Jesuit community at Belvedere, guided him through the preparation for his end. Fr Counihan's final visits to Kevin Barry in Mountjoy are recorded in the rector's archives of Belvedere College, and, although these are no longer extant, Fr Counihan's memoir of Kevin's last days are found in the *Belvederian* of 1921.

Counihan was not yet ordained when Kevin attended the school. He taught Kevin maths and chemistry and he was his rugby coach but, above all, he was his mentor and a guide. Tom Counihan told my grandfather Jim O'Donovan that he saw Kevin as unemotional – even though he was good-natured and full of fun, he was 'a dour kind of lad ... once he got down to something he went straight ahead'.[134]

Another Jesuit at Belvedere, Tom Ryan, remembered Kevin's 'special quizzical smile' and how, when he was talking, he would bend his head slightly and look up at an angle with that smile. 'He was a natural leader and drew others to him without effort but never put himself forward.'[135] W. C. Fogarty was Kevin's French teacher:

134 Information from Tom Counihan to Jim O'Donovan, GOD, DOD, p. 41.
135 *The Belvederian*, 1970.

Fogarty's nose is long
Fogarty's nose is long
It would be no disgrace
To Fogarty's face
If half of his nose were gone.

From prison in his last days, Kevin asked Tom Counihan: 'Please remember me to M. Fogarty.' Other teachers were Richard Campbell who, we learn from *A Portrait of the Artist*, was called 'Lantern Jaws' by the boys. Campbell is mentioned only briefly in *A Portrait of the Artist*, as Stephen imagines becoming a Jesuit priest himself and experiences the 'mental sensation of an undefined face or colour of a face … eyeless and sour-favoured and devout, shot with pink tinges of suffocated anger'.

The famous photograph of Kevin wearing a trench coat with the collar turned up and a slither of hair flicked over his forehead, the photograph from which the unknown artist painted the portrait that hung in my father's study, first appeared in a group photograph in the *Belvederian* in 1919, titled 'Pillars of the House'. That trench coat may be the one he wore at the ambush on 20 September 1920. In it he looks not just worldly, but giddy and eager to get on with being in the world.

Kevin Barry's friendship with Gerard McAleer

Kevin Barry's closest friend in the last four years of his life, outside of his political activities, was Gerry McAleer. He was the last of Kevin's friends to see him before his execution in Mountjoy on 1 November 1920. McAleer was from a prosperous family in Dungannon, County Tyrone, where his parents owned the Commercial Hotel along with an auctioneering and undertaking businesses. Gerry's daughter Evanna Kennedy described the hotel to me as 'the Catholic one'.[136]

Kevin and Gerry's friendship is cemented into a windowsill from the hotel in Dungannon, in which, while the concrete was still wet, Kevin carved out his name: 'K. Barry'

136 Interview with Evanna Kennedy, 2019.

Windowsill from the McAleer family's hotel in Dungannon, inscribed by Kevin Barry in 1918. Kind permission of Evanna Kennedy. Photo by Síofra O'Donovan, 2019

Going to Dungannon for diversions became a fairly regular venture for Kevin and Gerry. The motor car that belonged to Gerry's older brother's friend Sam McManus was always being borrowed to 'collect commercial travellers from the Belfast train, or to follow the hearse at funerals'.[137] Kevin loved Dungannon, which had also been the home town, for some time, of Thomas Clarke, one of the executed signatories of the Proclamation of the Republic in 1916. Kevin wrote to Kitby on one of his visits: 'Got several great motor drives last week. The motor man and I are great pals because he is a Meath man and looks down on all Northerners. The longer I stay in the town the better I like it.'[138]

In another letter, he has written a postscript thanking Kitby for her letter and for the 'few bob' for the bicycle chain that broke as he rode to Pomeroy that cost him four shillings.[139] He either forgot the 3d. stamp, or he had spent all his money. In any case, the postman charged his sister. In the same letter, he wrote, 'I hope none of the family were hurt at the recruiting meeting', a reference to the Republicans who went to disrupt conscription meetings at the time.

---

137 O'Donovan, p. 39.
138 Letter from Kevin Barry to Kathleen Barry. From the Kevin Barry estate.
139 O'Donovan, p. 39.

Gerry did not really understand why Kevin had made friends with him. His reasoning is amusing. 'Perhaps it was because of my northern accent, or because we shared the name Gerard.'[140] He spoke about Kevin with an air of self-deprecation, believing that his friend was brighter than he was – Kevin was always in honours classes, while Gerry was in pass. They both, however, went on to study medicine together at UCD, and Gerry would become an air commodore of the Royal Air Force and an honorary physician to the Queen of England, never knowing that Kevin was involved in the IRA. His daughter Evanna Kennedy told me that her father only learned from my father in 1988 that 'Kevin Barry had killed a British soldier. He was very shocked.'[141] At the time my father interviewed Gerry McAleer, he was a retired air commodore and PMO. 'The family was very nomadic, and international. This is why Daddy had little awareness of what happened to Ireland in its newest Free State years.' One of his daughters, Niamh, was born in Egypt 'in the desert'.[142]

Gerry McAleer had digs with Mrs Tipping on the North Circular Road while he was at Belvedere.

In a letter to Gerry from Mountjoy, on 1 October 1920, Kevin congratulated him on passing his exams and joked that he himself had 'stuck' or failed. 'You are all swanky second medicals now', he wrote. 'By the way, tell Mrs. Tipping I'll settle up with her when I get out, if I ever do. The missus was up today. She is looking awful … '.[143]

Evanna Kennedy went to see Mrs Barry with her father on Molesworth Street during the late 1940s, when she was young: 'It was important to Daddy to see her. We also visited the Jesuit priest [most likely Tom Counihan], in the 1960s in Milltown Park. He was covered in snuff, all down his frock vestments. [144]

....

140 Gerry McAleer told this to my father in 1988.
141 Interview with Evanna Kennedy, 2019.
142 Ibid.
143 Letter in possession of Evanna Kennedy.
144 Interview with Evanna Kennedy, 2019.

Rugby

Photo by the Keogh Brothers. Kevin Barry in rugby uniform, Belvedere, 1918.

Gerry described Kevin to my father as 'a fairly solid fellow, broader than I was. We were both forwards in rugby. He was a demon for eating chocolate bars at school. He would eat it morning, noon and night.'[145] Their friendship was partly forged in rugby. In 1917, Kevin, as a substitute on the Junior Cup Team, beat Blackrock College, which Gerry said was a miracle in those days. The *Belvederian* of 1917 noted: 'K. Barry (forward) – though rarely brilliant always plays a good, hard game; a fair tackier; works well in the scrum'.[146] Gerry had 'improved considerably during the year; dribbles very well, but did not shine out much – handicapped, doubtless, through want of knowledge of the game' – a want of knowledge more than made up for subsequently. Eugene Davy, later to have a brilliant international career, was a year or two younger than Kevin and Gerry, but secured his place on that junior team as scrum half – 'watches the ball very keenly and frequently comes round on the opposing half'. Kevin was Secretary of Rugby and a full member of the team. Later, in 1919, the *Belvederian* reported that Kevin, as forward, 'deserved his place, showed great dash, and tackled like a demon. This player improved very much during the season. A useful hooker in the scrum.'[147]

The team photograph by the Keogh Brothers, published in the *Belvederian* in 1919, is one of the best-known pictures of Kevin. Wearing the black-and-white striped jersey of the college, he looks young and eager. He may have played cricket too, as if it was not ironical enough that Kevin, a devout young Republican, played rugby. He also played hurling

145 Gerry McAleer told this to my father in 1988.
146 *The Belvederian*, 1917, p. 119.
147 *The Belvederian*, 1919.

in the same season, 1918–19, and Gerry McAleer and Eugene Davy were pioneers of Gaelic games at Belvedere.

In the 1919 *Belvederian*, in which those iconic photos of Kevin were first seen, there is a 'Middle II', a topical humorous rag written by the students about life in Belvedere. There is nothing here to reflect a posse of revolutionary students.[148] Nor in the beautifully printed *Belvederian*, published in the summer of 1919, with its 'union notes of the year' and its profiles of past pupils – priests and judges, and, of course, successfully conscripted young men who had been at the Front and returned, after Armistice Day. There was news of a Lieutenant Jock Burke, who turned up safe in Dublin, having been presumed dead.[149]

Kevin Barry's essays

Kevin's essays at Belvedere are full of doodles, which must have been scribbled in the margins after he received his grades. Around his Latin exercises, in black ink, is written

'UP the Republic!'[150]

Other doodles reveal his infectious humor. Doodles on the side margins of his essay on the minor characters in Shakespeare's *Henry V*, show Kitby 'at 50', plump and strict looking with a young boy at her Victorian skirts begging from her with a jam jar, saying, 'Please can I have more!' to which Kitby's speech bubble replies, 'Put that up at once!' Another is of Shel, 'at 48', saying to her young boy, 'I'm sick of you! Why can't you behave?' It was when I first found these drawings in his essays in the UCD archives[151] that I saw Kevin's mischief. I could see him at the kitchen table in 8 Fleet Street, mocking his sisters as they fussed around him. Whether Kitby and Shel ever saw these doodles or not, neither of them would have known that Kevin would never know them at the ages

148 http://digital.ucd.ie/view-media/ucdlib:39119/canvas/ucdlib:39565

149 http://digital.ucd.ie/view-media/ucdlib:39120/canvas/ucdlib:39568

150 http://digital.ucd.ie/view-media/ucdlib:39113/canvas/ucdlib:39443

151 'Exercise copy book', held by UCD Archives. © Public domain. Digital content: © University College Dublin, published by UCD Library, University College Dublin <http://digital.ucd.ie/view/ucdlib:39112> Dated 1917–1919.

of forty-eight and fifty. He would be a memory, enshrined in a ballad that none of them would sing.

In an essay titled 'The Freedom of the Press' Kevin writes that 'it is the unwritten charter of Liberty that newspapers and journals should be allowed to give undiluted truths as well as free opinion. The censorship of the press is a thing which England always called into use, when in a tight corner. In the reign of Charles it was even in use and again in the reign of George I. However here in Ireland censorship does not trouble us much as the censor cannot stop tongues or letters and the place being so small news travels more quickly. In fact there are quite a few papers being printed that the censor never hears about.'

Kevin's essays are always flippant, and rarely backed up by example or reference. He got 50 per cent for this essay. He says things like 'I could give any amount of examples to illustrate this but I will conclude … '.

Eoin Dudley Edwards, another former student of Belvedere, described the atmosphere at the school as 'one of a master-pupil conspiracy of irony rather than the crass indoctrination of crude nationalism'.[152] Essay titles like 'Freedom of the Press', 'Prejudice' and 'The Causes of Revolution' do not indicate that the fathers of Belvedere were on mission to suppress freedom of speech, or to indoctrinate the pupils with colonial or Home Rule narratives – far from it, in fact. However, Belvedere did have its share of students whose parents were loyal to the Crown, as the war memorial in the courtyard shows.

Kevin saw racism as an intrinsic aspect of colonialism. In an essay on prejudice, a subject topical at Belvedere during the Great War, Kevin argues that prejudice 'is a subject on which every Irishman should be able to discourse eloquently. This refers to all educated Irishmen who are able to compare the prejudice which all these countrymen suffer to that which oppresses other men.' There were two classes of prejudice which, combined, form the origin of very many of the world's greatest wars and slaughter. 'That of the white man against his coloured brother, for brother he is whether black, red or yellow, and that of the white man against his fellow white man of a

152 O'Donovan, p. 34.

different nation.'[153] In the context of prejudice in the United States, he observed that 'American people as a whole look down on the black-man as a work beast, as an animal without a soul. A white American refuses to travel or eat with a negro. Even for the slightest offence he is punished and in former days and even latter, the blackman has been "lynched by the mob" of "Superior white men".' While it is so unfortunate that Kevin uses a derogatory word for black Americans in his writing, he is, in his own way, passionately defending them. His view may have been unusual for his time, but the language unfortunately wasn't. Kevin's mother may have had significant influence on Kevin's attitudes. The Barrys had been in business in the city for many years and had good relations with Freemasons and Jews, all of whom lived around the South Circular Road, called by Dubliners at the time, 'The South Circumcised Road'.

Mrs Barry's grandson Michael O'Rahilly remembered being with her in 1945 at her apartment in Molesworth Street, in a beautiful recollection that again displays her open-mindedness:

> She sat me on the windowsill [of her Molesworth Street Apartment] when I was small. She pointed towards the Dáil, to the statue of Queen Victoria which was still there, then in 1945. She showed me what it all meant. She showed me the Orange Lodge 'Portico' and told me who the Freemasons were. She said that three groups of people were very kind to her in Dublin after Tom Barry [her husband] died – the Masons, the Quakers and the Jews. They all helped her in the dairy business. She was a very gentle soul, very devout. Clarendon Street [Church] was her gateway to God.[154]

My father felt that Kevin had got his tolerance from his mother 'who, as a businesswoman in the city for many years, had especially good

---

153 Sean Cronin, essay quoted in Kevin Barry, National Publications Committee, 56 Grand Parade, Cork, 1965, p. 10.

154 Interview with Michael O'Rahilly, 2019.

relations with Freemasons and Jews. There were always Protestant families in the Tombeagh area, the nearest being the Thorpes.'[155]

Kevin's revolutionary tone is turned up in a later essay:

> ... the very men who were always shouting for unity are the men who will not unite at this critical moment and the Hottentots, the Rainbow chasers and the 'grasshoppers' were first to respond to the appearance of a Dillonite bishop ... No matter how bleak things look at present a brighter day is coming and if everyone does his share, instead of submitting to present circumstances, instead of being satisfied with present conditions, there is no doubt but that 'at a no far distant date' we may be celebrating our——[a note in Kevin's handwriting follows: 'Deleted by censor'].[156]

The essay received a mark of 40 per cent, and beside this section of the essay, is written 'piffle' – possibly by the teacher. An essay on 'Imagination', however, received a mark of 85 per cent. Its final statement reads:

> 'Certain it is that the Irishman is much more imaginative than the phlegmatic Sassanach.'

Kevin's political convictions are most evident in his essay, written between 1918 and 1919, on 'Revolution' – by far the most structured and well argued of the essays written while he was at Belvedere. He divides his points into Causes, Objects, Remedies and Effects. As for the cause of Revolution:

> nine times out of ten the cause is bad government. In the history of every country there has been a period of oppression and tyranny, a period of despotic rule by monarch or ministers ... at length a time came when the people decided that they would stand it no longer and a revolution took place. If it were successful everything

---

155 O'Donovan, p. 41.
156 Cronin, pp. 10–11.

was all right. If not, it was only deferred for a few years so that in the end the people triumphed.

Kevin is referring here to 1916, and the deferral to which he referred was the very war that he was engaged in, on the streets of Dublin. Meanwhile, he still took the time to do his homework. "The great remedy for revolutions is to use an English made Irish bull, a preventative. Revolutions may be very easily prevented … by a constitutional government by the representatives such as was supposed to have been the case in England.'

Towards the end of the four-page essay he wrote: 'Of course I do not include the revolutions of S. America – no sane person would call them revolutions.' But the word 'S. America' is crossed out and '1916' is written over it in pencil. The next three lines are entirely crossed out. The essay is signed in his Irish name, Caomhín de Barra, in Gaelic script. 'I believe they are merely got up to save the people from being bored, just to keep things humming in the land of "ennui".' It seems a flippant statement from a revolutionary that he would conclude that people invented revolutions to keep boredom at bay. In fact, it entirely contradicts the original premise of the essay. One wonders, could he have decided to temper himself by the end of this essay, intending to keep the ferment of his own revolution as quiet as possible in the Belvedere classroom? The blue pencil mark of the teacher's verdict was 60 per cent.

At the back of an exercise book dating from around 1918, there is an interesting, more poetic reflection on the nature of card playing, followed by something that appears to be a confessional letter, or a diary entry. From this, we see how romantic Kevin was.

To the puny objectors against cards, which bring out all man's bravest passions, she would reply that man is a gaming animal, that he is always trying to get the better of someone and that his passions cannot be more expanded than on a game of cards.

Kevin continues with this possibly secret admission:

> She said also that cards are only a temporary illusion, a mere drama, a kind of dream. Fighting, battling but no bloodletting … that last game I had with my sweet cousin (did I tell you how foolish I am) I wished it lasted forever. We neither lost nor gained anything … '. [157]

<hr />

157 'Exercise copy book', held by UCD Archives. © Public domain. Digital content: © University College Dublin, published by UCD Library, University College Dublin <http://digital.ucd.ie/view/ucdlib:39112>

Chapter Five

'A GILT-EDGED CAREER'

When Kevin joined the C Company of the 1st Battalion in 1917, they laughed at his Belvedere cap, and fully expected the thrill of being a Volunteer to quickly wear off for this middle-class boy. The cap is still in Belvedere College, sitting in a glass cabinet along with some of his copybooks. Triona Maher had some of these, and many of them ended up in the UCD archives. Kevin's square, slanted oak writing desk on skinny legs is also still at Belvedere. The cap was 'a great joke [to the C Company] and they decided it was a flash in the pan and they would keep him until he got tired of it.'[158] Kitby's tone, however, is full of admiration when she describes Kevin's easy and impressive integration into life as a Volunteer:

> … as in everything else, he had a gilt-edged career. Most important people noticed him and liked him. Peadar Clancy and he were very close friends. He seemed to be able to wangle himself into odd little actions and engagements both in Dublin and at home in Carlow.[159]

Peadar Clancy had served as a Volunteer in the Four Courts garrison in the Rising and was imprisoned afterwards until 1917, when he came home to open a drapery business called The Republican Outfitters at 94 Talbot Street in Dublin. It became a secret meeting place for the IRA.[160]

---

158 KBM, WS 731, BMH.
159 Ibid.
160 *Dublin's Fighting Story 1916–21, Told by the Men Who Made It*. Introduction by Diarmuid Ferriter, Cork: Mercier Press, 2009.

Perhaps it was, as my father said, 'the temperate attitude of the Jesuits that acted as a counterbalance to the ferment of revolution'. Tony Woods, then a staff captain in the Irish Volunteers, caught the atmosphere of the city: 'Between the scraps, it was an extraordinarily unreal war, part-time civilians and youngsters pitched against a real army.'[161]

When Kevin joined the Volunteers in Parnell Square in 1917 it was during his second year at Belvedere when he was fifteen, in middle grade honours intermediate. Although he was laughed at in the beginning, Kevin 'proved regular in attendance ... so they gave him the mobilisation job'.[162]

He was made mobilisation officer for rote marches and Sunday morning parades. My father noted how uncanny it was that the 'good fathers' of Belvedere did not know Kevin had been part of the 'unreal war' for most of the time that he had been mentored by them at Belvedere. Kevin's capacity for compartmentalising the different parts of his public and secret lives was proving to be astounding.

Conscription, by this time, was rapidly going out of fashion. Sean Prendergast, 1916 veteran and Captain of the C Company of the 1st Battalion, Dublin Brigade, noted in his witness statement that by 1917, young men and boys couldn't be 'coerced to fight for an alien country which had kept our country in bondage for the past 700 years'.[163] They joined the Irish Volunteers instead. By the beginning of 1917 in Dublin, the 'Battalion and the Dublin Brigade staffs [of the volunteers] ... threw themselves into work with increased vigour and unbounded zest'.[164]

161 Uinseann Mac Eoin, *Survivors*, Dublin: Argenta, 1980, p. 314.
162 KBM, WS 731, BMH.
163 Sean Prendergast, WS 755, BMH, p. 220.
164 Ibid.

This was where Kevin Barry and Frank Flood met again after attending the O'Connell Schools together briefly in 1913. They both joined the C Company, 1st Battalion, in the Dublin Brigade.

The 1917 Roscommon by-election

Prendergast was, at this time, conscious of the 'altogether too sensitive prying eyes of the Castle Authorities. [However] all the other elements worked in our favour – the Roscommon election, fought by Count Plunkett, whose father had been a Signatory of the Proclamation of Easter Week in 1916 and also executed.'[165]

When the Irish Parliamentary MP James Joseph O'Kelly died in 1917, there was a by-election held in Roscommon, just nine months after the Rising. Count George Plunkett, the father of Joseph Mary Plunkett, who had been executed in 1916, ran as an independent candidate and won the seat of Roscommon North. At his victory party in Boyle he announced his decision to abstain from Westminster. This election, was, according to Prendergast, bringing in the 'new spirit' of the 'Living Republic'. In other elections, the Volunteers 'threw themselves into the public manifestations exhibited which to them meant the continuation of the work left unfinished in 1916. Vindication of the men of Easter Week. The voices of the people of Ireland were being raised on behalf of Ireland's sovereign right to be free – her right to be an Irish Republic. The torch was lit.' He describes how there were few hamlets, villages, parishes or towns in Ireland where a republican flag was not flying. 'It was the flag raised in Easter Week.'[166]

The 1917 East Clare by-election took place after the death of Willie Redmond, the Irish Parliamentary Party MP who had been killed in action in the Great War. Eamon De Valera, the only signatory of the Proclamation of Independence in the Rising who was not executed, won the election and took the seat. The canvassing campaigns for this and other by-elections at the time brought Volunteers from Dublin to different parts of the country to canvass with other Volunteers. The cars driven down from Dublin often bore the number plate 'IR1916', 'a practice contrary to the law. The

---

165 Prendergast, WS 755, BMH, p. 222.
166 Ibid., p. 224.

Volunteers' presence greatly affected electoral results. 'Much of the propaganda on our side … was directed against the British Government and British Authority, in favour of the Easter Week Rising 1916. "Sinn Fein Abú", "An Phoblacht Abú", "Up Sinn Féin", "Up the Republic" rang far and wide in Ireland.'[167] Meanwhile, in Belvedere College, Kevin Barry was writing such slogans in the margins of his essays.

Imprisoned Electoral Candidates

Elections also brought the imprisoned men into the public eye. Most of the candidates selected were volunteer officers who had participated in the Rising and were still in jail. Slogans such as 'Vote for McGuinness, the man in jail for Ireland', and 'Vote for De Valera, the man in jail for Ireland' were employed. In the Longford election on 9 May 1917, Joseph McGuinness, the Sinn Féin candidate, was serving a sentence in Lewes Jail for his part in the Easter Week Rising. A poster depicting a man dressed in convict garb was extensively circulated. He was elected, on a recount, by a majority of thirty-seven.

In June 1917, the British government opened the prison doors and 'Ireland rejoiced at their homecoming, we in the Volunteers felt that we were on the march again.'[168] Michael Collins made his way home from Frongoch internment camp in Wales and, with his fellow Volunteers, he set about retraining and reorganising those secret armies for the coming war. At the same time, the British authorities swiftly announced 'The Irish Convention', which was to 'try and settle the Irish question'. It took place in Trinity College on 25 July 1917 under the chairmanship of Sir Horace Plunkett. Sinn Féin, although invited to send delegates, boycotted the event. Sean Prendergast claimed it was an attempt to throw the blame on the Irish people for not settling 'their own affairs and to make it appear that the British, the sponsors of the expedient, were actually bursting to do justice to Ireland … the real reason was to undermine the Republican Movement.'[169] The bitter, salient tone is palpable. Predictably, the British

167 Prendergast, WS 755, BMH p. 225.
168 Ibid., p. 224.
169 Ibid.

Authorities went on to arrest Volunteers for drilling, making speeches and holding parades: 'Sinn Féin halls and other public halls were continually under their surveillance. And the jail doors were flung open to receive Sinn Féiners, so that some, for the second time, became "guests of His Majesty".'[170]

Sinn Féin clubs, of which hundreds sprang up around the country towards the end of 1917, began to attract more and more members. In October 2017 Eamon De Valera was elected President of Sinn Féin at the National Convention. Sinn Féin pledged to achieve a republic. In November 1917 J. P. Farrell MP advised 'young men to keep away from Sinn Féin and its policy'. He said 'it was the Irish party saved them from conscription.'[171]

Hunger Striker Thomas Ashe

Hunger striking became a powerful tool for political prisoners. The deaths of Thomas Ashe and Terence MacSwiney (who died a week before Kevin was hanged) made international news and had a profound influence on the Indian struggle for Independence. Jatindra Nath Das, the Indian Bengali activist and revolutionary who died in Lahore jail after a sixty-three day hunger strike in September 1929 was, like Thomas Ashe, forcibly fed. 'Ireland awakened to a new life, a new resurgence. Indignation, resentment and protestation were expressed by the people of Ireland against the machinations and wickedness of the British Authorities.'[172]

Patrick Berry, who was a prison warder in Mountjoy Prison from 1906 to 1922, dealt directly with the hunger striker Thomas Ashe. He saw many prisoners there, including Countess Markiewicz. He stated that things got very busy in the prison from 1917 when many prisoners were brought in, including Thomas Ashe, Austin Stack, Fiona Lynch, Phil Shanahan, Alec McCabe and John O'Mahoney:[173] 'They went on hunger strike and on a Saturday afternoon they were told that if they did not take food they would

---

170 Prendergast WS 755, BMH, p. 225.
171 Ferriter, *A Nation and not a Rabble*, p. 170. Notes on UKNA CO 904/21, RIC Office, Dublin Castle, Crime Dept. Special Branch, 'United Irish League, Meetings etc'.
172 Prendergast, WS 755, BMH, p. 242.
173 Patrick Berry, WS 942, BMH.

be forcibly fed. On that Saturday afternoon I was put in charge of the cell oc-cupied by Thomas Ashe' (B.2). He describes how a Dr Dowdall forcibly fed Ashe. Berry told Ashe to 'give the doctor a bit of his mind'.[174] The doctor re-quested that Ashe take his food voluntarily to which Ashe replied 'No'. Then the doctor said 'If not I have no other alternative but to feed you forcibly'. Thomas Ashe then said to the doctor he would go down to posterity crowned with the blood of innocent Irishmen on his soul. Dowdall fed him through the mouth then and after that Ashe walked back to his cell.[175]

Thomas Ashe died from being force fed on his hunger strike in Mountjoy in 1917, having been transferred to the Mater Hospital.

> They thought they would never get him out quick enough as he became very ill as a result of the forcible feeding by Dr Lowe which had not been done properly. He died that night in the Mater Hospital. An Inquiry was held at the City Morgue.[176]

Berry was sent for by the governor, and was promised a bright future if he gave 'suitable' evidence.

> The following morning I was brought down with other warders and things went on smoothly until my evidence came on. I re-member Maud Gonne MacBride was there and a good many sym-pathisers. I gave my evidence as I knew it and when I came to the remark Ashe made regarding the blood of innocent Irishmen going down to posterity there was applause in the Morgue with the result that the meeting ended in confusion.

Later, Berry's account turns to Kevin Barry, describing his involvement with the failed escape plan masterminded by Brigadier Dick McKee.

Thomas Ashe's death by hunger strike in 1917 resulted in a carefully choreographed funeral that 'led to the establishment of formal military

174 Ibid., pp. 5, 6.
175 Ibid.
176 Ibid., p .7.

structures for the Volunteers over the following six months and the formation of the Dublin Brigade.'[177] Richard Mulcahy was commanding
officer. Michael Collins, who was at the graveside of Ashe, had founded
the General Headquarters Staff and was the Volunteers' new Director of
Organisations, using the Irish Republican Brotherhood network to place
activists in the right positions.

Kevin Barry and the H Company

The C Company quickly became the H Company, one of the biggest
units in the Dublin Brigade, brimming with doctors, students, tradesmen, labourers, grocers and journalists. In 1918, Seamus Kavanagh
was Captain of the H Company. Tommy McGrane was 1st Lieutenant.
Bob O'Flanagan, Frank Flanagan, Matty McGrane, Joseph Sweeney,
Sean O'Neill, Tom O'Brien and John O'Connor were other prominent
members. It was, as O'Neill called the H Company, 'Brains and brawn'.
John Joe Carroll, a member of the H Company, was three years older
than Kevin and lived until 1987. My grandfather Jim O'Donovan interviewed him in 1960.

> He struck me as a very intelligent, upright young lad, full of life
> and very fond of sport, always wore a trench coat with belt and
> epaulets on each shoulder. He was a first-class Volunteer and it
> wasn't long till he was promoted Section Leader.[178]

The H Company met in the O'Flanagan Club in Ryder's Row,
off Bolton Street, in the Tara Hall in Gloucester Street, and at 44
Rutland Square, which is now Parnell Square. In 1914 the first plans
for the Easter Rising were hatched at 25 Rutland Square, which was
also used to enlist Volunteers and train them to use arms. 44 Rutland
Street, where Kevin joined the Volunteers, was later renamed the
Kevin Barry Memorial Hall and is now used by Sinn Féin as a book-
shop and offices.

177 Ferriter, *A Nation and not a Rabble*, p. 173.
178 O'Donovan, p. 45. See note [8] Liberty, April, 1960.

Kevin was quickly perceived as a dedicated, competent Volunteer, so 'they made him NCO to relieve him of the gruelling work. He made a deep and lasting friendship with Bob Flanagan, Company 1st Lieutenant … '.[179]

Although it is hard to imagine Kevin as being shy, Bob O'Flanagan, a prominent member of the H Company and one of Kevin's closest friends since he joined the Auxiliary C Company, described Kevin to my grandfather in 1960: 'When he was not actually drilling, he was standing near the wall, looking a rather lonely figure.'[180]

Kevin would come home late on a Saturday afternoon after a rugby match or hurling game to find a pile of mobilisation orders. Kitby remembered how he would have a hurried meal and would 'set out on his bicycle to deliver them. At that time H Company seemed to have no particular territorial location because, although most of the men lived on the north side, some of them outside the northern side of the city, some of them in Finglas, there was one of them living in the tramway cottages in Dartry … he would come home some time after 11pm, to be up next morning for the parade at 8am.'[181] Kevin would take the bicycle out of 8 Fleet Street to deliver mobilisation orders to Volunteers. Parades went out early at 8 o'clock on Sunday mornings, 'so after a night of dancing that might have been a strain.'[182] As Kevin went on to university, dancing and drinking would become his greatest source of amusement, in parallel with his rapidly advancing military career.

The Irish Republican Brotherhood

Since 1858 The IRB had been committed to founding an Irish Republic, and to that effect a complex web of clandestine connections was developed to bulwark the organisation. Michael Collins, as Director of Organisation, with his great skills in administration, used the IRB to develop a network of prominent activists placed in key positions in the same way that Thomas Clarke had the IRB infiltrate the Irish Volunteers

179 KBM, WS 731, BMH.
180 Information from Bob O'Flanagan to James O'Donovan in 1953.
181 KBM, WS 731, BMH.
182 Ibid.

in order to move forward the plans for the 1916 Rising. He put his volunteers 'in a position to complete by force of arms the work begun by the men of Easter Week [1916]'.[183]

In 1918, Kevin was put forward by the Clarke Luby Club to join the IRB, by his close friends Sean O'Neill and Bob O'Flanagan in the H Company. At sixteen, he was the youngest ever member of the IRB. Being a member of such a secret organisation might explain Kevin's ability to compartmentalise his life into the areas of 'student' and 'soldier'.

By the beginning of 1918 the British establishment was on the hunt for raids and arms stashes. Arrests for drilling, unlawful assembly and violations of the laws of sedition, were frequent. Volunteers often refused to recognise the courts. Brigadier Dick McKee, who was shot dead at Dublin Castle in 1920 after the Bloody Sunday massacre, administered the oath to officers and section commanders in the H Company. In Kevin's case, Peadar Clancy administered the oath at 14 North Great George's Street.[184] Kevin would have already known about the oath 'as it was discussed in the IRB circles prior to the Volunteers knowing'.[185] The oath that was taken was this:

> I, A.B., in the presence of Almighty God, do solemnly swear allegiance to the Irish Republic, now virtually established; and that I will do my very utmost, at every risk, while life lasts, to defend its independence and integrity; and, finally, that I will yield implicit obedience in all things, not contrary to the laws of God [or 'the laws of morality'], to the commands of my superior officers. So help me God. Amen.

In yet a later version it read:

> In the presence of God, I, ... , do solemnly swear that I will do my utmost to establish the independence of Ireland, and that I will bear true allegiance to the Supreme Council of the Irish Republican

---

183 O'Donovan, p. 43.
184 Sean O'Neill, WS 1,154, BMH, p. 5.
185 Ibid.

Brotherhood and the Government of the Irish Republic and implicitly obey the constitution of the Irish Republican Brotherhood and all my superior officers and that I will preserve inviolable the secrets of the organisation.[186]

The German Plot

In May 1918, the British military web was tightening under Lord French when seventy-three Sinn Féin leaders were arrested off the coast of Clare for what was known as the 'German Plot'. Ostensibly a bid to destroy all 'pro-German intrigue' in Ireland, it only served to swell the increasingly negative attitude towards the British. The Chief Secretary's Office was warned: 'If you merely imprison these men, deport them to England and hush the whole thing up – the course of action adopted with the arrested suspects after the 1916 rebellion – you will make things worse.'[187]

One of the arrested men, Tom Dillon, was a colleague of my grandfather's and was brought to Gloucester. They had both, at this time, been working on explosives: 'We got some results in getting tri-nitro cresylic acid, but it needed a research chest to produce it.'[188] When Dillon was arrested, he left instructions with my grandfather to 'clear the laboratory and remove all traces of our work'.[189]

The arrests brought protests. Despite all these attempts to push back the tide that was already turning (seditious songs were banned, a film about Thomas Ashe was censored), the Volunteers were now a well-organised structure with a GHQ. Sinn Féin was also becoming very adept at collecting donations – £42,612.16 up to 30 June 1918, according to the Chief Secretary's Office.[190]

---

186 Dr Mark F. Ryan, *Fenian Memories*, Edited by T. F. O'Sullivan, Dublin: M. H. Gill & Son Ltd, 1945.

187 United Kingdom National Archives, Kew (CO, 906/34 James O'Mahony to Edward O'Farrell, 18 May 1918.

188 James L. O'Donovan, WS 1713, BMH, p. 3.

189 Ibid.

190 UKNA CO 904.23 Sinn Féin Activities: SF funds, 1917–18.

The Conscription Crisis

In April 1918, under the Military Service Bill, the British government extended conscription to Ireland. Home Rule was declining in popularity. Three by-election results in 1918 warned of this, and that March the leader of the Home Rule Party, John Redmond, passed away.

The same month, the German offensive on the Allies brought on the urgency of the revision of the Military Service Bill. 'Even the Catholic Hierarchy labelled conscription "an oppressive inhuman law".'[191] The newly arrived Lord Lieutenant, Lord French of Ypres, a war veteran himself, would have several attempts made on his life during the War of Independence, until he was replaced by Lord FitzAlan-Howard, a Catholic. Lord French's sister, Charlotte Despard, supported Sinn Féin, much to his embarrassment.

The *Manchester Guardian* prophesied that the British Government was preparing to do 'Some very evil work in Ireland … [and would produce an Ireland] more alienated than any with which this country has had to deal with since the Rebellion of 1798'.[192]

De Valera had prepared a statement to Woodrow Wilson – 'Ireland's case against Conscription' – in which he insisted it was 'a battle for self-determination and the fundamental principles of liberty'.[193] Overall conscription roused the Irish people 'to a high pitch of enthusiasm to fight the conscription menace',[194] and the major effect was the rapid increase in the size and organisation of the Volunteers in many parishes.

However, 'the government abandoned the threat of conscription, partly because the war in France was going better, and replaced it with a new voluntary recruiting campaign with the aid of well-known Nationalist MPs in uniform'.[195] In August 1918 Kevin Barry was on

191 O'Donovan p. 47.

192 Ibid.

193 Maurice Moynihan, *Speeches and Statements of Eamon De Valera 1917–1973*, Dublin: Gill & Macmillan, 1980, p.12.

194 James Sullivan, WS 518, BMH.

195 O'Donovan, p. 47.

holiday with Gerry McAleer. In his letters home, he made reference to the Sinn Féin activists who came along to infiltrate and disrupt the recruiting campaigns.

Over 11,000 signed up for conscription within three months. The Great War was battering the Nationalist Party down. Its organisation was fraying at the edges and a vacuum emerged that would be filled by those it condemned. A general election took place in 1918, a month after the end of the war. Many of the returning soldiers did not return in time to vote and the new electoral register gave the franchise to 1,931,588 Irish people, including 800,000 women.

The result was devastation for the Nationalist party. Sinn Féin won seventy-three seats, unionists twenty-six and the IPP just six. Sinn Féin had won three quarters of the Irish seats at Westminster. De Valera defeated the Nationalist leader, John Dillon, in East Mayo. On 21 January 1919, Dáil Éireann was established and committed to being an independent parliament that would elect its own ministry. For the rest of 1919, Sinn Féin would push to secure Ireland's right to self-determination at the Peace Conference at Versailles. Once the Dáil Ministry was established the Volunteers took an oath of allegiance.

Some time in the winter of 1919/20, Kitby recalled Kevin coming home after the mid-week parade to find her waiting up for him to share supper. 'We took the Oath tonight,' he said, referring to an oath of allegiance to Dáil Éireann, Government of the Irish Republic.

'Good!' said Kitby. 'You're in a real army now.'

'I don't know. But I'll tell you one thing. When this damned Dáil takes dominion Home Rule, they need not expect us to back them up.'[196]

Kitby remembered the conversation vividly, and brought it up with Michael Collins in 1922 in the context of the Anglo-Irish Treaty, which was to spawn civil war between those for and against the agreement trotted out by Lloyd George.

'Mick listed a number of very fine soldiers who supported it and said: "How do you know your brother would not have supported it too?" I

----

196 KBM, WS 731, BMH.

told him this little story and, with characteristic generosity, he said: "That is good enough. I won't say any more."'[197]

Kitby's friendship with Michael Collins lasted until he was assassinated during the Civil War at an ambush in Béal na Bláth in West Cork, by the pro-Treaty IRA. Kitby would 'cry buckets' for him, despite their being on opposing sides in the Civil War that followed the Anglo-Irish Treaty in 1921.

C. S. Andrews, otherwise known as Todd, who was one of my grandfather Jim's closest friends, gives an evocative description of when he took the Oath of Allegiance to Dáil Éireann in the autumn of 1919 in an atmosphere of 'solemnity' in the Ballyboden Library. 'It was anything but an ordinary parade of the Company. Coughlan warned us that we were undertaking a serious obligation. He suggested that anyone who had doubts should "fall out". Nobody did.'[198]

Andrews, in fact, felt sorry he took the oath, as he felt that no organisation outside of their own should have any say in the Volunteers' activities. 'In 1919 parliamentary democracy was a word not so often heard used. The only democracy we knew of was British democracy and that had less than nothing to recommend it to us.'[199] He spoke bitterly about Lloyd George's poor view of Republicans. He quoted Lloyd George's son as saying: 'He [Lloyd George] was quite willing to let them have what they seemed determined to become, an impoverished semi-peasant community with their peat fires and untrained bogs and dreams of glory seen in a fine mist of alcohol.'[200]

Raids and Ambushes in Dublin

Sean O'Neill, a Lieutenant of the H Company, was with Kevin as he went on to stage raids in the greater Dublin area. At that point, Peadar Clancy had given the Company permission to conduct such raids after they had got a Lewis gun for £34 out of Ship Street Barracks, the first

---

197 Ibid.
198 Andrews, p. 120.
199 Ibid.
200 Ibid., p. 121.

weapon this Company had seized. 'Kevin carried it wrapped in newspapers on a Sunday evening to Davy Golden's home on the South Circular Road. The money to purchase it came from Phil Shanahan, J. J. Walsh and the Company Officers.'[201]

O'Neill remembered that 'the most earnest, intelligent lads were picked out and underwent a special course of training as potential NCOs. Kevin was appointed left Section Commander in the No. 2 Section. Up to this, Kevin was hardly noticed. But you could always see a young boyish smiling face on parade, one who gave no trouble and [who] always had that smile for every volunteer in the unit.'[202]

Kevin, now a member of the Clarke Luby Club in the IRB, 'started to do things in real style. We carried out several raids for arms [with] sanction from Peadar Clancy. The raid on the Shamrock Works, Brunswick Street (now Pearse Street) yielded a Morris-Tube rifle.'[203]

Kevin got a few punctures on the way to Wolfe Tone's grave in Bodenstown. 'The whole column was black from the dust. [Kevin's] whole worry that day was to get to Bodenstown and when we were washed and dried on tea, mixed with leaves, brambles and stick ashes, he was still smiling.'[204]

Throughout 1919 the H Company had marches, drilling, training and camp at Ticknock in the Dublin mountains. O'Neill always enjoyed Kevin's company. 'Kevin entered into every devilment, pinching cakes ... '.[205] There was another raid at Shamrock Works, Brunswick Street, where they got a Morris Tube rifle. At the Markes Fireworks Makers on Capel Street Kevin and the younger men flirted with the reception girls while Golden and O'Neill searched the place for arms. Tommy McGrane, 1st Lieutenant, had no time, according to O'Neill, for these frivolities.

No. 25 Parnell Square was a venue for céili dances, which 'later in the evening would give way to swinging girls and "foreign" music, all of which

---

201 O'Neill, WS 1,154, BMH, p. 3.
202 Ibid.
203 Ibid., p. 5.
204 Ibid., p. 3.
205 O'Donovan, p. 44.

infuriated Mícheál Ó Foghludha, master of ceremonies, who would try to stop the band.'[206] Even so, Bob O'Flanagan observed that the dancers, including Kevin, went to six o'clock Mass on their way home.

However, according to Andrews, 'there was relatively little activity by the IRA in Dublin until late in 1920, apart from the General Strike and a day of national mourning for Terence MacSwiney. Life in the city was normal except for the curfew which lasted from midnight until sometimes 5am. The citizens suffered little inconvenience in going about their business. The theatre and picture houses were open. Football matches were played … in Dalymount, Jones Road and Landsdowne Road and there was racing. I doubt if the horsey people were aware that there had been a 1916 Rebellion.'[207]

---

206 Ibid.
207 Andrews, p. 159.

Chapter Six

THE STORMY CAMPUS

Todd Andrews maintained that everyone in UCD knew of his IRA connections: 'I played cards with Cooney [who was also in the IRA] and saw a lot of him but we never mentioned our membership of the IRA. This attitude was indicative of the extreme secrecy which was the strength of the IRA and which distinguished it from all previous separatist movements in Ireland.'[208]

In 1919, Kevin Barry was awarded a Dublin Corporation scholarship to UCD. In 1917 and in 1918 he had got senior grade honours while he was at Belvedere. Nobody in the Barry family had become a doctor before, but his maternal aunt Margaret Dowling, known as 'Aunt Maggie', had a fierce determination to pursue a career in medicine. Although she did not become a doctor, she trained in St John's and Elizabeth's Hospital in London and went on to become the first matron of the Bon Secours Hospital in Cork.[209] (After Kevin's execution the British prohibited the printing of IRA memorial cards, but a few were printed in secret and Aunt Maggie Dowling kept hers with her to the end of her days.)

University life was highly politicised when Kevin entered it. As far as Todd Andrews was concerned, the Literary and Historical Society at UCD was run mainly by 'the sons of Castle Catholics and the detritus of the Irish Party, downright frivolous in character. It was a mere training ground for lawyers and careerists who were waiting for the coming of Home Rule, who regarded the IRA as gun bullies and even murderers.'[210]

Kevin's subjects at the faculty of medicine were botany with James Bayley Butler and zoology with Dr George Sigerson (1836–1925) (who

208 Andrews, p. 158.
209 Information from Dorothy Dowling, 2020.
210 Andrews, p. 133.

was already very old and 'could scarcely be heard'[211]), and he had Professor John A. McClelland for experimental physiology.

A new student at UCD described the dissecting room at Cecilia Street as a room 'lined with small slate-topped tables each bearing its load of gruesome flesh and having around it its particular coterie of interested searchers. Bright green paint on the walls, socialist red paint on the chairs and stools, furnish a certain amount of noble splendour to this apartment of science.'[212]

Jim O'Donovan, my grandfather, had graduated from UCD with a chemistry degree not long before Kevin enrolled, and he was still doing postgraduate study there. In 1917 Jim had come into contact with committed Republicans and this set the course of his life. His professor of chemistry,

Kitby Barry with aunt Maggie, who became Sister Cecelia, matron in the Bons Secours Hospital in Cork. She may have influenced Kevin Barry to study medicine.

Hugh Ryan, became his mentor and master in a 'growing expertise as a chemist, specialising in the manufacture of explosives'.[213] My grandfather used to work late in the university laboratory at Earlsfort Terrace. He describes in his own witness account how he made 'poison gas, tear-gas and things like that. I took it that we were going to use these gases, and I did not think very much of the possibilities, but I learned from Dick Mulcahy ... that what we were really working on was to take safeguards against poison gas, the use of which, during the imminent imposition of conscription, was expected.'[214]

They also worked on helmets, goggles and masks that would absorb the poison gas. My grandfather seemed to have a penchant for botched experiments, and one of the first of these happened at this time when one

211 O'Donovan, p. 57.

212 Ibid.

213 David O'Donohue, *The Devil's Deal, The IRA, Nazi Germany and the Double Life of Jim O'Donovan*, Dublin: New Island Books, 2009, p. 7.

214 James L. O'Donovan, WS 1713, BMH, p. 8.

of his experiments 'blew up and I got all the gas on my face. I thought I was blinded but fortunately, after about 20 minutes I found I could open my eyes. I could thus lay claim to be the first poison gas casualty in Ireland if not the only one ever recorded.'[215] Professor Hugh Ryan (1873–1931) knew very well that my grandfather was working on these gases, but pretended he knew nothing about his work.

Thus, it would seem the professor was more than willing 'to look the other way when IRA work was going on in his chemistry department'.[216] There could have been great potential for my grandfather to be arrested but, due to the unstated collusion of his mentors and the laboratory assistants, he never was – at least, not in UCD at that time. The college authorities 'were none the wiser about the events … and the existence of a bomb maker in their midst'. [217] My grandfather went on to become 'a front line fighter and a key back room strategist, developing new types of explosive drives for use in the war of independence',[218] and this led to him becoming the Director of Chemicals for the IRA GHQ.

Jim O'Donovan and Kevin Barry would never meet each other, despite sharing the same *alma mater*, the same political convictions and the fact that Jim went on to marry Kevin's sister Monty, my grandmother. They had the same professor for chemistry, Hugh Ryan. Todd Andrews, who was very close friends with Jim, recalled how, at that time (1919) the first-year medicals, engineers and chemists took their chemistry lessons together in a large lecture theatre at Earlsfort Terrace. Kevin Barry and Andrews would have attended these lessons simultaneously, although they were not acquainted. An incident occurred when Professor Hugh Ryan was lecturing on ketones. The door of the lecture theatre was pushed open and a voice shouted 'Up National – Trinity are here!', at which the entire theatre of students ran out to witness a big mob of Trinity students singing 'Rule Britannica' and 'God Save the King', waving Union flags, celebrating the Armistice. Out came a mob from UCD shouting: 'Up

215 Ibid.
216 O'Donohue, p. 8.
217 Ibid., p. 9.
218 Ibid.

Dev!' and 'Up the Republic!' The Trinity students retreated along the Green and 'every messenger boy from around was armed with stones to fling at them'.[219]

Todd Andrews, Frank Flood and Kevin Barry were all at UCD at the same time. Andrews did not know Kevin so well 'because he was a rugby player and a Jesuit boy. I knew he was one of "us" although this fact in no way helped to foster our acquaintance ... there were a number of students who were known to be IRA men but unless they were in the same Battalion or Company, they never spoke or associated with one another.'[220]

If Gerry McAleer did not indeed know about Kevin's IRA activities, he also did not know how much Kevin drank. Gerry was not a drinker. 'They [Kevin and Charlie O'Neill, a close mutual friend] were great dancing people ... I never bothered my head going to dances but Kevin and Charlie, and one or two others had nights out in those "low down" dance halls. If they drank, it was damn little or nil.'[221] Charlie, who was also from Dungannon, shared digs with Gerry.

The Great War had killed a generation of young men, so when it came to Kevin enrolling at UCD on 13 October 1919 to study medicine, the university was bursting at the seams. As my father astutely observed, 'Those who had been too young to offer themselves as cannon fodder were clamouring for higher education.' The enrollment for First Year Medicine was 193, thirty-two of them women.

It was here that Kevin's dancing took off in the dance halls of Dublin. Dancing, drinking, betting and flirting were to become some of Kevin's favourite pastimes in his short university career. A UCD student, Honoria Aughney, met Kevin at a céili. They were dancing to 'The Siege of Ennis', a dance in which you change partners, and Kevin said, 'I didn't know the Carlow girls knew anything about dancing', to which Honoria answered, 'and I didn't know the rugby players knew anything about it either.'[222] In fact, she didn't even know that Kevin himself was from Carlow.

....

219 Andrews, p. 135.
220 Ibid., p. 158.
221 Gerry McAleer to my father, in 1988. O'Donovan, p. 50.
222 O'Donovan, p. 55.

Kevin also loved betting. I found his racing card from the Metropolitan Baldoyle Races for Saturday, 10 May 1919. It is full of scribbles on the back about major sea routes, including the Suez and Panama Canals, and distances by sea between America, England, New Zealand and Hong Kong. I wonder if this was preparation for a geography exam.[223]

The Curfew

Dancing hours were cut short by the curfew. Erskine Childers [224] wrote in the *London Daily News* at the time:

> Take a typical night in Dublin. As the citizens go to bed, the barracks spring to life. Lorries, tanks and armoured cars muster in fleets and when the midnight curfew order has emptied the streets – pitch dark streets – the weird cavalcade issue forth to the attack. Think of raiding a private house at dead of night in a tank (my own experience), whose weird rumble and roar can be heard miles away. A thunder of knocks: no time to dress (even for a woman alone). No warrant shown on entering, no apology on leaving if, as in nine cases out of ten, suspicions prove to be groundless and the raid a mistake.[225]

Robert Erskine Childers, a Wicklow Protestant from Annamoe, educated at Cambridge, wounded in the Boer War, turned away from the British Empire to support Home Rule.[226] He wrote popular spy stories (including *The Riddle of the Sands*, published in 1903). He also published *The Framework of Home Rule* in 1911, calling for the restoration of a parliament to Dublin. he would go on to strongly oppose the Anglo-Irish Treaty of 1921. When he was executed on 24 November 1922, at the Beggars Bush Barracks in Dublin, he shook hands with

223 http://digital.ucd.ie/view-media/ucdlib:39121/canvas/ucdlib:39607
224 Childers, who was born in England and brought up in County Wicklow, had done some gun-running with his yacht the Asgard for the Volunteers in 1914. He was executed in 1922 by the anti-Treaty side.
225 Taken from a letter in Triona Maher's private estate by Donal O'Donovan.
226 O'Donovan, p. 55.

the firing squad before he was shot.[227] His final words, spoken to the firing squad, were: 'Take a step or two forward, lads, it will be easier that way.' He was buried in the Beggars Bush Barracks, but in 1923 his remains were exhumed and reburied in the republican plot at Glasnevin Cemetery. As a child, my father used to make me carry the wreath for his commemoration. I remember the gloomy graveyard in November, and my father at his graveside speaking piously about another dead hero of his.

Curfew, of course, put the Volunteers at a great disadvantage. The Crown forces were the only ones allowed on the streets between midnight and 5am. Prendergast noted that it 'lessened the time at our disposal for carrying out night ambushes. We had but a bare hour and a half at night. It must be said of most of the men who were giving service while on duty they took their work seriously and were obedient to all orders. Off duty, many of them sociable, gay and full of life.'[228]

Volunteers' entertainment

Prendergast gives us one of the clearest pictures of Dublin's social life in 1919/20. He takes a measured, sober account of his view of the drinking habits of the Dublin Brigade, stating that they mostly abstained from intoxicating drinks, admitting, however, that 'Some there were who loved their drink ... Cases were uncommon of men who did and would get top heavy at times, but few people could admit that any of our men were drunk or resorted to drink when on duty.'[229]

While the men may not have drunk heavily on duty, Kevin's letters reveal somebody who thoroughly enjoyed drinking. He observed 'the bright congenial atmosphere of the ceilidhe hall or dance halls, in some cases dark, smoke infested billiard saloons and the dark confines of the picture houses that were "aids" to keep up the spirits.'[230]

....

227   Jim Ring, 'Childers (Robert), Erskine (1870–1922)', Oxford Dictionary of National Biography. Oxford: Oxford University Press, 2004.
228   Prendergast, WS 755, BMH, p. 473.
229   Ibid.
230   Ibid., p. 474.

Despite the fact that such places carried the risk of 'prying eyes' and raids by the British forces, Volunteers like Kevin went along and did it anyway. The Savoy Billiard Rooms beside the Gresham Hotel, Wilson's Billiard Rooms, the Tobacconists on North Frederick Street and the infamous Mattassa Coffee and Ice Cream Saloon in Marlborough Street, where Prendergast observed the men having a 'cup of coffee or bovril or a mineral or a portion of ice cream … to steal a few peaceful moments in company.'

The Grafton Picture House was a favourite of Kevin and Kitby Barry's. In Dublin, the theatres had full houses – the Gaiety, The Queens, the Tivoli, the Theatre Royal, the Empire, La Scala and the Abbey where the likes of *The Colleen Bawn* and *The Bohemian Girl* were performed by The Gilbert and Sullivan Company.

The Mattassa Coffee House had a large IRA clientele, according to Prendergast. Frank Flood, Kevin's close friend in the H Company and a fellow member of the clandestine Clarke Luby Club, had been in the Mattassa Coffee House with friends the night before an ambush he and his company carried out in 1921, which led to his execution. After the raid on the King's Inns on 1 June 1920, Kevin took the Lewis gun over to his place in Fleet Street and then 'adjourned to our usual spot in Matassa's, Marlboro street for coffee, etc.'[231]

Prendergast wrote nostalgically about these haunts:

> If the walls of that place could only speak, what stories would be unfolded, what pictures would be painted, history would be made; in such moments we were not conspirators or conspiring. Tommy McGrane, Frank Carberry, Dinny Holmes, Sean Nathan, Paddy Kirk, Tom O'Brien, oh the names were legion. Sad and pleasant memories.[232]

Todd Andrews and his crew lunched in Roberts Cafe on Grafton Street: 'two rolls, a butter and a bun or baked beans on toast. Roberts became a sort of club for us and we got to know the waitresses very well.'[233]

---

231 Sean O'Neill, WS 1,514, BMH, p. 6.
232 Prendergast, WS 755, p. 475.
233 Andrews, p. 138.

Even with the curfew imposed in February 1920, Dublin still spilled over with life. 'Meet at the Grafton Picture House', read an advertisement on the street. Kevin frequently met friends there. In a letter to his friend Bapty Maher (who later married Kevin's sister Shel Barry), at Christmas 1919, he wrote from the family home in Tombeagh, Co Carlow:

> A Chara dhil,
>
> I wrote you a letter about a month ago and I don't know if you ever got it as I'm not sure if I put the right address on it. Anyway how are you since I saw you last? You might write to a fellow you know, now and then, and say how things are. Now answer this soon and answer it to 'my town house' as I'm nearly fed up here … yours to a cinder, Kev.[234]

Three weeks later, he still had no answer from Bapty, by which time he was back up in Dublin at 8 Fleet Street.

> How the devil are you at all? You know you might write to a fellow once in a while. I wouldn't mind me not writing because I'm very busy, pictures, National Library (ahem) and Grafton (5–6pm), but a fellow like you – a bloody gentleman of leisure, you know it's unforgivable.
> By the way that bloody bastard never came with the suit with the result that I have to borrow one for a dance tomorrow night. Write and tell him that I say he's a ——so and so etc.
> When will you be up in town? You ought to come for a ceilidhe (College of Science) on the 30th Jan … Yours 'til hell freezes, Kevin.[235]

Again, nobody would know from letters like these that Kevin was, by this time, up to his neck in the war against the British. Nobody knew that by November that very year he would have become one of the most

---

234 By kind permission of the Kevin Barry Estate.
235 Ibid.

iconic martyrs of the Irish independence movement, and that his signature 'Yours 'til hell freezes' would become part of his mythology.

Another letter to Bapty around that time reveals how he went to the Commerce dance on Wednesday night and hardly got a wink of sleep since. Miss Brown and Miss Flood had visited Fleet Street separately and 'the missus' went to see Mrs Doyle of Westpark House. He tells Bapty to 'mend the Darracq'. Bapty was a brilliant mechanic, and could drive without using the clutch in the days before synchromesh gearboxes. His motoring skills were greatly appreciated by the Barrys in Tombeagh – he lived in Athy, County Kildare, and would often take a motor car over to the Barrys. Kitby was known to have rescued Kevin with Bapty's car from drunken sprees in Glendalough, when the bicycle just wouldn't do it.

The picture we get of Kevin is not one of a dour, sober Volunteer. There is no hint of his single-mindedness. Like every other student, he was determined to enjoy himself. And he liked girls. He didn't just dream about them, as he seemed to do in his Belvedere exercise book, when he wrote about a cousin he played cards with. In this letter he wrote to Bapty Maher, he told him that he 'never cursed as much in my life as coming up with dear Mrs Bannerman. A peach of a tart got into the carriage and was swinging the glad on me the whole time and I had to look virtuous while my face was blue with supported curses. Excuse scrawl, K.G.B.'[236]

But all the fun took its toll. He failed his medical exams at the end of the academic year of 1919-/1920. The board failed seventy-three candidates in mid-June 1920. Honoria Aughney, who had danced with Kevin at the céilí, passed. Gerry McAleer failed. Kevin's military and social lives had begun to eclipse his academic life. It is not surprising, since he was in the vanguard of the King's Inns Raid on 1 June 1920 – the first major raid he had taken part in, for which he received an unwritten commendation from his superiors.

---

236 Letter from Kevin Barry to Bapty Maher, 1919. By kind permission of the Kevin Barry estate.

The King's Inns Raid, 1 June 1920

Sean O'Neill, Lieutenant of the H Company, liked to attend céilís, like many of the young 'We came to be known as eye-wipers, Kevin included.'[237] Around 1919, the company got their first Lewis gun in a raid 'for 34 pounds out of Ship Street barracks. The money to purchase the gun was subscribed by Phil Shanahan, J.J. Walsh and the company officers.' On a Sunday evening, Kevin carried it, wrapped in newspapers, to Davy Golden's home on the South Circular Road, where his uncle Pat lived. This was around the same time that Kevin was accepted into the Clarke Luby Club of the IRB, the youngest ever member.

Kevin was to be involved in a raid on the King's Inns, on the heels of his medical exams in the early summer of 1920. He missed an exam because of it. The King's Inns was at the very heart of the British military enterprise, an outpost of the garrison in the North Dublin Union. After its smooth accomplishment Kevin earned the first ring in his military halo. He was no longer the Belvedere boy of the H Company of the 1st Battalion of the Dublin Brigade, wearing the cap they all laughed at. He was a young soldier with experience in military planning, raids and ambushes. He was the one who wore the uniform, the one I had seen in a photograph that passed through my childhood – Kevin wearing his Volunteer uniform, with his leg up on a chair, his arm resting on his thigh with a revolver in his hand. He is wearing a hat with a band and a brim, and he looks as proud as punch. To me, he was my uncle-hero.

Dublin, and the whole of Ireland, had been sliding out of British control since the winter of 1919/20, according to Prendergast.[238] The war was no longer one in which pockets of IRA men attacked RIC men. It was now a war waged against British troops utilising an increasingly sharp intelligence system masterminded by Michael Collins from GHQ. But nobody wanted a battle at the King's Inns. 'Our GHQ had learnt through the Intelligence Department that although the Inns

237 Sean O'Neill, WS 1,154, BMH, p.3.
238 Prendergast, WS 755, BMH, p. 230.

were well guarded, militarily discipline was not so strict as it was in other outposts.'[239]

It was the fact that it was not so well guarded that gave the masterminds of the plan the possibility 'to get a good knowledge of the position from the outside, while the plans of the inside of the building were obtained, and studied by Dick McKee, our Brigadier, and Peadar Clancy, our Vice-Brigadier.'[240] Nobody was to be harmed in the raid.

My father noted that when 'Brigadier Dick McKee and Vice-Brigadier Peadar Clancy had studied the drawings of the interior, a plan was made allowing seven minutes for the whole operation.'[241] That all depended on good weather, and on good men to get the arms. There was a green in front where soldiers would sit with their girlfriends. Civilians, if careful, could mingle with them and, in that way, they could get close to the guardroom. However, if it rained, that was not going to be possible as the soldiers would be in the guardroom, which was where the arms were kept.

As for the men who were to perform the raid, they were 'picked from "H" Company to go on it, including the O/C., S. Kavanagh. It was their job to get the arms.'[242]

Kevin Barry was with his friend Frank Flood on this raid. The sun shone on 1 June and the chosen men from the 1st, 2nd and 3rd battalions, under the command of Peadar Clancy, left 46 Parnell Square in staggered little groups.

Joe Dolan approached the sentry guard at the door that led in from Henrietta Street, distracted him with a question and rapidly disarmed and imprisoned him. 'Not a simple thing to do, for the solider was a "distinguished Service" man who had served at the front.'[243] A party under Section Commander Fitzpatrick strolled on to the green and pretended to play cards. The soldiers on the Temple Green were quickly taken prisoner to stop them going to assist the sentry. They were marched into

239 Denis Holmes, *Dublin's Fighting Story 1913–21, Told by the Men who Made it.* Tralee: The Kerryman, 1948, p. 131.
240 Ibid, pp. 131–2.
241 O'Donovan, p. 59.
242 Sean O'Neill, WS 1,154, BMH, pp. 5–7.
243 Holmes, p. 133.

the building. The girls they were talking to were placed under an armed guard outside.[244]

Dolan went in and disconnected the telephone lines. Denis Holmes and his party entered at the front and another section made their way to the back to carry out the raid on the guardroom at the left of the building. In Holmes's words, Kevin Barry, 'a mere youngster compared to most of us, showed the courage and daring of a born soldier. Barry had never been on an important operation before this raid. I had drilled Kevin when he joined the C Company of the 1st Battalion in 1918. All of us older volunteers loved the boy, for he was gay and enthusiastic, and yet very serious in his devotion to the cause and in his rigid attention to orders.'[245]

Kevin Barry, again according to Denis Holmes, came out of the guardroom with a Lewis gun in his arms. 'His boyish face was wreathed in smiles, as he said to me: "Look Dinny, what I have got." I could not help laughing even in that moment and thinking that he looked like a child clasping a new toy in his breast.'[246]

Meanwhile, Sean Prendergast of the 1st Battalion was ready with his men on Henrietta Street. Paddy Kirk had another party of men form a cordon across the street. Holmes proudly declared that 'it was Kevin Barry who, in a moment of doubt, stepped forward and led the section into the building. Had it not been for his action in steadying one of the officers and leading the rush, the work of all the other men might have gone for nothing.'[247]

Sean O'Neill, who was also in that section, saw that Kevin had carried out the Lewis gun, noting that this was his second time to get one. 'He also got the Corporal's uniform, which was afterwards dyed green.'[248]

After the raid, the car, commandeered from the rear of the British Army and Navy Canteen Board Stores in Aungier Street and driven by a D. Golden of the H Company, took the rifles to the GHQ, which was off

244 Ibid.
245 Ibid.
246 Ibid., p. 134.
247 Ibid.
248 Sean O'Neill, WS 1,154, BMH, p. 5.

North Great Charles Street and Rutland Street.[249] The only hiccup was the tin hat that fell out of the cab while they made their escape. That was the reason for the rapid infestation by the British military on the north side of the city, searching for the arms dump.

There had been only four on the raid: Kevin, Frank Flood, Paddy Kenny and Sean O'Neill. According to O'Neill, they got a Volunteer in the H Company, Sean Flood, known as 'Brasser', 'to yoke up his cab. He drove to 609, N.C. Rd. with the four of us in the cab. We used this cabman on several occasions such as this and had christened him "Skin the Goat".'[250]

The raid yielded twenty-five rifles, two Lewis guns, a large quantity of ammunition and other military equipment. The whole operation had taken just five or six minutes. The next night the rifles taken in the raid were brought to 44 Parnell Square and divided among the units in the 1st Battalion that had been on the raid. Kevin and Frank picked their own rifles. O'Neill remembered that Kevin marked his with two marks and Frank with three. 'Frank took the bayonet with the curl on the boss. I got the Corporal's ground sheet and still have it. We took Kevin's rifle over to his place in Fleet St. and then adjourned to our usual spot, Matassa's, Marlboro St., for coffee etc.'[251]

The excitement at Mattassa's Coffee and Ice Cream House was palpable. It is hard to forget Holmes's description of Kevin grinning ear to ear in the guardroom, carrying out the Lewis gun, saying to Holmes, 'Look Dinny, look what I have got' … like a child clasping a new toy to his breast.' The image endures because it captures Kevin's boyishness, the excitement he had about being on a real raid. The youthfulness of the soldiers is again striking. Prendergast watched them slide into their military activities with ease, as Kevin did, despite the fact that 'they had little knowledgeable military training, certainly not anything like the training of those arrayed against them. One of their big advantages in their favour was that they were disciplined and orderly to an uncommon degree, they

249 Ibid., p. 6.
250 O'Neill, WS 1,154, BMH, p. 6.
251 Ibid.

were game and eager to fight and they would go to any length to prove their loyalty to our cause.'[252]

The King's Inns raid gave the Volunteers a huge boost. O'Neill said that having found the raid 'turned out to be so easy, we started to look out for a similar job for ourselves. M. Douglas, "G" Company, told us about a lorry of British troops who came every Tuesday and Thursday morning between 8 and 9 am to Monks Bakery, Upr. Church St.'[253]

He was referring to the next raid, the one that would define Kevin Barry's short career, which would involve more men and far more meticulous planning. O'Neill and the Company decided that this would be a 'pudding', and decided to do the job. It would not be for another four months, in September 1920, and it would be the raid that would change everything for Kevin Barry.

....

252 Prendergast, WS 755, BMH, p. 333.
253 O'Neill, WS 1,154, BMH, p.6.

Chapter Seven

THE CARLOW BRIGADE

Back to Tombeagh

The King's Inns ambush was the making of Kevin Barry. His courage outshone that beaming grin and his Belvedere cap, a badge that had him cast in the wrong light as a lily-livered middle-class boy when he first joined the Volunteers. Kevin was growing up. That summer he would lounge about on the sofa in the Glendalough Hotel with girls, getting 'rotto', then falling off his bike on the way home to Tombeagh.

After the King's Inns raid, Kevin went back to Tombeagh for the summer holidays as he always did, to help out his brother Mick on the farm. Mick was quieter than Kevin, and most of his time was devoted to the farm, but he was also, at this time, Battalion OC with the Company in Carlow. 'Shel [Barry, Kevin's sister] was in the local branch of the Cumann na mBan. There were always transactions with the Carlow Brigade, procuring and carrying arms and messages from Dublin to our home.'[254]

Life was very different at Tombeagh. There was no motor car, apart from when Bapty Maher would lend them his. 'Bapty had been a great friend of Kevin and Mick's, played rugby into his 40s. He was larger than life, a wild man.'[255] Bapty Maher would later devote his time and energy to his infamous public house and undertaking business in Athy, County Kildare. Known as 'Bapty's', this pub's clientele 'only entered the premises after 11pm, and drinking would go on all night'.[256]

Pat O'Gorman was Kevin's close friend in Hacketstown and his family had a car service there. Later, it was in one of the O'Gorman's

---

254 KBM, WS 731, BMH.
255 Interview with Michael O'Rahilly, 2019.
256 Information from John Maher, grandson of Shel Barry and Bapty Maher, August 2019.

cars that Eamon De Valera would be driven from the Barry home at Tombeagh, which he frequently used as a safe house during the War of Independence. 'There was a secret attic room at Tombeagh, which De Valera was too tall to fit into. He was given a different room at the back of the house, and always left instructions to the girls to have his boots polished, and left outside the door in the morning.'[257] De Valera would take a stroll up the lane in the evenings, at dusk, dressed as a woman. The lane to the Dowling household at Drumguin, where Mrs Barry had come from, was a mile long. De Valera took his stroll with her brother, Michael Dowling.[258] Tom Molloy, another friend of the Barrys, was the guard on the drive who hid in the ditch. He was arrested at one time and taken to Baltinglass where he was interrogated, and then released. Not being the most secretive person, many in the company were concerned about what he would reveal. Kevin Barry junior recalled Tom Molloy frequently 'coming out of the ditch covered in muck' when the coast was clear. There is a photograph of Tom Molloy with Kevin and Michael Barry taken that summer of 1920, sitting on top of Lugnaquilla in County Wicklow, the sun shining and the clouds spinning across the sky over them.

There was no electricity at Tombeagh and it would be a long time until Michael Barry would have the place electrified under the rural electrification scheme. Dr Michael O'Rahilly remembered Michael Barry as 'a very quiet man. He had no chip on his shoulder. He took life as it came. As regards rural electrification – it was a long time before Mick got the house wired as he'd no money.'[259]

Michael Barry is remembered by Tom Kehoe cutting turf on Kehoe's bog in Rathmore, in Knockananna, County Wicklow.

'He was tall with a hat, and used to cut the turf with Fie Dowling, who was a distant cousin of his. He'd bring the turf back to Tombeagh on a horse and cart. Michael Barry was fond of my father, Simon Kehoe. They'd meet up at fairs in Hacketstown.'[260]

....

257 Interview with Michael Moriarty, grandson of Michael Dowling, 2020.
258 Ibid.
259 Interview with Michael O'Rahilly, 2019.
260 Interview with Tom Kehoe in Knockananna, July 2019.

Kevin Barry junior speaks of his father Michael Barry as being 'much more reserved [than Kevin]. He had much more responsibility as the older son, holding the fort here at Tombeagh. Shel was here as well of course.'[261] Shel would run the farm almost singlehandedly when Michael Barry was imprisoned in Lincoln prison for a year from December 1920.

Nana Dowling

When Kevin came home from Dublin to Tombeagh, Nana Dowling was part of the household, as she had been since 1908, when Kevin's father Tom Barry died, just a year after the death of her husband, James Dowling. Before she married, she was Ellen McCardle from Drumguin, the neighbouring townland to Tombeagh, just up the lane. She had a cackle of sisters, Mary, Ann and Catherine, the daughters of Patrick McCardle, a strong farmer who died in 1882. Kevin was around his grandmother at Tombeagh through the very formative years of six to twelve, when it was decided that he should attend the O'Connell Schools in Dublin. After this time he came to Tombeagh during school holidays. When he was at Belvedere, secretly flinging off his cap to embrace life as a Volunteer, Nana Dowling was still living in a little room upstairs at Tombeagh. As a child, I was fascinated by the tales I was told about Nana Dowling. My aunt, Sheila Hannah (née O'Donovan), said that 'she had the second sight. She could see funerals before they happened.'[262] Nana Dowling was a formidable woman who may have had a tendency to see things that may not have been there – which, of course, might indicate that she had dementia in later life. By the summer of 1920, Nana Dowling was no longer at Tombeagh. She had passed away that March.

Kevin in the C Company, Carlow Brigade

After King's Inns, Kevin was probably brimming with confidence. What he got up to that summer in Carlow would certainly suggest that. He was as keen to be involved in raids and drills around Carlow as he was to be jumping on his bicycle for drinking expeditions in Glendalough and Aughrim.

261 Interview with Kevin Barry junior at Tombeagh, 2018.
262 Interview with Sheila Hannah by DOD, 1996.

During that summer of 1920 he was attached to the C Company of the 3rd Battalion in the Carlow Brigade, under Matt Cullen, chairman of Baltinglass no. 2 Rural District Council, who farmed at Kilcarney.

My grandfather interviewed Matt Cullen in 1952. He was determined, at this time in his life, to write a book about Kevin Barry, and he dedicated a number of years to it. The book was never published, and the manuscript has disappeared, but my father drew extensively from Jim's research and interviews for his own book about Kevin Barry. Matt Cullen told my grandfather that in the summer of 1920, Kevin was 'involved in raids to get arms from loyalists' homes in the area, cutting telephone lines to the police and army barracks, and intercepting the mail, tracking how much the police knew about the Carlow Brigade. When the C Company failed to capture the barracks in Hacketstown Matt Cullen and Dan McDonnell consulted the 'Twelve Apostles' (Michael Collins's assassination squad), who were happy that the barracks be captured. However, the Company were told they had to foot the bill. They came up with an elaborate plan to fundraise through a travelling theatre company. One night would be dedicated to raising funds for the Volunteers.'[263]

Although the actors were very willing, the audience had no idea that this was a front for funding an attack on a barracks by the local IRA men. We don't know what play or which acts were performed, despite the show being well advertised. Matt Cullen continued:

> We appointed Kevin Barry to get up on the stage. He made a very appropriate speech on our behalf and his own, thanking the show people for their kindness in giving us the night. And for their performance, and thanking the people for attending in such numbers.[264]

It is not surprising they got Kevin up on the stage, since he was so charismatic and full of mischief. He was in full swing that summer. Apart from helping his brother Mick on the farm at Tombeagh, he was having a whale of a time. There was no sense that that summer in

263 Interview with Matt Cullen by Jim O'Donovan, quoted in O'Donovan, p. 53.
264 Ibid.

Tombeagh was a sombre one, dictated by the raids, drills and police tracking he and the C Company were conducting. It was a summer of jaunts and expeditions across Carlow and Wicklow. Kevin and Pat O'Gorman were often out in Glendalough and Glenmalure, over the mountains and back through Rathdrum to stop for a drink at the Woodenbridge Hotel (where Eamon De Valera spent his honeymoon in 1910). Pat O'Gorman told my father how he and Kevin were drinking at Woodenbridge when Michael Barry came along and suggested they take the train from Woodenbridge. Pat asked the train driver Jim Haynes when he was going.

'Ah,' he said, 'I'm supposed to go now when this Dublin train passes, but you don't mind that. I see you're having a drink. Go up and finish your drink. I'll hold on.' So we put the bikes in the guard's van and were carried back to Tinahely. We didn't pay either ... '.[265]

Pat and Kevin also drank at Richardson's Hotel by Glendalough Lake, preferring it to the Royal Hotel, which was full of Dubliners. These day-jaunts became longer than a day. Kevin refers to a friend from Coolmana near Tombeagh who was ostensibly a week late for his dinner. Kevin's letter to Bapty Maher shows just how much fun they all had that summer:

> It was a bloody pity you didn't come yesterday. We had a good day [so good] that my ruddy head is singing like a top and my eyes are all bloodshot. I got rid of Mike and spent the day with Gorman, but I'll never touch a drop again as long as I live. We stopped in Tinahely, Aughrim, Woodenbridge, Avoca, Rathdrum and Laragh going and ditto coming back. I wasn't in the Bed or anywhere else. I was laying on the sofa in Royal Hotel [Glendalough] with a Belgian girl drinking. We held up the car for 1½ hours while they were looking for us and we made them stop in Rathdrum one hour, Woodenbridge ½ hour and Aughrim 1½ hours so it was 1.30 before we got to Hacketstown. We had to lift Gorman out of the car and carry him home. He was absolutely rotting. I fell off

---

265 Interview with Pat Gorman by Donal O'Donovan, 1988.

the bike twice on the way home and I was up all night drinking water. Damn booze anyway.

Yours till I'm qualified K.G.B.[266]

He goes on to mention Peg Scully, who told him that he made a speech about Medicals and Gorman made one about Clerical Students. He said he was 'f———-d' if he remembered. Regarding the same drinking expedition, he wrote to his school friend Leo Doyle.[267] In this letter, he apologises for not greeting him in Hacketstown with Fr Dunne, 'but as I was drilling a company of rebels I didn't like to speak to you as Fr Matt might not be pleased.'[268] Fr Matthew Dunne was a friend of the Doyles and the Barrys – the problem was that he was a Chaplain in the British Army. This letter is also full of drinking bravado, and had another reference to Pat O'Gorman having to be lifted out of the car. 'I also met two university girls, but there was a dud crowd down from Dublin.' Kevin states that he will be up in Dublin 'in about a week and I'll see you some evening outside the old College … ',[269] so the letter would have been written in late August 1920. At the end of this letter, he describes the political situation around Carlow.

'There's hell around here. 30 houses raided, 2 men arrested, 1 wounded and about 40 men "sleeping out". There are 6 men arrested in Baltinglass and 30 more lorries have arrived from the Union from the Curragh [in Kildare, a military base].'[270]

He signs off again with, 'Yours till I'm qualified (*ad saecula saeculorum*), Kevin.'[271] He would have been preparing (or not) for the resits of his medical examinations at UCD, which he had failed in May.

266 Letter in possession of Triona Maher in 1989, O'Donovan, p. 63.
267 Letter in possession of Mrs Cecil Van Cauwelaert, who was a sister of Leo Doyle, as referenced by O'Donovan, p. 64.
268 Ibid.
269 Ibid.
270 Ibid.
271 Ibid.

Pádraig Ó Catháin, Adjutant of the Carlow Brigade, described Carlow in 1920 as 'a difficult year'.[272] Raids and arrests and sentences depleted company, battalion and brigade staffs. 'The house of a Volunteer was burned at Clonmore, ... two shops that Volunteers worked in were burned in Tullow following an ambush in which two police were killed, and two Volunteers were killed at Barrowhouse in a badly sited ambush. A clinician alleged to be consorting with the Tans was shot dead in Borris and a Tan was badly wounded outside the Barracks.'[273]

As if this wasn't enough, some of the Carlow Volunteers conscientiously objected to some military orders so that the Volunteers lost their Intelligence Officer (Conkling), the Quartermaster (P. O'Toole) and the Adjutant. But it was intelligence work that was emphasised then, with the aim of capturing documents. 'The police went from plain capers to figures in an effort to evade us, but they determined 'exact times and areas of the night Lancia car patrols which they sent out.'[274] Raids and ambushes were continually plotted and carried out due to the need to acquire ammunition, of which there was a shortage and so, overall, there were no large-scale military attacks in Carlow in 1920. It would change in 1921 when the Volunteer forces were more organised and attacks were made at Bagenalstown Barracks and on concentrations of Black and Tans in Carlow, Tullow and Borris, but only when they could determine the points at which the British presence was most vulnerable.

My grandfather noted in his witness statement that at this time the authorities knew that chemicals were being made into explosives and so they tightened up on all the raw materials. 'We had to have recourse to gelignite and things used in quarries, and then replace the small sources of chemicals and try to work up something on a big scale in the way of importing.' He met Peadar Clancy and Dick McKee in the summer of 1920 to discuss how to proceed.[275]

....

272 Pádraig Ó Catháin, Adjutant of the Carlow Brigade, WS 1,572 BMH, pp. 8–10.
273 Ibid.
274 Ibid.
275 James O'Donovan, WS 1713, BMH, p. 8.

The Active Service Unit

In any case, a plan was brewed that summer to capture a barracks in Hacketstown. That plan failed, however. The two active service unit agents positioned in Knockananna in Wicklow (where they were from), the half-brothers Mick McDonnell and Tom Kehoe, were part of Michael Collins's assassination team, known as 'The Squad', and later as 'The Twelve Apostles'.[276] In 1917 Tom Kehoe had set up an ordnance factory under cover of a bicycle shop in Aungier Street. With a lathe and hand drill he manufactured weapons and hand grenades and later made a foundry at Parnell Street in Dublin where grenades were cast, including the 'number 9' and the GHQ grenade.[277] It is not impossible to imagine that he would have worked with my grandfather.

Tom Kehoe, known as 'Long Tom', was, as well as being an assassin and a munitions manufacturer, an accomplished pianist. 'He played his Percy French numbers on the piano while whooping it up with [the British] in the lounge of the Liverpool Hotel.'[278]

By 1919 Michael Collins had tightened intelligence operations with his staff. The Intelligence Department was by this time highly organised. 'Former and serving British soldiers of RIC men, tradesmen, ladies and maids, taxi men, business men, postmen, British agents and others provided vital information upon which the IRA intelligence department depended to build its massive data-base.'[279] This forced the British to draft in agents from England, the Middle East and Russia, the Cairo Gang, so-called because of their intelligence work in the Middle East and because they met at the fashionable Cairo Café on Grafton Street in Dublin. This brainchild of Sir Henry Wilson was drafted in to eliminate Dáil Éireann, the IRA and its intelligence networks. 'Organised on continental lines,

---

276 James Slattery, WS 445, BMH, referred in his witness account to the formation of 'The Squad' p. 2.

277 *Cnoc an Eanagh, The Hill of the Marsh, Stories of Knockananna from Yesteryear*, Government of Ireland, 2006. Chapters on the Military: Tom Kehoe and Mick McDonnell, by Shay Courtney, p. 103.

278 Ibid., 104.

279 Ibid., p. 105.

with separate HQ and sub-HQs, they [the Cairo Gang] secretly entered the city, singly, in pairs, or with their wives as cover, living in guest houses, hotels, flats and boarding houses in the city.'[280]

Both McDonnell and Kehoe were involved in the failed ambush on Lord French in Ashtown which was investigated by Resident Magistrate Alan Bell. Twelve attempts had been made on French's life, all planned by the Dublin GHQ in attempts to oust the head of the British military administration in Ireland. This attempt, involving McDonnell and Kehoe, took place on 19 December 1919, and also involved Dan Breen, who had started the War of Independence when he killed an RIC officer at Soloheadbeg. In March 1920 Tom Kehoe attacked Bell as he descended from a tram and dragged him to the footpath, where Mick McDonnell executed him on the spot.[281] Kehoe himself met a violent death 'within two years in the Black and Tan struggle and in the Civil War'.[282]

The Attempted Burning of Aghavannagh Barracks, July 1920

In July 1920, Kevin and Michael Barry, along with Matt Cullen in the C Company, were instructed by GHQ, through Mick McDonnell and Tom Kehoe, to burn down Aghavannagh Barracks, a military barracks built in 1804, which was to be occupied by British troops. It had been used as a hunting lodge by Charles Stewart Parnell and later became John Redmond's home. In the summer of 1920 it was occupied by William Redmond, MP for Waterford, his sister Johanna, and her husband Max Greene.

Fourteen members of the C Company in Carlow cycled to Aghavannagh, including Mick McDonnell and Tom Kehoe of the ASU, Michael and Kevin Barry and Matt Cullen. The description of the attempted raid was given to my grandfather by Matt Cullen in 1952 and this account was corroborated by his grandsons Brendan and Matt, who still live near Tombeagh. Cullen spoke to his grandsons at length about the incident at

---

280 Courtney, ibid., p. 105.
281 Ibid., p. 104.
282 Holmes, *Dublin's Fighting Story, 1916–21*, 2009 edition, Introduction by Diarmuid Ferriter, Cork: Mercier Press, pp. 246–47.

Aghavannagh. Alice, his daughter-in-law, described Cullen as 'a quiet man who later became a District Court Clerk and a commissioner for oaths, and would do anything to help anyone. He told me the story of the raid of Aghavannagh many times and, when he recalled Kevin, and he'd had a drink or two, he would cry. He married Julia Donoghue in November 1920, and was imprisoned in Mountjoy not long after that for a year.'[283]

The sergeant in charge of the barracks at Knockananna was sympathetic to the IRA, according to Courtney. This is Matt Cullen's direct account as it was told to my grandfather in 1952:

> When we arrived there every place was barred but in the back there was a door with a small pane of glass in it; it was broken and Kevin Barry got in through it, head first. Inside he found Captain Redmond [William Redmond, son of John Redmond] with a large club raised to strike him, but the sight of Kevin's automatic vanished the pluck of the Captain. As soon as he got his speech he enquired our business.[284]

Mick McDonnell told him their intention was to burn down the barracks. William Redmond apparently lost his speech again and a 'female came on the scene giving out plenty of abuse at the thought of the dirty Irish attempting to interfere with the residence of the late leader of the Irish people'.[285]

This female was, according to Con Foley of Knockananna, the housekeeper of Aghavannagh, who had a lot of sway. In his account, told to him by his father Patrick Foley, a Sinn Féin judge during the War of Independence:

> It was a wild, wet night in July 1920. Matt Cullen, Kevin and Michael Barry and the others came to barracks at Aghavannagh on a fleet of bicycles. Kevin was the leader, he broke in through a back

283 Interview with Alice Cullen, Síofra O'Donovan, 3 July 2019.
284 O'Donovan, p. 67.
285 Matt Cullen to Jim O'Donovan, 1952.

window and was confronted by the housekeeper forcibly when Kevin told her they were going to burn down the barracks. She gave him powerful verbal opposition and she was an able dealer. I don't know her name but she was well able to hold her corner. The lads stopped and thought about what they were about to do. And whatever she said to them, they agreed not to do it.[286]

Redmond had asked Kevin and the rest of the Company to review the house and its valuable furniture and paintings. He claimed not to know that the British troops were going to garrison there, and assured them as an MP that he would have serious discussions with those responsible if such a thing were attempted. But according to Con Foley, it was the housekeeper who made the strongest case against the burning of the barracks.

It is possible that this housekeeper implored Kevin and the other men of the C Company not to burn the house down because it was a building that Parnell had lived in, and he often hoisted the green flag with the harp, the symbol of Irish freedom from 1798, from the roof. Parnell's grandfather had acquired the property after the British War Office left in 1825. He had been the ground landlord. When he used to come to stay at Aghavannagh to do some hunting, he would be greeted along the road as he approached the building, by fires in the field and candles lit in the windows of the houses. As the instigator of land reform in Ireland, he may have been the very excuse that the housekeeper at Aghavannagh used to push Kevin and the C Company boys back out the window through which they came.

Kevin, Matt and Michael discussed the situation among themselves, and decided not to burn the house down, but told Redmond that they would hold him responsible if the barracks came to be occupied by the British troops. They threatened to have him shot if it did. Aghavannagh was occupied by the Auxiliaries a year later, but Redmond was not shot.

....

286 Interview with Con Foley at his home in Knockananna, County Wicklow, July 2019.

After Aghavannagh Barracks had passed out of the hands of the Redmonds it became an An Óige youth hostel until 1998. It was run by the Cullen family during the 1960s and it is now in the hands of the McCardle family, who occupy it as a family home and run a bed and breakfast. It is an austere but somehow elegant building with beautiful rose bushes in the front garden. The children of the present occupants play in and around it, gently distracting from the heavy history of this building and the valley, which has barracks dotted all along the Military Road, built at the time Michael Dwyer was hiding in the mountains, spearheading his guerrilla campaign. It is hard now to imagine that wild night in July 1920 when Kevin Barry and his company cycled up the drive to burn the building to the ground. Thanks to the Company's willingness to compromise with the formidable housekeeper, the barracks still stands.

On the way home under the moonlight at Ballygobbin, the boys in the Company rested, looking at the mountains and the moon. Kevin said, with typical breezy magnanimity: 'God, wouldn't this make you proud to die for Ireland.'[287]

Tom Kehoe, today

There is a signpost in Knockananna for the 'Birthplace of Mick McDonnell and Tom Kehoe'. Following the direction of the sign down the country road, there is no further indication of where the birthplace is. I flagged down a pick-up truck at the end of the lane and the driver told me emphatically that the half-brother of Tom Kehoe, also called Tom Kehoe, lived in the house with the black gates. I followed his directions and met this Tom Kehoe, who tentatively greeted me across the yard, behind the black gates. Once I showed him a copy of my father's book, and explained why I was there, the black gates swung open.

Tom Kehoe was born in 1936. We got on like a house on fire. Over tea, he told me all about Michael Barry cutting turf in the bog overlooked by his kitchen window. He brought me to Aghavannagh Barracks,

287 O'Donovan, p.69.

Con Foley and Tom Kehoe in Knockananna. Photographed by Louise Hogan, 2019

leading the way in his little black car, pelting down the country roads. I felt that evening as if we were following in the footsteps of our ancestors, as we drove up the tree-lined drive where they would have cycled that wild wet summer evening up to the imposing barracks, which is now draped with climbing roses. Entering the barracks by the back door, I was led into the hall by the McArdles, who now own it, to the cold stone hallway where Kevin Barry met Redmond holding a mallet, and retorted with his rifle. There he would have met the 'hysterical housekeeper', who is perhaps the one to thank that the barracks was not burned down. The kitchen is now a brightly painted room with a glass door that opens out on to the beautiful herb gardens in front of the house. We agreed that it was good the house had not been burned down. The present owner showed me a picture of the green harp flag that Parnell hoisted from the barracks, all the way back in the 1870s when fires were lit in the little valley to welcome him when he came for a few quiet days of hunting in the forests around.

At some point during that summer, in late July, Kevin got a bit bored in the countryside. He missed dancing in the Dublin halls. He wrote a letter to friend called Jack saying he hoped 'you are not affected by the trouble these Sinn Féiners are causing. There is no news of any interest here. I came home here about three weeks ago, got fed up and returned to town. I had a hell of a great fortnight. Stopped with another fellow all the time and was drunk every night with the result that I'm a nervous wreck. I met Paddy Nugent several times at the Empire [dance hall]. By the way are you still backing horses … I've given it up since yesterday. I backed Cooldrinagh at the Curragh. Straight tip – 3rd at evens. Now I'll have to shut up. Yours 'til hell freezes, KGB.'[288]

Kevin certainly came back to Carlow after his brief visit to Dublin. His activities with the C Company continued all through that summer. My father noted, however, that 'although British troops were everywhere to be seen more of the King's soldiers were being killed in Mesopotamia … and [the British military presence] was not enough to stop English tourists from spending their holidays in Ireland.'[289]

My father was also told by Matt Cullen that, by the end of that summer, there was a C Company excursion to Glendalough in a charabanc. Matt Cullen said 'it was to be our last enjoyable day'.[290]

Con Foley remembered his father telling him how, at this time in 1920, he was sitting in his house at Knockananna, when he saw two men on the road. 'One had a motorbike, and their accents were British. He heard them say: "Do you want to call up now? This is where Foley [Patrick Foley] lives?" My father shot up the road out the back to O'Shea's pub in Aghavannagh and talked to the owner, Mrs O'Shea, giving her the instruction that "you saw nothing, you know nothing and you heard nothing." My father made himself so scarce that those undercover agents never found him. Nobody called to him.'[291]

At the end of the summer, a general parade was called for the C Company at the field in Hacketstown, to collect arms from the area. Kevin, Michael and Matt Cullen drove out in Michael's pony and trap to the New Line to cut the telephone poles. The next day they raided Jones's of Woodside for arms, got some guns, and then went to the Church of

288 By kind permission of the Kevin Barry estate.
289 O'Donovan, p. 68.
290 Ibid.
291 Interview with Con Foley, 2019.

The Aghavannagh Barracks, now a private home. Photographed by Louise Hogan, 2019

Ireland rectory and surrounded the Reverend Charles Stewart Stamford Ellison's house. Matt Cullen told my grandfather that 'Kevin Barry, Mike McDonald and myself were refused admittance, demanded that the door be opened, then saw the minister let down the window and fire from a shotgun point blank range at us.'[292] Nobody was injured by the irate minister, but Kevin replied with an automatic and the others with revolvers, through the window. The reverend kept firing as they got cover, and they too kept firing. Matt Cullen said they could not afford to lose so much ammunition, nor did they want to shoot the reverend dead. They decided, instead, to take the gun from the minister without his knowing. But the military got there first.

The C Company, with Kevin, raided a mail car that night, hoping to intercept police reports of C Company activity. Control was tightening, and they knew it. Kevin then had to go back to Dublin to sit his repeat medical exams. His military activity continued in Dublin, and put a spanner in his academic work for good. Before he left Tombeagh for Dublin, he cycled ten miles to Tuckmill to see the Doyle cousins – Mr and Mrs Doyle who lived with their six children in a crossroads shop. When Mary Doyle opened the door, Kevin said, 'You don't know me, Mrs Doyle, but I know

292 Interview with Matt Cullen by James O'Donovan, 1953.

you. I am Kevin Barry of Tombeagh.'[293] He took the children over the wall and up the field to see the pony and foal. Mrs Doyle had thought a lot of Kevin and 'the manly way he introduced himself'.[294]

Matt Cullen stayed at Tombeagh the night before Kevin left Carlow for the last time. 'When we got up that morning, we played some hurling. He left quickly that evening on the train from Rathvilly, and events worked quickly after that.'[295]

The Templemore Miracles

One August night in 1920 'wild scenes were witnessed in Templemore … as the Northamptonshire regiment carried out reprisals following the killing of RIC District Inspector Wilson by the IRA. Houses were attacked, shops looted and the town hall was a burned down.'[296] As has often happened in Ireland, Our Lady came to the rescue, with reports of 'supernatural manifestations and cures' at Curraheen near the village of Gortagarry. Statues of the Virgin Mary at places such as the Templemore Barracks were seen to be bleeding tears. James Walshe, a young local farmer, saw statues and holy pictures in a newsagent's house begin to bleed. Overnight, Templemore became a place of pilgrimage.

The roads to the town were blocked with farm carts, ass carts, outside cars, Fords and bicycles. Such traffic had never been seen, even for the races. Pilgrims slept in the streets and wretches past help were dragged to the newsagent's shop in the hope of a miraculous cure. An old soldier who had been shot through the right knee at the Battle of the Somme regained the use of his leg. A harnessmaker was relieved of his sciatica, and a girl in the last stages of consumption rose from her stretcher and walked. Or so it was said.[297]

During the Templemore 'crisis' – which went on throughout the summer of 1920 – Kevin would have seen cabs full of pilgrims leaving Hacketstown.

293 O'Donovan, p. 70. Information from Brigid and Joe Doyle to my father, 1988.
294 Ibid.
295 Interview with Matt Cullen by James O'Donovan, 1953.
296 O'Donovan, p. 74.
297 O'Donovan, p. 75.

In Rathvilly near Tombeagh, Tom O'Gorman from Hacketstown 'drove full hackney cars of pilgrims to Templemore twice a day'.[298] Despite this strange hiccup in the emerging war and the bizarre handling of it by the IRA, the latter were not deterred. Moving and bleeding statues are not an unknown phenomenon in Ireland or, indeed, at other places of pilgrimage in the world. Not long after Kevin's ambush and arrest on 20 September 1920, the IRA activity in the Templemore area quickly resumed. There was an attack on a group of RIC men at Goldings Cross RIC barracks on the pilgrimage route, killing Constables Noonan and Flood and wounding two others. Travelling pilgrims were stopped by the IRA and ordered to take the bodies of the two dead constables with them. The IRA continued the surge of war across the country. *An t-Óglach* exhorted: 'His strongholds must be attacked, his forces surprised and disarmed, his communication interrupted, interfered with, his supplies cut off in every part of the country with such persistence, speed and ubiquity that he will not be able to get his "system" established anywhere.'[299]

Whether the Templemore Virgin Mary liked it or not, a full-scale guerrilla war was in full swing.

---

298 O'Donovan, p. 75.
299 O'Donovan, p. 75.

Chapter Eight

WAR

Unrest in Mesopotamia

Although British troops were frequently around Carlow, especially towards the end of that summer of 1920, far more troops were being killed in Mesopotamia, where the Iraqis had been violently demonstrating against British rule since May 1920. At the San Remo Conference in April 1920, Britain obtained the Mandate for Iraq, which was then called Mesopotamia. They also obtained the Mandate for Palestine. The British rid themselves of former Ottoman officials in Mesopotamia and replaced them conveniently with their own officials. With reason, the Iraqis feared that they were being annexed to the British Empire.[300]

Armed revolt broke out in late June 1920, just at the time Kevin was in Carlow with the C Company, plotting the burning of Aghavannagh Barracks. Ayatollah al-Shirazi issued a fatwa stating that it was the duty of Iraqis to demand their rights, and this seemed to encourage armed revolt.[301] By late July, armed tribal rebels controlled most of the mid-Euphrates region.[302] The success of the tribes caused the revolt to spread to the lower Euphrates and all around Baghdad.

British War Secretary Winston Churchill authorised immediate reinforcements of aircraft in Iraq, shifting the advantage to the British and ending the revolt. Although '[T]he use of poisonous gas was never sanctioned',[303] Churchill was 'strongly in favour of using poisoned gas

300 Tripp, Charles. *A History of Iraq*. Cambridge: Cambridge University Press, 2007, p. 41.
301 Ibid.
302 Report on Mesopotamia by T.E. Lawrence, *The Sunday Times*, 22 August 1920.
303 Anthony Clayton, 'Deceptive Might': Imperial Defence and Security, 1900–1968', in Judith M. Brown and Wm. Roger Louis (eds), *The Oxford History of the British Empire, Volume 4: The Twentieth Century*, Oxford: Oxford University, 1999, pp. 280–306.

against the uncivilised tribes; it would spread a lively terror.'[304] He ordered a large-scale bombing of Mesopotamia, with an entire village wiped out in forty-five minutes.

Dublin Castle reshuffles

Resistance to British rule was intensifying in Ireland, albeit not on the same scale as in Mesopotamia. By mid-1920, Republicans had won control of most county councils, and British authority collapsed in most of the south and west, forcing the British government to introduce emergency powers. In early 1920 Sir Hamar Greenwood MP became Chief Secretary of Ireland. Major General H. H. Tudor was replaced by Sir Joseph Byrne as the head of the Royal Irish Constabulary. General Sir Frederick Shaw was replaced as General Officer Commander of the Forces of Ireland by Sir Nevil Macready, who was then Commissioner of the Metropolitan Police in London.[305] Macready demanded high compensation for this post – table money of £1,500, special pension rights and disturbance money of £5,000. Winston Churchill said the payment could not come out of his budget, but all of Macready's demands were met in the end. Churchill reported to King George V: 'Mr. Churchill with his humble duty to Your Majesty has thought it proper to offer the Command in Chief of Ireland to Sir Nevill [sic] Macready, who he believes will be willing to undertake this most critical and difficult of tasks … '.[306] Macready's posting would seal Kevin Barry's fate.

By May 1920, Macready gave a full account to the Cabinet of the situation in Ireland, with detailed references to military and police requirements, 'in view of the present state of disorder'. The minutes and results of the meeting are discussed below.

'I cannot say I envy you for I loathe the country you are going to and its people with a depth deeper than the sea and violent than that which

---

304 Shashi Tharoor, 'In Winston Churchill, Hollywood Rewards a Mass Murderer', in The Washington Post, 10 March 2018.
305 O'Donovan, p. 71.
306 Ibid., PRO WO 32 4815.

I feel against the Boche,'[307] Macready wrote to Ian Macpherson, Chief Secretary for Ireland since 1919. Macready's intention was to bring 'order' to Ireland, yet he was inexperienced in such matters and brashly castigated the Dublin administration for the 'crass stupidity which is so often found among police officers who have not been carefully selected'.[308]

Churchill and Ireland

Winston Churchill had a long and complicated relationship with Ireland. When Lloyd George was voted in as British PM in 1918, Churchill was given the War Office and the Air Ministry.[309] Although his attentions were cast as far afield as Mesopotamia and Egypt, he was always fixated on the Irish problem. His attitude became increasingly aggressive and his strategic developments increasingly brutal. Tensions were rising in May 1920, when Churchill argued for the establishment of a special tribunal to try murders. 'It is monstrous that there have been some 200 murders and no one hanged.'[310] Churchill was keen to see IRA men hanged, and his frustration was soon ended. He said to Lloyd George, 'You agreed six or seven months ago there should be hanging.'[311]

Yet Winston Churchill claimed to have a particular fondness for Ireland, and disliked anyone suggesting that he was Hibernophobic. His earliest memories of the country were when his father, Lord Randolph Churchill, was an aide to John Churchill, Winston's grandfather. Randolph lived in the Phoenix Park with his American wife Jennie and two-year-old Winston. The family socialised with Catholic clergy and had every sympathy for tenants oppressed by Irish landlords.[312] However, Churchill opposed Gladstone's 1881 Land Act as communistic.[313]

....

307 Information from Keith Jeffery, 'Macready Sir Cecil Frederick Nevil, first baronet (1862–1946)', in *Oxford Dictionary of National Biography* (online ed.), Oxford: Oxford University Press, p. 261.

308 Ibid.

309 Paul Bew, *Churchill in Ireland*, Oxford: Oxford University Press, 2016, p. 94.

310 Ibid., p. 95.

311 Ibid.

312 Ibid., pp. 15–16.

313 Ibid., p. 19.

When it came to Dan Breen's shooting of two policemen in Soloheadbeg, County Tipperary, on 21 January 1919 at the beginning of the War of Independence, Churchill expressed disdain for all this 'organised baboonery'. In 1918 he had failed to accept that Irish public opinion had shifted towards Sinn Féin and away from the Irish Parliamentary Party.

The Black and Tans

The British Army was stretched very thin by the ongoing insurgencies in Iraq and the impending coal strike in the UK in September 1920. India was, for now, quiet enough after the brutalities at Amritsar. The Secretary to the Cabinet, Sir Maurice Hanley, said that terror must be met with greater terror. The Restoration of Order in Ireland Act, passed in August 1920, conferred powers on the military administration in Ireland to intern anyone without charge or trial for an indefinite period, to try any prisoner by court martial and with no legal advice (except in cases that required the death penalty), and the suppression of coroners' inquests. It gave the Black and Tans the opportunity of 'striking down in the darkness those who struck from the darkness', and it gave the administration a mechanism for dealing with rebellious civilians. Kevin would be the first of these to have a court martial since 1916.

The Black and Tans were English recruits to the RIC. Their name derived from the shortage of dark green uniforms, which meant the recruits were issued with a mismatched combination of dark green tunics and khaki trousers. In March 1920 the first recruits arrived. Their pay was ten shillings a day. They had no guerrilla training but were soon supplied with regular RIC rifles and machine guns, fortified barracks and transport by their new chief, Major General H. H. Tudor. By the end of May 1920, 351 evacuated barracks had been destroyed and 105 damaged by the IRA. Fifteen occupied barracks were ruined and twenty-five damaged. Over 500 RIC men resigned in June and July 1920, but the flow of recruits from England compensated for this loss. By the time Kevin Barry was arrested 2,000 Black and Tans had reinforced the 8,000 members of the RIC, and Gormanston barracks became the Black and Tan depot in Dublin. [314]

----

314 O'Donovan, p. 73.

'The summer of 1920 saw 1,300 RIC either resigned or retired and by the autumn, the numbers were below 10,000. But by the end of that year it was back to 12,000 as the Auxiliaries and the Black and Tans bolstered them.'[315] They had been recruited too quickly, without proper training. The majority were unskilled or semi-skilled workers, and skilled manual workers (36 per cent) made up the rest. They were not men with criminal records, but 'a collection of British and Irish ex-servicemen who had been hardened by First World War service had no monopoly on brutality'.[316] One former Black and Tan said, 'We were mercenary soldiers fighting for our pay, not patriots willing and anxious to die for our country, our job was to earn our pay by suppressing armed rebellion, not die in in some foolish forlorn hope.'[317]

The Auxiliary forces

Churchill's measures did not stop at the Black and Tans. At a ministerial conference in the Cabinet on 11 May 1920, he submitted a scheme to raise a special Emergency Gendarmerie that would become a branch of the RIC. Cabinet notes from that date reveal that mechanical transport was required to 'render the existing military forces more mobile'.[318] In view of the deficiency of troops, Macready was reported to have the utmost regard for the War Office exigencies. But how would they deal with the present emergency in Ireland? It was then that Churchill, as Secretary of State for War, submitted to the Cabinet a scheme for raising the Special Emergency Gendarmerie. They discussed the need for wireless telegraphy operators, who were difficult to recruit quickly, and the RIC and Dublin Metropolitan Police needed at their disposal a small staff, including a first rebate intelligence officer.

The proposal was referred to a committee chaired by Macready, which initially rejected Churchill's proposal, but two months later, in July, the Police Adviser to the Dublin Castle administration, Major General H. H. Tudor, justified the scheme.[319] Tudor's 'Auxiliary Force' would enlist for a

---

315   Ferriter, *A Nation and Not a Rabble*, p. 193.
316   Ibid., p. 197.
317   Ibid.
318   Crown copyright, Cat Ref CAB/23/21.
319   Memo dated 6 July 1920, CAB/23/21.

year, their pay would be £7 per week (twice what a constable was paid), plus a sergeant's allowances, and they would be known as 'Temporary Cadets'. At this time a London advertisement for ex-officers to manage coffee stalls at £2 10s. a week received five thousand applicants.[320]

The Auxies were intended to be an elite cadre[321] operating counter-insurgency units independent of other RIC formations. Recruiting began in July 1920, and by November 1921, the division was 1,900 strong. Divided into companies (eventually fifteen of them), each about a hundred strong, heavily armed and highly mobile, they operated in ten counties, mostly in the south and west, where IRA activity was greatest. They wore either RIC uniforms or their old army uniforms with appropriate police badges, along with distinctive Tam o'Shanter berets. They were commanded by Brigadier General Frank Percy Crozier. According to Bew they were 'formidable adversaries to the IRA, by the simple expedient of borrowing the method of assassination with rather better weapons'.[322]

When the first 500 Auxies arrived at the North Wall in Dublin at the end of July 1920 they went straight to the Curragh military camp in County Kildare. Their Tam o'Shanter berets sported the crowned harp badge of the RIC. Initially, their tunics, breeches and puttees were khaki, and they wore a bandolier across the chest, a belt with a bayonet and scabbard, and an open black leather holster for a revolver on the right thigh. Crozier came back from service with the Polish Army against the Red Army to command the Auxiliaries. 'Crozier is variously described as a reformed alcoholic, an Orange firebrand, and a volatile and excitable Irish officer [who] resigned in disgust in February 1921, having met and admired Kevin Barry in Mountjoy.'[323]

Churchill was the driving force behind the recruitment of the Black and Tans and the Auxiliaries. Sir Henry Wilson, who appeared to be more moderate, criticised their brute force and was apparently horrified by the

---

320 Bew, p. 95.
321 Ferriter, *A Nation and not a Rabble*, p. 198.
322 Bew, p. 95.
323 O'Donovan, p. 76.

sacking and burning of Balbriggan, Dublin, in September 1920. This was the first major reprisal after the IRA killed Head Constable Peter Burke. As locals saw it, the town was sacked by drunken men – the Black and Tans. Twenty-five houses were burned to the ground. Henry Wilson wrote in his diary at the time: 'Churchill saw very little harm in this, but it horrifies me.'[324] He considered the British were behaving as badly in Ireland as the Germans had in Belgium during the Great War.

Sir Henry Wilson disagreed with Churchill's plan to arm '20,000 Orangemen to relieve the troops from the North'.[325] This would mean 'taking sides', possible civil war and savage reprisals, great tension with America and open rupture with the pope. 'Winston does not realise these things in the least and is a perfect idiot as a statesman.'[326] According to Bew, 'Churchill was much more responsible for the heavy-handedness of the Black and Tans in the south and the "B-Specials" in the north than Henry Wilson, who was a critic of both forces.'[327]

However, there was logic to Churchill's terror tactics. More severe methods were needed to manage the Irish. He believed it would take 100,000 troops to make them loyal to the Crown again. The British military presence in Mesopotamia and Egypt was already costing the British taxpayer £51.5 million in 1920–21 alone and the 'Irish troubles' were costing the taxpayer £20 million a year.[328]

Sir Henry Wilson wrote in his diary on 7 July 1920: 'Macready has asked for another three battalions and a brigade head-quarters. I at once wired approval, but added that I hoped that these incessant demands would make us impotent in all other theatres … we would be faced with grave difficulty in Ireland when winter set in as to barrack accommodation.'[329]

---

324 Ross O'Mahoney 'The Sack of Balbriggan and Tit for Tat Terror', in David Fitzpatrick (ed.) *Terror in Ireland*, Dublin: The Lilliput Press, 2012, p. 164.
325 Bew, p.95.
326 Ibid.
327 Ibid.
328 Bew, p. 97.
329 Major General Sir C. E. Callwell, *Field-Marshal Sir Henry Wilson – His Life and Diaries, Vol. II*, London: Cassell and Company, p. 251.

Wilson was very concerned that General Macready and other authorities were miscalculating the situation in Ireland. When he expressed this to Lloyd George, he referred to 'his amazing theory that someone was murdering 2 Sinn Féiners to every loyalist the Sinn Féiners murdered'.[330] Lloyd George 'seemed to be satisfied that a counter-murder association was the best answer to Sinn Féin murders. A crude idea of statesmanship, and he will have a rude awakening.'

He went further in confronting Lloyd George's 'suicidal' policy in Ireland in a conversation with Lord Duncannon, noted in his diary that July. He told him that if he were in the House of Commons he would 'March down to Lloyd George and say: "You have two courses open to you. One is to clear out of Ireland and the other is to knock Sinn Féin on the head. Before you do the latter, you must have England on your side, and therefore you must go stumping the country explaining what Sinn Féin means."'[331]

The situation in Ireland was spiralling into chaos, as 'Sinn Féin are steadily getting the upper hand, and unless this Cabinet acts soon all this will spread to this country'.[332] Wilson understood that the seeds for civil war were being sewn in Ireland. He knew that 'striking darkness with darkness' struck too many nerves in the Irish system and that the sacking of Balbriggan and Cork by the Black and Tans might make matters worse. In Ennistymon, Lahinch and Miltown in Clare, twenty-six buildings were burned down in reprisal for an ambush in Rineen, in which a police tender was attacked and a district inspector was killed. This occurred on 20 September 1920, the day that Kevin Barry and the H Company ambushed Monk's Bakery in Dublin. The death of hunger striker Terence MacSwiney, Lord Mayor of Cork, and the hanging of Kevin Barry, who was just eighteen years old, would turn public opinion against the British. Yet it was Wilson who threatened to resign if Kevin Barry was not hanged. On 20 September his diary entry is about his lunch at the Ritz with Lord D'Abernon to discuss the future of Poland, Russia, Germany and France. He noted disdainfully in his diary that the sacking of Balbriggan

330 Ibid.
331 Ibid., p. 254.
332 Ibid.

had been 'carried out without anyone being responsible. Men were murdered, houses burned, villages wrecked'.[333]

Wilson despaired that neither 'Lloyd George nor Bonar Law had the faintest idea of what to do ... Lloyd George has never shown any sign of governance since the Armistice, and this Irish affair is typical of his ideas of governing.'[334]

Some have viewed Wilson as moderate, and others have criticised him harshly as 'a schemer, driven by an endless and indefatigable malice. His attempts to organisationally dehibernicise the British army were successful. It was an act of political vindictiveness and tribal spite, which reached its culmination with the laying up of the regimental colours in Windsor Castle on 12 June 1922.'[335]

Wilson was shot dead by two Irish ex-servicemen outside 36 Eaton Place, London, on 22 June 1922. He had been targeted by Michael Collins because of his role as security chief for the new Northern Ireland government.

The Black and Tans on the Street

Courts martial were now frequent proceedings. General Macready told the Irish Situation Committee of the British Cabinet on 26 September 1920 that thirty-one people had been court-martialled the week before, sixteen for being in possession of arms or documents, and sentences ranged from a £2 fine to two years' hard labour. In the following weeks there were up to almost 100 courts martial, with seventy-one convictions. Macready reported that he was of the opinion that 'under the surface the situation is developing against the extremists'.[336]

Out on the streets, military presence was becoming more visible. C. S. Andrews first encountered the Black and Tans in December 1920 after a Company meeting in St Enda's. 'We heard first one, then another and still another volley of rifle shots ... we ducked into the woods and waited for further developments ... two lorries manned by the infamous

333 Ibid., p. 263.
334 Diary entry for 29 September, Callwell, p. 264.
335 https://www.irishtimes.com/opinion/an-irishman-s-diary-1.1084480
336 O'Donovan, p. 77.

Black and Tans crammed with prisoners drove by.'[337] They recognised the prisoners as members of the Fifth Engineering Battalion of the Dublin Brigade, who had been on unarmed manoeuvres in the Dublin Mountains when the Tans appeared and opened fire. 'We suspected, almost certainly wrongly, that the Tans received their information from St Columba's College – a bastion of the ascendancy.'[338] St Columba's College, in Rathfarnham, Dublin, is said to be the Eton of Ireland.

My father interviewed Mags Leonard, the daughter of Edward Charles Stewart Proctor, Kevin Barry's chosen guard in the condemned cell in Mountjoy until the time of execution. Mags was a child during what she called 'the Troubles of 1919–21'. Her father spent a lot of time with Kevin Barry, from 21 September to 1 November 1920 when he was hanged. Mags Leonard saw Maud Gonne McBride and Countess Markiewicz on hunger strike outside the prison 'on a little bed', later to be 'whooshed away down the Prison Avenue on to the North Circular Road'.[339]

Mags Leonard lived by the Prison Avenue and she used to go to the little shop on Glengarrif Parade to buy the soldiers cigarettes for a price. 'The soldiers would be in the port holes at the back of the prison and they'd roll down their puttee on the leg and drop it down and roll up their message in it with their money and we would get them their cigarettes and they'd give us two shillings. We used to sit and watch who was coming on duty. I remember the lorry loads of prisoners coming from the Four Courts or the GPO. Their parents and family would come up and give them cigarettes, chocolate, whatever and they were all shipped off to the Curragh. They were all very young men, standing in the lorries.'[340]

Later, she remembered walking in procession on a Sunday, and how 'the Black and Tans liked to see us all dressed up. We had snaps taken with them. They'd ask our parents could they take us for a walk. They wore black trousers. They were fierce, but I was a child and I didn't know.'[341]

....

337 Andrews, p 157.
338 Ibid.
339 Donal O'Donovan interview with Mags Leonard, 1988.
340 Ibid.
341 Ibid.

By the time Kevin got back to Dublin from Tombeagh in September 1920 the British Army numbered 40,000, the RIC with the Black and Tans 10,002, the Auxiliary Division 591 and the Dublin Metropolitan police 1,141– thus about 50,000 armed personnel were in operation. Yet Todd Andrews claimed that 'there was relatively little activity by the IRA in Dublin until late 1920 … except for the curfew which lasted from midnight until 5 am. Theatres and picture houses were open. Football matches were played before big crowds in Dalymount, Jones's Road and Lansdowne Road, and of course there was racing. I doubt if the horsey people were aware that there had been a 1916 rebellion; they may have associated it with Fairyhouse Easter Meeting which took place on the same day.'[342]

Ultimately, it was General Macready, the self-confessed Hibernophobe, General Officer Commanding the Forces in Ireland, who was 'the man who in effect signed Kevin Barry's death warrant – a man who was well aware of the "propaganda value of the soldier's ages"'.[343] He informed Sir Henry Wilson on the day that Kevin's sentence was pronounced that of the three men killed during the ambush that had resulted in Barry's arrest, two were nineteen and one twenty years old. 'So if you want propaganda there you are.'[344] In fact, Private Harold Washington was only fifteen.[345]

When a telephone message was sent from Dublin District of the British Army to General Macready in General Headquarters, the transcript relayed to Macready outlined that six armed civilians attempted to hold up a party of the Duke of Wellington's Regiment that morning of 20 September 1920, that they had opened fire killing one soldier and badly wounding two others. Macready made up his mind at once, in a note to Lieutenant Colonel H. Toppin, Assistant Adjutant General, in Dublin District Headquarters: 'Colonel Toppin. Try for murder.' It was already the end for Kevin Barry.

342 Andrews, p. 158.
343 O'Donovan, p. 71.
344 Fr Brian P. Murphy OSB, *The Origins & Organisation of British Propaganda in Ireland 1920*, Aubane Historical Society, 2006.
345 http://news.bbc.co.uk/2/hi/uk_news/northern_ireland/1596618.stm

It was an intensifying war, and from the perspective of the average IRA volunteer on the street it was war, not terrorism. 'As IRA violence continued, it appeared to many in London that Britain was countenancing a dirty war of "reprisals" in Ireland as the only viable response.'[346] In the C Company of the Dublin Brigade Prendergast observed the escalation of 'the first shock of the intensification the guerrilla warfare, and particularly the street warfare'.[347] The Crown of force onslaughts were more frequent now, and so 'the Dublin Brigade could be said to be feeling its sea-legs. We were meeting the worst period in our existence then as the forces of the Crown demonstrated their strength and prowess by sheer brute force … the next the I.R.A. by ruse, subterfuge or stratagem engaged in some daring exploit, the urge in each case being to exact an influence on the situation then prevailing.'[348]

Each company had its own system of ambush groups, acting independently of each other, and 'no operation of a military nature was to be carried out within the immediate neighborhood of certain buildings that were being utilised as Dáil Éireann or I.R.A.'[349] G.H.Q. had to give special permission for certain areas to conduct ambushes. It was an 'unwritten law to respect territory that was considered to be invulnerable to our side, so signally implied in those orders'. [350] In terms of distributing ammunitions, 'men armed with revolvers were placed with men armed with grenades or convenient thereto in order to act as protection when the attack was delivered. Sometimes the grenade men were armed with revolvers.'[351]

By this time, my grandfather was Director of Chemicals in the IRA GHQ. There is a group portrait of the IRA GHQ by Leo Whelan hanging in the Collins Barracks National Museum. 'Frozen in time, the IRA leaders looked out from the group portrait with resolute, fixed expressions.'[352]

346 Prendergast, WS 755, BMH, p. 332.
347 Ibid.
348 Ibid, p. 431.
349 Ibid., p.432.
350 Ibid.
351 Ibid.
352 O'Donohue, *The Devil's Deal*, p. 12.

It is a dark, sultry portrait of men in black suits and white shirts. Michael Collins looks straight at the painter with his arm back on the chair, ready for action. My grandfather peers out from a dark corner, looking very serious indeed. Whelan found the canvas rolled up in his studio some time in the 1940s, long after Ireland's independence had been won. Yet for some, like my grandfather, independence was far from 'won'. He would not rest until he saw the north of Ireland cradled back into the whole of the island of Ireland. Whelan painted a singular portrait of my grandfather that hung in my father's study for years, beside the oval portrait of Kevin Barry in his trench coat. I was always a bit afraid of my grandfather with his stern, angular face and the stories of the German spies he hid at home. My father called his study 'The Republican Plot'.

My grandfather Jim ODonovan and grandmother Monty with my sister Kristin.

Jim O'Donovan, Director of Chemicals, IRA GHQ, War of Independence.

Chapter Nine

MONK'S BAKERY

Maybe the only person who knew Kevin was going to die in 1920 before he was even arrested for the ambush at Monk's Bakery was Eileen Dixon, a close friend of the Barrys. She lived in Sandycove and would spend evenings in the Barry drawing room in Fleet Street. Part of their entertainment would come from Eileen's ability to read tea leaves and palms. One evening in 1920, she took Kevin's palm. She stopped, and looked up at him.[353] 'You should be dead,' she said. The story of her reading of Kevin's hand was one that gripped me as a child. I could see Kevin in the sitting room in 8 Fleet Street, bemused when Eileen Dixon told him he was going to die. He just didn't mind, I was sure of it. Eileen was known to the Barrys as Chimo, and before she went on to become a doctor, she dabbled in a bit of palmistry.

We don't know how anyone in Kevin's family reacted to this shameless but accurate prediction. Kevin's life line on his palm was extremely short, and Eileen had never seen one this short before. We can imagine, from the tone of Kevin's letters and from his ability to compartmentalise his life, that he would have laughed it off. Perhaps Kitby, who knew the extent of his involvement in the War of Independence, would have felt an ominous shiver if she'd been in the room. I am fairly certain that this was around the time that Kevin had come back up from Tombeagh to sit his repeat exams at UCD.

Kevin had an exam scheduled for 20 September 1920, the very day that he was to take part in the ambush at Monk's Bakery. By this time, he had already sat his repeat exams in experimental physics, theoretical chemistry, practical chemistry, botany and zoology in the Examination Hall at

353 Information from Helen Moloney to Donal O'Donovan, O'Donovan, p. 56.

Earlsfort Terrace. In the meantime, the H Company were hatching a plan. Dick McKee told his men at a meeting in the billiard room at 41 Parnell Square, 'I believe this company is going to carry out a job. There is one word of advice I would like to give you, that is to remember that these men in the lorry are six feet above you, and the best of luck to you.'[354]

Kevin, when he heard of the plan, wanted nothing more than to be in on the action, even though he had left his revolver at Tombeagh. Kitby recalled how Kevin, in mid-September, had 'come up from Tombeagh to do the exams. He had left his revolver at home. When he heard about this action, he insisted on being allowed to take part. His officers, Seamus Kavanagh, Tommy McGrane and Bob Flanagan, were very reluctant to allow this on account of the exam that day. But he persuaded them that it would be all over and done with long before two o'clock. His station in the action was on the pathway outside the entrance to the bakery. His job was to keep the lorry covered.'[355]

Reconnaissance

A plan to ambush Monk's Bakery, on Church Street, Dublin, was hatched when, according to my father, a report came in that a Lancashire Fusilier in the North Dublin Union had smuggled two rifles out of the premises.[356] The bakery was carefully observed by H Company's John Joe Carroll, who had been in the King's Inns raid with Kevin Barry, and James Douglas of the C Company for two or three days, at 11 am, when the bread deliveries were made. Carroll carefully made a map of the bakery from his observations. He noted that Mr Molloy and Miss Byrne took care of the telephone, Dublin 1084. They were in an office on the left-hand side of the building, along with the manager, Mr Feely. Opposite them was a door that led down a corridor to the bread shop on 38 North King Street,

354 Sean O'Neill, WS 1154, BMH, p. 7.

355 KBM, WS 731, BMH.

356 However, Captain Seamus Kavanagh does not mention any incidence of arms being smuggled by the Crown Forces via Monk's Bakery. My father, who seemed to take his information from *The Liberty* April edition in 1960, went on to claim that John Joe Carroll, who had done the original reconnaissance with James Douglas, managed to get a 'Canadian Ross Rifle for one pound'. O'Donovan, p. 79.

which would be the retreat route.[357] John Joe Carroll and James Douglas figured this was an easy ambush. The IRA desperately needed arms, and this would be, they hoped, a simple operation. Carroll consulted Captain Seamus Kavanagh of the H Company. It was observed that 'the party came in a lorry and comprised 1 officer and a driver in the cab, 1 N.C.O. and 8 privates in rear. The lorry came from the Royal [now Collins] Barracks [now the National Decorative Arts and History Museum], then garrisoned by the 2nd Battalion, Duke of Wellington's Regiment.'[358]

Captain Kavanagh went to make his own observations when Carroll and Douglas informed him of what they had seen. Usually, an officer and a soldier went into the bakery, while the other troops got off the lorry and went into the shop opposite the bakery for cigarettes and sweets. (The owner of this shop was to become the unwitting catalyst for Kevin's capture.) That security was lax was duly noted. The lorry was habitually loaded with bread hampers from the bakery while the troops all boarded again for the lorry to return to the barracks via North Brunswick Street. Kavanagh went back to the bakery to do more reconnaissance. On the morning of 13 September, he went down to Church Street at 10.50 am and studied the activities, noting the lorry arriving that day at 11.05 am from North King Street. He felt assured that the daily routine was fixed and reliable: 'in fact, my informant's report was correct in every detail.'[359]

Kavanagh paced out the distances and then went into the bakery to speak to the foreman carpenter, J. J. Moore, whom he knew. He explained the mission, and Moore obligingly showed him the whole building. He noted again the line of retreat that Carroll had noted: through a yard at the back there was a passage that led to the bread shop in North King Street. He would place men in the yard, and a man or two in the shop. 'In a loft overhead, there was a window overlooking the spot where the lorry stopped, where I first considered placing a man with grenades in case the surprise I had planned did not materialise.' But he rejected that plan, due to the potential danger of the grenades for his own men.

---

357 O'Donovan, p. 79.
358 Seamus Kavanagh, WS 493, BMH, p. 1.
359 Ibid., p. 2.

Kavanagh then interviewed his commanding officer, Commandant Tom Byrne O/C 1st Battalion. He was doubtful if permission would be obtained to conduct this ambush, since it was not in the H Company's area, and crossing territorial lines with another Company's area was not encouraged. Fearing the plan would be rejected, he approached Peadar Clancy, who 'had a soft spot for the H Company',[360] and Kavanagh was brought before the Brigadier, who cross-examined him about the whole plan, and about the men who would be on the operation. Most of these had been on jobs before, including the raid on the King's Inns the previous June. The H Company men on this operation included Kevin Barry, Frank Flood and Tom Kissane.[361] When Clancy gave him a wink and a nod on the way out of the meeting, he knew the plan would be approved.

The H Company paraded as usual on Thursday night, 16 September, at 41 Parnell Square. However, the chosen men were not to be told about the plan until Sunday, 19 September. There were twenty-four men. Section Commanders were T. Staunton, Sean O'Neill, Bob O'Flanagan, Frank Flood, M. Higgins, C. Robinson and D. Golden. Squad leaders were P. Kenny, P. Young, D. MacDonagh and Kevin Barry. J.J. O'Carroll and Tommy Kissane were among the Volunteers. The van was to be driven by D. Golden with J. Carrigan. On the evening of Sunday, 19 September, the men were mobilised at 41 Parnell Square and instructed to report to The O'Flanagan Sinn Féin Club on Ryders Row at 9 am the following morning. Nobody was to carry anything that would identify him.

At this meeting on 19 September, Kavanagh called Kevin Barry aside and asked him about his exam the following day, to which he responded, 'Oh, that will be all right.' Kavanagh told him he didn't want him to miss another examination, knowing as he did that he had already missed one on the day of the King's Inns raid. Kevin asked, 'How do you think I could sit for an examination, knowing this job is on and me not on it? Why, there might be another machine gun for "H" Company, and I'd hate to miss it.'[362] Kavanagh saw the look of bitter disappointment on Kevin's face when

360 Ibid., p. 3.
361 Ibid., p. 4.
362 Ibid., p. 6.

he told him he could not take part, so, he conceded and even made sure to tell Dr McKinney, who taught at UCD, to help Kevin in case he missed his exam. McKinney had helped Kevin when he missed his exam when he was on the King's Inns raid. Since that raid on 1 June 1920, it seems that nothing was more important to Kevin than being a soldier. Kavanagh wrote in his statement: 'I can never forget the look of delight on Kevin's face when I told him he could come on the job.'[363]

Not only was the plan important to Kevin, Kevin was important to the H Company. His capability as a soldier was indispensable, and Kevin knew it. He was willing to gamble his medical training. 'On Monday, 20th September [1920], Kevin was to sit for an examination at 2 o'clock. He had come up from Tombeagh some days before and, on instructions, had not stayed at home [but] with [our] uncle, Patrick Dowling, 58 South Circular Road.'[364]

On the evening of 19 September Kevin had his dinner with Kitby and his mother at 8 Fleet Street, and not at Pat Dowling's. This would be his final meal with them. Kitby and Mrs Barry were going to see the Dixons in Sandycove after dinner. Kevin did not go, of course. He was in great spirits, singing 'The South Down Militia' with Kate Kinsella as they went out the door.

> You may talk about your King's Guards,
> Scots Guards an'a',
> Your Back and Tans and Kilties
> An' the fighting forty-two
> Also our brave Auxiliaries
> A most ferocious band
> But the South Down Militia
> is the terror of the land.[365]

---

363 Ibid.
364 KBM, WS 731, BMH.
365 Written by Peadar Kearney, who wrote the national anthem of Ireland. O'Donovan, p. 80.

Monday, 20 September 1920

On the morning of 20 September, when all the men reported in at 9 o'clock sharp to the O'Flanagan Sinn Féin Club on Ryders Row, Kevin wasn't there. He was ten minutes late and, according to my father, Kavanagh bawled Kevin out of it and said, 'Well, this is the only gun I have for you!' The gun he was given would be another contributing factor to Kevin's downfall. Kevin had told Kavanagh that he had had to go to UCD to make 'everything right about his examination', but in fact he had been to Mass on Clarendon Street to receive Holy Communion. Each man had already been issued with a revolver and six rounds, and some had been issued with grenades. Kevin Barry's revolver, a short Webley, had already been issued as he was late. Instead, he was given a .38 Mauser Parabellum. It was made in 1915, and numbered RJR 995 KN2.[366] 'Kevin was not pleased about it, and the other Volunteers chaffed him about it.'[367] Kevin had left his own revolver in Tombeagh, not knowing that he was going to take part in this ambush.

Kavanagh drew out the plan on a blackboard and marked each man's position. He pointed out where the lorry would stop, marked X. He selected Lenehan's public house as a suitable command post from where he could observe enemy movements. From there, he would join the action, along with Frank Flood, Liam Grimley and Mick Robinson, all UCD students. J. J. Carroll and others would enter the bakery from the North King Street entrance. Sean O'Neill, second in command, section leader Kevin Barry and second lieutenant Bob O'Flanagan were to follow the lorry into Upper Church Street and hold up the soldiers. Kavanagh was to give the signal by taking out his handkerchief and pretending to wipe his mouth or blow his nose. Then, the men were to close in on the lorry, draw their guns and shout 'Hands up!'[368]

As my father said, 'It was a simple plan. Occupy the bakery, isolate the short street of Upper Church Street – fifty-seven yards precisely, as the Royal Engineers cartographer calculated it later from the court martial;

366 MS 8043 NLI R/O 2609.
367 Kavanagh, WS 493, BMH, p. 7.
368 Kavanagh, WS 493, BMH, p. 8.

close in on the lorry and disarm the men on it. It had worked at the King's Inns; it should work again.'[369]

'If the plan went successfully and the British surrendered, the Volunteers covering the sides of the lorry were to keep the troops covered; the men at the rear of the lorry were to disarm the British and load the rifles into the waiting van.'[370]

Kavanagh was prepared for the plan to fail, and with that in mind he had instructed the Volunteers to open fire and evacuate the area without any signal. This is an important point, as the Barry family were highly critical of Kavanagh for not blowing a retreat whistle. They would not talk to him when they met him in public. It was not the first time somebody would be shunned by the Barrys after Kevin's death. Grief has its casualties and its culprits.

By 10.50 am everyone was in position, mingling with the crowds on Church Street, hiding their revolvers in newspapers or coats, mooching around for a whole hour because the lorry was late. 'Bob O'Flanagan bought a newspaper and we read it in Nth King Street.'[371] O'Neill and O'Flanagan moved slowly to the corner of Upper Church Street. The atmosphere was very tense as the lorry finally turned the corner on to North King Street at 11.20 am, 'crammed full of troops'.[372] The back of the lorry was let down. There were about twenty men and it worried Kavanagh. Frank Flood turned to Kavanagh and said it was 'going to take twice as long to collect all those rifles!'[373] At that point, they felt like they were in for a fight. Bob O'Flanagan moved in, his gun under his coat. Kavanagh was getting ready to give the signal from where he was. He 'could see Kevin Barry at "D" position, calmly pretending to read a paper, but another man was popping his head round the corner and drawing back. Frank Flood said, "If that fool doesn't stop popping his head around the corner, he will have us all spotted and we'll have to fight our way out".'[374]

....

369 O'Donovan, p. 82.
370 Kavanagh, WS 493, BMH, p. 8.
371 Sean O'Neill, WS 1,154, BMH, p. 8.
372 Ibid.
373 Ibid.
374 Ibid.

The troops remained in the lorry and just one private went into the bakery. Kavanagh estimated there were about fifteen in the lorry. He waited to see if they would get out and buy sweets and cigarettes in the shop, as they usually did. Flood then pointed out to Kavanagh that the Volunteer at the corner talking to Kevin Barry was looking anxiously in their direction. Kavanagh took out his handkerchief and gave the signal, saying, 'We'll move in the name of God.' Another said 'Amen'.[375] Kevin Barry still had the paper in front of him. Lieutenant Bob O'Flanagan was moving along with Sean O'Neill. Kevin Barry was to follow the lorry, with these two men, into Upper Church Street and hold up the soldiers while the rest of the Company would enter the bakery by the side entrance on North King Street. The plan was to disarm the men in the lorry, withdraw and take the ammunition.

Kavanagh and his men advanced as the others surrounded the lorry. 'One of the Volunteers (not Kevin Barry), probably as a result of over-anxiety, ran out in front shouting "Hands up" and fired.'[376] Since O'Neill describes this part of the operation in his statement, it seems that it was he that shouted 'Hands up'. In his witness statement he said that Bob O'Flanagan asked him to do this as he could shout louder than O'Flanagan.[377]

According to O'Neill, none of the troops in the lorry made a move. Privates Henry Washington, Matthew Whitehead, G. Dalby, P. Newton and M. Clearly all had rifles and rounds. Private Thomas Humphries was in the front with Private C. Barnes, the RASC driver.

'They were sitting around the edges of the lorry,' Bob O'Flanagan told my grandfather, in 1953. 'They had their rifles between their knees.'[378] O'Neill gave the order for them to drop their rifles and they obeyed, keeping their hands up for about ten seconds but then, seeing that there was only one man at that point covering the lorry, they grabbed their rifles and there was a shot. Then there were more shots.

---

375 Kavanagh, WS 493, BMH, p. 11.
376 Ibid.
377 O'Neill, WS 1,154, BMH, p. 8.
378 O'Donovan, p. 83.

The window of Clarke's dairy next door was shattered by a bullet. Mrs Clarke moved a baby in a pram to the back room. In a flat at 114 Church Street Mrs Chatham collapsed on the floor in fright. Sergeant Archer Banks, Duke of Wellington's Regiment, who was NCO in charge of the ration lorry, was down the passage of the bakery when he heard gunfire, 'about ten shots'. He was unarmed. Two shots were fired at him and he ran into the office where he saw an armed man in a blue serge suit. He went to hit him but was hit himself by a revolver. He ran out of the bakery and got a loaded rifle from Private Cleary.[379]

O'Neill was now at the side of the lorry, hoping that more men would arrive quickly, but then all he could see was the muzzle of a rifle over the side of the lorry 'Did you ever look down the muzzle of a rifle, especially with a man behind the trigger? It appears to grow bigger and bigger and you can take it from me I never want to look down one again in similar circumstances.'[380] Then he started to fire at the troops and as this happened he saw Bob O'Flanagan get shot in the head. He described what happened to my grandfather: '[I was shot] by one fellow sitting with his back to the cab. He seized his rifle, raised it and fired. He's the fellow that got me. The discharge from the rifle set fire to my cap and the bullet took part of my skull.'[381] He retreated. O'Neill saw him getting into a cab at Mary's Lane, not knowing he was wounded.

In Sean Cronin's account of the Church Street ambush, a 'ricocheting bullet hit Sean O'Neill. Harry Murphy was wounded. Tom Staunton and John O'Dwyer had their hats shot off. The men with the grenades feared to use them lest they maim or kill their own comrades.'[382]

Bob O'Flanagan made his escape as 'bullets were digging up the street. A hawker in a pony and trap suddenly wheeled into the line of fire out of North King Street. At Church Street Chapel I saw a man with a cab and hailed him. Jimmy Moran ran all the way after me with my cap, which

379 Court Martial Documents http://digital.ucd.ie/view-media/ucdlib:39126/canvas/ ucdlib:39627 also in MS 8043 NLI .

380 O'Neill, WS 1,154, BMH, p. 9.

381 Bob O'Flanagan to Jim O'Donovan, O'Donovan, p. 84.

382 Sean Cronin, p. 15.

The scene at Church Street after Kevin Barry's arrest on 20th September 1920 at around 1pm.

had dropped on the street. He was afraid my name was on it. Part of the scalp was in the cap.'[383]

O'Flanagan went up Jervis Street to the hospital with Jimmy Moran, who gave a sworn statement for the court martial, where a student poured iodine into the wound and stitched it while Frank Flood was in the waiting room covering the entrance.[384] He spent two months in hiding after that. John Joe Carroll found his way out through a door in the bakery which led out on to North King Street via the bread shop. 'When the girl at the counter saw me she nearly fainted. I put my gun in my pocket and left the shop. The area was surrounded by several hundred troops and everybody in the vicinity was held up and questioned. When I got as far as Bolton Street, I realised I had left my cap behind.'[385]

Although his cap was found, no arrests were made of the staff at Monk's Bakery. Kavanagh wrote, 'As we left Church Street, Mick Robinson almost fell over a bicycle left abandoned by someone in the road. I can still

383 Ibid.
384 O'Neill, WS 1,154, BMH, p. 10.
385 O'Donovan, p.85, ref Liberty, 1960.

hear his swearing heartily and Tom Kissane laughing equally heartily. I saw section Commander Higgins firming from his position at 'B', covering our retreat until we got round the corner.'[386]

They went to the Capuchin church and said a prayer of gratitude 'for coming out of that hell alive', and then saw another party of British troops and auxiliaries cordoning off Monk's Bakery. A shop owner ushered them in and let them upstairs to observe from the window. O'Neill wanted to go back to the scene and leave the revolvers in the shop but the lorry had moved off quickly. At that point they heard that a man had been found under the lorry and had been taken by the British.

It might have been as they were running that Kevin was spotted under the lorry. Sergeant Banks wrote in this testimony for the court martial that he saw a man under the lorry with a pistol, told him to come out and raise his hands, dropping his pistol when Banks told him to. 'I told the accused to get into the lorry. He did so. There were no other civilians around the lorry.'[387] One of the soldiers, Private Harold Washington, had been shot dead. Two others, Privates Marshall Whitehead and Thomas Humphries were both badly wounded, and later died of their wounds.

In her witness statement Kitby said that Kevin told her later at the court martial that 'The British soldiers were all back in the lorry and the man in charge [Sergeant Banks] had his foot on the wheel to get in. This was when a woman on the opposite side of the street shrieked out "There's a man under the lorry!" Kevin then tried to escape through the wheels on that side but the soldiers tumbled out of the lorry and he was captured.'[388] Kevin told this to Kitby during the court marital on 20 October in the yard of Marlborough Barracks. It was the first time she had seen Kevin since the 19 September dinner.

Decades later, my father gave a lift to a neighbour who was waiting for a bus in Bray, County Wicklow. When my father told him he was writing a book about Kevin Barry, John Doyle told him that he had

386 Kavanagh, WS 493, BMH, p. 13
387 Court Martial Documents http://digital.ucd.ie/view-media/ucdlib:39126/canvas/ ucdlib:39627 also in MS 8043 NLI.
388 KBM, WS 731, BMH.

been working in a shop called Kavanagh's, beside Lenehan's pub (where Kavanagh and Flood hid before the ambush), in 1920. That he now (in 1988) was an old man who lived behind our family home was some coincidence. I remember him standing at the 45A bus stop in his dark green overcoat. He had thick spectacles and was bald, except for a crescent of thin black hair. Mr Doyle knew the woman who had seen Kevin under the lorry – Mrs Garrett, who owned a coal and vegetable shop on the corner of Church Street and North King Street. Kitby mentions in her statement months after Kevin's execution, 'We were most distressed to hear that this woman had been driven mad and was in an asylum as a result of the blame attached to her by her neighbours.'[389] However, Kevin himself was convinced there was no malice on her part, only concern that 'the man' under the lorry would be injured. Indeed, he would be, but not by the wheels of the lorry. Mr Doyle dispelled the myth of Mrs. Garrett's madness to my father. He claimed that she was already quite old, and died naturally after that. There had even been rumours that Mrs Garrett herself had ended her days by being run over by a lorry.[390]

The problem all along, had been with Kevin's revolver, the .38 Mauser Parabellum. This gun had just been reconditioned and it jammed on the third round.

'He knelt down beside the lorry, discarded the round, fired another one with which he claimed to have killed one of the soldiers. He was amused at the evidence given [at the court martial], in which they were unable to account for the death of this particular soldier [Private Washington]. He stood up after discarding the third round, he lifted a flap of the lorry, fired and got this man. The gun jammed again on the fifth round. He knelt once more, but this time it was more difficult.'[391]

O'Neill, who had escaped with a scrape from 'a bit of the wall which was struck by a bullet',[392] noted also that it was when Kevin's gun had jammed that he dived under the lorry. He said that only one shot had

389 Ibid.
390 O'Donovan, p. 88.
391 KBM, WS 731, BMH.
392 O'Neill, WS 1,154, BMH, p. 9.

been fired from Kevin's gun. 'You can understand about a parabellum if you have not all the ammunition with the same mark and date it causes a jam.' He then stated that they would never make that mistake again.

The Barrys blamed Captain Kavanagh for failing to blow the whistle, yet Kitby said in her statement that it may even have been hearsay that there was to be a whistle blown, because, as she noted herself when she talked to Kevin in the yard of Marlborough Barracks during the court martial, he never mentioned it. Kavanagh was emphatic in his statement that there was an agreement that if there was trouble, a whistle would not be blown. The trouble was that Kevin had vanished and nobody had seen him being picked up by Sergeant Banks and thrown into the lorry beside Privates Whitehead, Washington and Humphries of the Duke of Wellington's Regiment. He went straight to the North Dublin Union.

Captain Kavanagh and Sean O'Neill went to the Barry's house at 8 Fleet Street, to break the news to his mother and sisters. He said 'they were broken hearted but stood up marvellously to this ordeal'.[393] Perhaps because the family could not forgive him for what they saw as his failure to warn Kevin to retreat, Kitby does not mention this visit in her statement, nor that he removed Kevin's rifle and equipment from the house for their safety. Kavanagh said that it was a great blow to his comrades to lose Kevin and that they quickly set about plans for his rescue.

However, on the afternoon of Monday, 20 November, nobody knew where Kevin was. His hideout, Uncle Pat Dowling's house on South Circular Road was raided – 'his Donegal tweed, a spare wristlet and good fountains pens were taken'.[394] That was all the Barry family knew. Kitby noted that it was interesting that it had been a military raid, and not one carried out by Auxies.

At about four o'clock on the afternoon of Monday, 20 September, Kitby was in the office on Abbey Street where she worked, with her boss, Ernest Aston. She had a phone call and was told about the raid on Pat Dowling's house. Aston sent her home, and on her way she bought the

---

393 Kavanagh, WS 493, BMH, p. 14 .
394 KBM, WS 731, BMH.

Evening Herald, which, as she said, 'contained a garbled account of the action'.[395] Kevin had also, of course, been missed at his final medical exam in UCD. Gerry McAleer had searched for him in the Aula Maxima, but he was nowhere to be seen. It was also Kevin's youngest sister Peggy's birthday, and 'a number of young people were to come to tea, including Kevin's closest friends',[396] one of whom was Gerry McAleer. During the party, Kitby and Mrs Barry left the party to search the streets of Dublin that night after curfew, calling to Kilmainham Gaol and Mountjoy to see if Kevin was there. 'I told mother and we made our plans to go ahead with the tea, dress in our best and make the rounds of the jails looking for information between tea time and curfew. We left the party in full swing and made the rounds without locating Kevin.'[397]

Kevin's sister Peggy remembered the day after his arrest, how her mother sent her up to UCD in Earlsfort Terrace to find him. 'I walked around it for about three hours and I think it was one of the most awful things in my life to have to go back and tell her I hadn't found him. Even after so many years [she wrote this in 1965], I am totally unable to see the whole thing objectively – to me it is still a very close, terrible and personal matter.'[398]

---

395 Ibid.
396 Ibid.
397 Ibid.
398 Information from Peggy Barry to James O'Donovan, O'Donovan, p. 58.

Chapter Ten

THE GOLDEN BULLET

W hen Kitby learned about Kevin being arrested from underneath the lorry at Monks' Bakery, she felt something had gone very wrong. 'From that moment I knew there was no hope. I knew by some obscure instinct that Kevin was finished. I had no knowledge of how or when he had been arrested, nor of any solider being killed and up to then, no prisoner had been executed since 1916.'[399]

Of course, she was right. The powers granted to the authorities could now be lethal to Kevin and other unruly 'civilians'. After it received the royal assent on 9 August, 1920, the Restoration of Order in Ireland Act (ROIA) enabled courts martial to pass a sentence of death by hanging. It gave the military the power to arrest without charge, detain without trial, have secret courts martial and suppress coroners' inquests. The *Irish Independent* had called it 'a measure for the creation of disorder, and anarchy, and the abolition of law'. These were indeed the predictions of Field Marshal Sir Henry Wilson, Chief of the Imperial General Staff, who had condemned 'unofficial reprisals' and sought a disciplined approach to dealing with the 'Sinn Féin rebels'. By the end of 1920, Wilson would write with despair in his diary at how 'he [Lloyd George], has handed over the Government to the "Black and Tans" until public opinion and the logic of facts have driven the Government to martial law for Munster, and in Mesopotamia, Percy Cox is trying to form an Arab Government, and in India, Montagu [sic] favours the rebels against the loyalists. No matter where we look, we find Lloyd George totally unable to govern.'[400]

....

399 KBM, WS 731, BMH.
400 Callwell, p. 275.

Statements and Reports Among the British Military

At Monk's Bakery Sergeant Banks had thrown Kevin into the lorry beside Privates Whitehead, Washington and Humphreys of the Duke of Wellington's regiment, and driven straight to the North Dublin Union. Kevin was jabbed by rifles in the guardroom of the barracks, but no harm came to him at that point. Banks reported, 'Pvt. Whitehead and Pvt. Humphreys had been wounded. I handed over the accused to the N.C.O. of the Guard. The wounded were taken away for treatment. Pvt. Washington was dead in the lorry.' Three rounds of ammunition from Kevin's pistol were taken, along with the pistol, to 'Adjt. 1st Lancs. Fusiliers'. Sergeant Banks left the North Dublin Union and went back to collect the bread from Monk's Bakery. Banks also stated that Kevin Barry said, 'We were after the rifles', and that he had been ordered by an officer to attack the lorry that morning. The statement is signed by Sd. A. Banks, L.Sgt. No. 4601932, 2nd Bn. The Duke of Wellington's Regt.[401] Private C. Barnes, the driver of the lorry, said in his statement that he took Kevin's pistol from the scene of the crime on Banks's orders and carried it with him in the lorry until they reached the North Dublin Union, where he saw the officer pull out the clip with three bullets in it, one of which was round, and one flat. He turned these over with the pistol, and returned with Banks to collect the bread from Monk's Bakery.[402]

The medical students in the Richmond Hospital to which the British casualties were removed gave the losses as three killed and seven wounded. There was still hope that Privates Marshall Whitehead and Thomas Humphries, both badly wounded, would survive. But they both soon died of their wounds. Bandsman Noble was carried to the Richmond Hospital by two civilians.[403]

....

401 Court Martial Documents http://digital.ucd.ie/view-media/ucdlib:39126/canvas/ucdlib:39627 also in MS 8043 NLI.

402 Private C. Barnes, R.A.S.C. driver, statement in Court Martial Documents http://digital.ucd.ie/get/ucdlib:39126/content

403 O'Neill, WS 1,154, BMH, p. 10.

At the GOC's office at Parkgate Colonel Toppin received a handwritten note from Major C. G. Hetherington, staff officer at GHQ:

'This is the only report I can find about the affair in Dublin on Monday. It should have gone to you before – not my fault! It is obviously very incomplete …'.[404] He may have been referring to the telephone report about the incident, or about the rushed note that Toppin had sent him the day before. Somebody along the line of enquiry had forgotten to have the witnesses sworn in, 'in accordance with GHQ instructions', according to Colonel S. D. N Browne of Dublin District. On Friday, 24 September, Colonel Toppin sent a 'secret and pressing' message to Dublin District enquiring about the 'Berry' case: 'The GOC desires that this case would be put forward in a thorough manner as soon as possible.'[405]

Captain R. S. Chomley, Adjutant for Major Lieutenant Colonel, Commandant 2nd Battalion of the Duke of Wellington Regiment, made a sworn statement from Collinstown Camp to Headquarters, 24th Infantry Brigade, on the day of the raid at Monk's Bakery. In this, he stated that Kevin was recognised by Privates Dalby and Cleary as being the man who shot Private Washington. The rest of the civilians had disappeared when the escort opened fire. He refers to one 'civilian' wounded, which must have been Bob O'Flanagan. 'Escort returned fire and hit one man. He screamed and was dragged away by his comrades. Sgt Banks came out of bakery, and saw the man under the lorry. Civilian came out under order, dropped his revolver, a German automatic on the ground.'[406]

When they arrived at the North Dublin Union, a patrol came out, the Sergeant (Banks) reported it to the Adjutant Lancashire Fusilier and the lorry driver handed over the prisoner's revolver. The prisoner

---

404 O'Donovan, DOD, p. 99, note File R.O 2609 Restoration of Order Section. O'Donovan noted that the R.O. 2609 File in the GOC's office at Parkgate and the Dublin District file 59/169/A1 were merged into one file: Kevin Berry – Civilian. It was this file that my grandfather 'appropriated' from Dublin Castle in 1921, and later donated to the NLI as a gift.

405 Ibid.

406 Sgt. R.S. Chomley Capt & Adjt. for Major Lieut-Colonel, Commanding 2nd B. Duke of Wellington Reg. sworn statement on 20.9.1920. R/O 2609/ MS 8043, NLI (2).

was put in Lancashire Fusiliers' guardroom while the wounded were taken by ambulance to King George V Hospital. An escort was provided by the Lancashire Fusiliers for the lorry's return to Collinstown, and notification had just been received that Private Whitehead had died in hospital from the effects of his wounds.

Lieutenant-Colonel F. J. Palmer R.A.M.C. described the condition of the wounded. 'He [Private Washington] was hit in the mouth and throat. Pte. Whitehead, Pte. Humphries and two bandsmen were wounded.'[407] He was called to see 'a seriously wounded man, Pte. Whitehead, operated on by Sir William Taylor', whom he assisted. In his assessment, the wound of entry was in the 'left lumbo [sic] abdominal region of the abdomen.' The bullet was lodged in the body and there was no wound of exit. When the abdomen was opened four perforations of the bowel were stitched up. 'Several bleeding vessels, which required tying up, and the abdomen was full of blood clots, scooped out with flat of the hand.'[408] No bullet was found at this time.

After this operation Private Humphries was operated upon. His wound of entry was in his right hip and had 'all the appearance of a wound of exit to the left of the umbilicous [sic]. No bullet was naturally found.'[409] These were his only wounds – in the caecum and in the transverse colon. He stated that all injuries were inflicted by the one bullet. 'In my opinion the bullet found by the attendant and handed to me could only have come out of Pte. Whitehead and was probably swept up unnoticed in a mass of blood clot during the operation.'[410] Later on the operating theatre attendant handed Palmer a 'golden-colored bullet which I now identify. It bore the marks of having been fired.'[411]

Captain Barrett, the Courts Martial Officer, had already, by 28 September, taken Palmer's statement at the King George V Hospital, saying he was 'handed a bullet found in the operating theatre after the

407 Statement by Lieutenant-Colonel F. J. Palmer, R.A.M.C., sworn statement L MS
      8043 NLI (2).
408 Ibid.
409 Ibid.
410 Ibid.
411 Ibid.

operation on the two deceased soldiers, a copper coloured pistol bullet.'[412] That same afternoon he had been in the North Dublin Union, to see Adjutant Lieutenant Lonsdale of the Lancashire Fusiliers and to examine the sealed packet containing the revolver and ammunition that had been taken from Kevin Barry there on 20 September. He compared the bullet he received from Colonel Palmer with those in the packet and deduced that the 'bullet is of the same calibre … I then sent for Armourer Sergeant of Lanc. Fus. and he said the same. Two of rounds in the packet are flat nosed and one is not. The flat nosed bullets have not been flattened after manufacture, but were cast flattened. The bullet found in operating theatre fits the pistol, Mauser automatic, 1915 pattern, giving evidence the pistol had been recently fired. There were six grooves in the barrel of pistol from the rifling and there are six grooves in the bullet found in op theatre.'[413] It all matched up.

Private Whitehead died 2.50 pm on Monday, 20 September, and Private Humphries died the following night at around 9 o'clock. On 22 September, inquests on the three British soldiers by the City Coroner, Dr Louis A. Byrne, brought in verdicts of death by bullets fired 'by persons unknown'.

Private Whitehead's given name was 'Marshall' rather than 'Matthew', as the official records of the Barry case erroneously state. Similarly, Private Washington, who was only fifteen at the time of his death at Monk's Bakery, was incorrectly named 'Henry', rather than 'Harold'.[414]

On 26 September, a very secret and urgent note came to Dublin Castle from Sergeant A. H. Bann, Court Martial Officer,[415] to the Chief Commissioner of the Dublin Metropolitan Police, regarding the shooting by civilian KEVIN BERRY at a lorry on Church Street on 20 September. Enclosed in this note were several documents: Statements by Captain R. S. Chomley, Sergeant Banks, Private Barnes

---

412 Statement by Captain A. H. Barrett, Courts Martial Officer, Dublin District, L MS 8043 NLI (2) 59/169 A.

413 Ibid.

414 See M. A. Doherty, 'Kevin Barry and the Anglo-Irish Propaganda War', in *Irish Historical Studies* xxxii (2000) [hereafter Doherty, 'Kevin Barry'], 219.

415 Statement from Sergeant A. H. Bann, Court Martial Officer, MS 8043 (2) 59/169A.

(the driver of the lorry who had carried Kevin's gun in transit), and statements by Privates Cleary, Newton, Smith and Noble, along with a sketch plan for the law officers. Sergeant Bann added that the statements comprised evidence from all persons in the lorry, and requested that the case be put up 'AS QUICKLY AS POSSIBLE TO THE LAW OFFICERS FOR A DETERMINATION'. In the bottom left-hand corner, beneath his address, Lr. Castle Yard, Dublin, was typed: 'Prosecute for Murder'.

Geoffrey Granville Whiskard ('Whiskers'), who was not generally well liked, informed General Macready's office, on behalf of Lord French, that 'His Excellency is advised that the offender in this case should be prosecuted by Court Martial for murder'. The decision had already been made, of course, on 20 September by the GOC.[416] Colonel Toppin had written by hand in black ink a letter to GHQ, Parkgate, dated 20 September. He gave a brief description of the incident at the 'North Dublin Union Bakery'. One soldier shot, two wounded. At the bottom he wrote 'Try for Murder'.[417]

Kevin's Affidavit

When Kevin was removed from the North Dublin Union, he was taken to the Bridewell prison for one night and then on to Mountjoy, where he would remain until he was executed, six weeks later. The decisions that were made for and about him were rapid, reflecting the chaos in the British Cabinet and the resolve of Churchill, Macready and, by default, Lloyd George, to deal firmly with these renegade 'civilians'. Sean O'Neill claimed that when Kevin got to the Union, 'they gave him a terrible grilling, pulled his arms from their sockets, blacked his eyes and practically left him next door to death trying to make him tell who was with him, but nothing passed his lips'.[418] However, Kevin's affidavit later showed that he was not as badly treated as O'Neill made out. My father said that 'had he been taken and interrogated by the Black and Tans or the

416 O'Donovan, p. 101.
417 Letter from Col. Toppin to GHQ 20.9.20 Ms. 8043 NLI (8).
418 O'Neill, WS 1,154, BMH p. 10.

Auxiliaries, it is doubtful whether he would have suffered only the injury which put his arm in a sling for three weeks.'[419]

Kevin's affidavit, which was not taken until 28 October – a last-ditch effort by the Barrys and by Kevin's solicitor, Sean Ó hUadhaigh, to publicise his case and garner more public sympathy – had no tone of victimhood, although his treatment in the guardroom of the 1st Lancashire Fusiliers was harsh enough:

1. On the 20th Day of September, 1920, I was arrested in Upper Church Street in the City of Dublin by a Sergeant of the 2nd Duke of Wellington's Regiment and brought under escort to the North Dublin Union. I was brought into the guardroom and searched. I was then removed to the defaulters' room by an escort, belonging to the 1st Lancashire Fusiliers.

2. After I was placed in the defaulters' room two commissioned officers came in. They both belonged to the 1st Lancashire Fusiliers. They were accompanied by three sergeants of the same unit. One of the officers asked my name, which I gave. He then asked the names of my companions in the raid or attack. I refused to give them. He tried to persuade me to give their names and I persisted in refusing. He then sent a sergeant … for a bayonet. When it was brought in the sergeant was ordered … to point the bayonet at my stomach. The same questions as to the names and addresses of my companions were repeated, with the same result. The sergeant was then ordered to turn my face to the wall and point the bayonet to my back. I was so turned. The sergeant then said he would run the bayonet into me if I did not tell. I was turned round again.

3. The same officer then said to me that if I persisted in my attitude he would turn me out to the men in the barrack square, and he supposed I knew what that meant with the men in their present temper. I said nothing. He then ordered the sergeant to put me face down on the floor and twist my arm. I was pushed down on the floor after my

---

419 O'Donovan, p. 91.

handcuffs were removed by the sergeant who went for the bayonet. When I lay on the floor, one of the sergeants knelt on the small of my back. The other two placed one foot each on my back and left shoulder, and the man who knelt on me twisted my right arm, held it by the wrist with one hand while he held my hair with the other to pull back my head. My arm was twisted from the elbow joint. This continued to the best of my judgement for five minutes. It was very painful. The first officer was standing near my feet, and the officer who accompanied him was still present.

4. During the twisting of my arm the first officer continued to question me as to the names and addresses of my companions, and also asked me for the name of my company commander and any other officers I knew.

5. As I still persisted in refusing to answer these questions I was let get up, and I was again handcuffed. A civilian came in, and he repeated the questions with the same result. He informed me that if I gave all the information I knew I could get off. I was then left in the company of the military policeman, the two officers, the three sergeants and the civilian leaving together.

6. I could certainly identify the officer who directed the proceedings and put the questions. I am not sure of the others, except the sergeant with the bayonet. My arm was medically treated by an officer of the RAMC in the NDU the following morning, and by the prison hospital orderly afterwards for four or five days.

Signed KEVIN GERARD BARRY

Declared and subscribed before me at Mountjoy Prison in the County of the City of Dublin this day 28th October, 1920.[420]

Kevin's uncle Pat Dowling went to visit him just before he was transferred to Mountjoy. Kevin complained to Pat about the pain in his arm after the interrogation.

....
420 KBM, WS 731, BMH.

Michael Knightly, member of the 'F' Company in the Dublin Brigade, Intelligence Officer to Michael Collins and a reporter for the *Irish Press*, stated in his witness account that Kitby came to see him the evening of the day that Kevin was arrested, presumably while she and her mother were searching for Kevin after Peggy Barry's birthday party. However, it is still unclear at what point Captain Seamus Kavanagh came to see Mrs Barry and Kitby at 8 Fleet Street, since he claimed to have told them himself about Kevin's whereabouts that afternoon, not long after the raid. In any case, Knightly claims he told Kitby that Kevin was unhurt but that he would likely be tried for his life, because 'two Tommies were dead'.[421]

Knightly was certain it was Kevin, because he had had it confirmed by Tom Kissane, who was also on the Monk's Bakery raid. Knightly had found Kissane very despondent that evening after the raid. 'I found him lying on a sofa, a very disappointed man. "I told Seamus Kavanagh," he said, on the way to North King St. "that the job would not be as easy as he thought, but he was of a different opinion".'[422] A colleague of Knightly's, Paddy Quinn, had seen Kevin being thrown into a lorry at the North Dublin Union. Knightly gave Kissane a description of Kevin, and Kissane confirmed that it was indeed Kevin Barry.

Within a few weeks, Knightly was arrested in a raid on 11 Great Denmark Street. 'I became friendly with my Warder and enquired if Kevin Barry was uninjured when brought to prison. He said no, that his arm was in a sling. It was obvious that poor Kevin had his arms twisted to get him to disclose information, and that he had held out against his torturers.'[423]

On the morning of Wednesday, 22 September, Kitby was summoned to 13 Fleet Street to see Paddy Flanagan, editor of *The Irishman*. His brother Bob Flanagan (sometimes called O'Flanagan), 1st Lieutenant of the H Company, was the one who had been seriously wounded in the ambush at Monk's Bakery. Paddy Flanagan told her that army orders were that 'none of us were to go near Kevin, that there was a hope that the British might feel that a mistake had been made and that only my

---

421 Ibid.
422 Michael Knightly, WS 835, BMH, pp. 2–3.
423 Ibid.

uncle and outside friends, who were not connected with the Republican movement, should visit him'.[424] He also told her that the case would be handled by GHQ, and that they would receive orders through him. In the meantime, they were not to show they were connected to Kevin because there 'was still the hope of confusing the British'.[425]

Mrs Barry was naturally desperate to see Kevin. She got permission from GHQ to visit Kevin in disguise, using the name 'Miss McArdle', her mother's maiden name. She wore clothes borrowed from neighbours and visited him on 1 October, accompanied by a family friend. Kevin refers to her visit in a letter to his friend Gerry McAleer, who visited Kevin quite frequently since he had no known associations with the IRA.

Mrs Barry was referred to in this letter as 'the missus' and Kevin noted that she was 'looking awful'. She must have been very distressed to find Kevin's arm in a sling after the ordeal that he certainly did not tell her about, but more so about his plight in general. Whether Kitby disclosed to her mother her own ominous feelings about Kevin's predicament, is unknown. Kevin had been attended to by Dr Hackett, the prison doctor.

Kevin was, as he almost always was, pretty cheerful, and went about making friends in the prison.

'Immediately after his arrival in Mountjoy he established himself with the warders by giving one of them a tip – Busy Bee – for the race that was to be run on the Wednesday.'[426] Kitby also recalled a story about another prisoner who had been on a raid in the mountains, and told a visitor that they were arresting 'all sorts of people now, they brought in one of their own last night by mistake, a fellow with a wristlet and his hair sleeked back'.[427] He was referring to Kevin.

As a remand prisoner, Kevin was entitled to have meals brought in by his family, but he was still very concerned about associating his actions with them. The authorities never knew that his real address was

424 KBM, WS 731, BMH.
425 Ibid.
426 KBM, WS 731, BMH.
427 Ibid.

8 Fleet Street. Kitby did not see Kevin until she met him in the yard at Marlborough Barracks, where the court martial was held on 20 October. Uncle Pat Dowling visited regularly from the time of Kevin's arrest, because he had no known Republican associations.

On 24 September Kitby's boss, Ernest Aston, told her that he went to Sir Hamar Greenwood with an introduction from Sir Henry McLaughlin, a prominent Freemason, 'a very decent man'. Greenwood told Aston that Kevin would be tried for murder. 'Mr. Aston had pooh-poohed the idea of Kevin being a murderer. He said to Greenwood, "The boy is only a child. I know him well." Greenwood said, "He may be a child in years, but he is a long time mixed up with that crowd."'[428]

Hunger Strikers

Meanwhile, the public eye was not on Kevin Barry, but on Terence MacSwiney, the hunger striker. Three days after the Restoration of Order in Ireland Act came in, Terence MacSwiney, Lord Mayor of Cork, was arrested on charges of sedition at a meeting in the City Hall. In mid-October, following his conviction, he went on hunger strike in Brixton prison. He was becoming an international sensation – a hero for the French and Italian socialists who showed solidarity for the Irish cause.

When MacSwiney died, Ho Chi Minh said that a nation that has such citizens would never surrender. The lead story in the Italian fascist newspaper *Popolo d'Italia* highlighted the MacSwiney story. In India, the War of Independence was getting attention from the sub-continent and MacSwiney's The Principles of Freedom were already influencing India's own efforts to break free of Britain. At the 1920 conference of the Irish Trades Union Congress, Shapurji Saklatvala brought greetings from India.[429] MacSwiney said, 'I am confident that my death will do more to smash the British Empire than my release.'[430] Kevin Barry's attitude was similar, as he faced the noose. As MacSwiney inevitably deteriorated, the Roman Catholic Church's Secretary of State revealed from the Vatican

428 O'Donovan, p. 138.
429 Ibid., p. 74.
430 Ibid.

that 300,000 Brazilian Catholics had demanded the pope's intervention on MacSwiney's behalf. A French newspaper headline read: *'Bravo, l'Irlande heroique: bravo le Lord Mayor de Cork'.*

In Brixton Prison, the guards used the tactic of tempting the hunger striker with food. There were, as there had been with Thomas Ashe, attempts at force feeding in MacSwiney's final days. On 20 October 1920, just twelve days before Kevin Barry was executed, he went into a coma and died five days later. His last rites had been administered by the Capuchin monk who had been to see Kevin Barry in Mountjoy.

MacSwiney was not the only hunger striker. Todd Andrews also went on hunger strike in 1920. First taken to the Bridewell, like Kevin, Andrews was relieved when the next day he was taken from that 'gloomy, obnoxious Bridewell to Mountjoy Prison'.[431] When Peadar Clancy encouraged Andrews to hunger strike he told him 'we were [to be] recognised as prisoners of war'.[432] Andrews, who was eighteen years old, and at UCD with Kevin Barry, was in the E Company of the Dublin Brigade. The *Evening Telegraph* had already reported that 'Christopher Andrews, a boy of eighteen, one of the worse cases on account of his youth and delicate health, collapsed a couple of days ago and was in a state of delirium.'[433] Dublin Castle was in disarray and tried to compromise with the prisoners even to the extent of offering political treatment, but 'Peadar Clancy showed his mettle. He realised that the British Government's nerve had gone.'[434]

They were released, but MacSwiney died and the public was outraged. Fearing large-scale demonstrations in Dublin, the authorities had MacSwiney's coffin sent to Cork, where his funeral was held at the Cathedral of St Mary and St Anne on 31 October, the day before Kevin's execution. He is buried in the Republican plot in St Finbarr's Cemetery in Cork. Churchill, who viewed hunger striking as a pathetic strategy, was quoted by the American journalist John Steele as having 'employed his cleverest verbiage in ridiculing

431 Andrews, p.144.
432 Ibid.
433 Ibid., p. 151.
434 Ibid.

the fast of the Lord Mayor of Cork, which brought loud laughter from his audience'.[435] Churchill believed it took more courage to endure trench warfare than to hunger strike. 'It was during the silly season that Mr MacSwiney assumed his determination to starve himself to death. If the government had given in to him, the whole administration of criminal justice would have broken down. MacSwiney did not want to die. The government didn't want him to die but he had many friends in Ireland who wished he would die. Now, after nine weeks of fasting, he still is alive.'[436]

The difference between hunger striking and fighting in the trenches, is the difference between violence and non-violence. Gandhi's hunger strike was based on the fundamental Hindu and Buddhist tenet of *ahimsa*, non-violence. 'It can be argued that the hunger strikers like Terence MacSwiney had more impact than the belligerent activities of the IRA, in compelling the British government to abandon its support of the terror tactics of the Black and Tans and seek peace with the Irish Republicans.'[437]

Cross Examinations

Todd Andrews recalled after an interrogation in which he was 'let off', that he came to the conclusion that the men who interrogated him were Englishmen who had 'formed in their mind an archetype of the IRA man wearing leggings and trench coat and cap with neither collar nor tie and who was … illiterate. I did not conform to that image. The fact that I was a university student added to their conception of respectability. On the other hand, the fact that Kevin Barry and Frank Flood were students didn't stop the British from hanging them.'[438] Kevin was not seen as a soldier, but as some random assassin on the street wearing a trench coat, carrying a revolver, who with malice aforethought committed an act of cold-blooded murder. That the British and the Irish were at war, was denied. It was all due to the 'baboonery' of the problematic Irish.

---

435 Bew, p. 116.
436 Wilson Papers, 26 July 1920, quoted in Bew, Gibbon and Patterson, p.1150.
437 *The Irish Examiner*, 'Death of MacSwiney had enormous significance as prisoners' hunger strike drew global coverage', Ryle Dwyer, 13 August 2019.
438 Andrews, p. 181.

On 30 September, Captain Barrett, the Courts Martial Officer, met Kevin Barry in a room in Mountjoy to be cross-examined by the sixteen witnesses who would be at the court martial. This would produce the summary of evidence that would be submitted by 4 October. Kevin asked twenty-six questions of just five witnesses. He asked Private Dalby:

Q: How was I dressed?

A: Raincoat, dark suit and a cap.

Q: What colour was my cap?

A: I don't know.

Kevin did not succeed in pointing out any major contradictions in the prosecution's evidence. Nor did he seem too bothered about trying to, since he examined only five of them. Kevin asked Sergeant Banks about his cap, and Banks said he was wearing a soft hat with a black band, not a cap.

The next witness to be cross-examined by Kevin was Bandsman William Smith, 'one of the fatigue men with the Lorry on the 20th September', who noted in his statement that Kevin 'Had not a hat on.' Cross-examined by the accused, he was asked:

Q: Were the three men who fired at the entrance of the passage from the street or at the entrance of the passage from the bakery courtyard?

A: They were at the entrance for the bakery courtyard.

Q: How long was it from the time of the first firing until you saw me in the lorry?

A: About 5 minutes.

Q: How far down the passage were you when the firing started?

A: About a yard or two.

Q: Did you go back to the street when you heard the firing start?

A: No.

Q: How much of the street could you see from your position?

A: I could see about eight or nine houses on the other side of the street.

Q: Could you see the lorry?

A: No.

One other witness present was R. F. Bridges, who had performed the post-mortem on the body of Private Washington.

> The bullet went back through the mount and passed through the spinal cord and lodged in the muscles of the back of the neck. The bullet was extracted. It was 450 pistol bullet, smashed up owing to its passage through the deceased. Then I took out the brain which was healthy. Death was caused by shock and haemorrhage following a gunshot wound, and death was probably instantaneous.[439]

It was for this that Kevin Barry would go down. He declined to ask this man any questions. Captain Barrett submitted 'in very secret' form, the summary of evidence to General Macready.[440]

Kevin's Lawyers

Kevin had sent out messages to everyone that he did not want to be defended. Kitby and Mrs. Barry were told to go ahead and see a Mr Duggan, who was acting under GHQ orders. 'At that time nobody recognised the court and for us this was the most nightmarish period of the whole business.'[441] Kevin was to be the first person to be court-martialled since 1916, under the ROIA. In any case, Duggan was to be 'in charge of defence'. He told Kitby on Saturday, 16 October, that the date was fixed for 20 October to have the court martial. A mere four days' notice was hardly giving a fair trial to Kevin, who was on a capital charge. It was as rushed as it could possibly be.

---

439 http://digital.ucd.ie/get/ucdlib:39126/content
440 O'Donovan, p. 101.
441 KBM, WS 731, BMH.

Duggan was not able to attend the trial on that day, because, as Kitby later discovered, he had to get married on that day, although he told her that he could not attend because he had to appear in another IRA case before the House of Lords. In any case, Duggan handed the case over to Sean Ó hUadhaigh, who would become a lifelong friend of the Barrys. 'No words could ever describe the comfort and strength that Sean Ó hUadhaigh exuded as compared with Mr. Duggan's legal personality.'[442] However, GHQ had already decided that Tim Healy, of Little Doyle and Woods, was to defend Kevin. He read the summary of evidence and he told her with tears that 'there was no doubt they meant to hang Kevin'.[443]

The only hope was that if Kevin could plead insanity he could not mount a defence, but this was abhorrent to the Barrys. 'I refused this [option] out of hand, without consulting anybody.'[444] Healy felt that Kevin would stand a better chance by being allowed to 'follow his inclination and refuse to recognise the court – thus throwing the onus of hanging an 18-year-old prisoner of war who had not been defended'.[445] He gave Kitby a long lecture about 'the essential badness of the English people', stating that Lloyd George was an 'unspeakable cad'.[446] She ended up trying to cheer Healy up, because she felt 'so sorry for an old man who could not understand a young soldier's point of view. He wept bitterly at the sadness of the case, and I could see that he thought there was something odd about me because I was not weeping too.'[447] In the end, through his hopelessness, he sent Kitby home 'laden with a hot-house fruit for Mother'.[448] Seán Ó hUadhaigh took over Kevin's case, meeting him for the first time just two days before the trial.

Now that Kevin's education was not the matter at hand, Kitby took to managing his affairs in this immensely difficult period in the Barry family's lives. Her mother never came with her on trips to lawyers. At this

442 Ibid.
443 Ibid.
444 Ibid.
445 Ibid.
446 Ibid.
447 Ibid.
448 Ibid.

point, Mrs Barry confined herself to the house, and went to see Kevin as much as she could in Mountjoy. But she did come to Kevin's court martial, along with Sean Ó hUadhaigh and Uncle Pat Dowling and Fr Augustine and Joe O'Farrell, a family friend who was in the 5th Battalion who had once delivered a bag of guns to 8 Fleet Street, and, of course, Kevin's dear friend, Gerry McAleer.

British Administration Communication over Kevin Barry Case

'His primacy lies in the decision of General Macready to try him for murder, thus reversing the policy followed after the 1916 executions.'[449]

General Macready received a letter on 5 October from Colonel Henry Davies Foster MacGeagh in the office of the Judge Advocate General, London. Kenneth Marshall, the Deputy Judge Advocate, was to be Judge Advocate at the trial. Macready was instructed to procure a barrister to assist in the case. It would be 'a convenience' if the trials 'could be fixed to begin early in a week so as to avoid, if possible, counsel being detained in Ireland over the weekend.'[450]

A letter dated 7 October 1920 from Parkgate, Dublin Admin GHQ, to Judge Advocate General, 68 Victoria Street, London SW1, included the summary of evidence and draft charge sheets for the case of 'Kevin Barry, Civilian to be tried by Court Martial in Dublin on charges of murder, requesting that Counsel for prosecution and a Judge Advocate may be appointed. Date of trial will be fixed on receipt of the Charge Sheet'.[451] The summary of evidence included all of the reports, sworn statements from witnesses, mostly soldiers, but also doctors who had dealt with the three dead soldiers, and the cross-examinations already mentioned. Captain Barrett had submitted in 'very secret', the summary of evidence to General Macready and assured him that Kevin's pistol and 'all relevant ammunitions' were in his possession. [452]

449 O'Donovan, p. 100.
450 O'Donovan, p. 101.
451 MS 8043 (3), and see Note from Jim O'Donovan in Files.
452 O'Donovan, p. 101.

The Charge Sheet, dated 15 October 1920, and signed at Dublin Castle by Colonel A. H. Spooner of the Lancashire Fusiliers [453] read:

The accused, Kevin Barry, otherwise Barry of 58 South Circular Road, in the County of the City of Dublin, is charged with:

> Committing a crime within the meaning of Regulation of the R.O.I.R., that is to say MURDER, in that he, at Dublin in the County of the City of Dublin, on 20th September 1920, feloniously, willfully and of his malice aforethought did kill and murder no. 46030001 Private Henry Washington, a soldier of His Majesty's Forces. Signed by Lieut Col. A.H. Spooner, Commanding the Lancashire Fusiliers.

There was an intense focus on Kevin Barry's case at Parkgate HQ. Throughout October reports were made daily and telephone messages were dispatched in this rushed preparation for the first court martial since 1916, and, inevitably, the first execution since that of Roger Casement in August 1916. Kevin Barry was going to be made an example of, used as a deterrent for further attacks on British soldiers and property. Communication was between about seventy British officials in Dublin Castle and the London Cabinet. Beyond the bureaucrats and officials were the warders, the chaplains, the guards and stenographers. The case against Kevin was being prepared carefully because it would test the newly made laws.

The choices for the members of the court martial team went on throughout October. Correspondence about civilian Kevin Barry, and the recruiting of those who were to make up the court martial team, went on throughout October. Macready wrote on 8 October that he 'requests that the names of a President, 5 members and 3 waiting members were to be submitted in 10 days' time'.[454] By 11 October, another SECRET note from the Under Secretary at Dublin Castle, Sir Hamar Greenwood,

---

453 MS. 8043 (8) NLI.
454 Ref 1057/ 168/AZ written and marked SECRET on 8 October 1920 by Major General Macready. This is in MS 8043 (8).

(referring to Gov. file 31707 containing the case of Kevin Barry), states that the Lord Lieutenant requested under Reg. 69 (5) of R.O.I.R.[455] to nominate Major Sidney Johnson Watts as a member of the court martial to be held for the trial of the accused, as he had legal knowledge and experience. Another letter marked SECRET[456] to the Judge Advocate from Parkgate HQ stated that Kevin Barry's trial was to be held on Wednesday, 20 October. This, as has already been seen, was conveyed to Kevin's then solicitor Eamonn Duggan as late as 16 October, leaving a mere four days for Kevin to prepare his defence.

The court martial team were Brigadier General Cranley Onslow, Officer Commanding the 25th Infantry Brigade, Major H. P. Yates of the 2nd South Wales Borderers, Colonel C. F. Phipps of the Royal Garrison Artillery, Col. E. Morton of the 1st Cheshire Regiment, Colonel F. C. Pilkington of the 15th Hussars, Colonel B. H. Chetwynd-Staplyton of the Cheshire Regiment, Major S. J. Watts of the Royal Engineers, and an Assistant Legal Officer, who was a barrister. It was a very distinguished and senior court. The court martial was to be conducted at the Marlborough Barracks, the newest of the Dublin barracks. Members of the public would be allowed to attend, depending on how much space was there, but they had to be searched by the officer commanding the 15th Hussars. The court was to be closed to the press until the trial began. It was a court that, despite the eminence of its personnel, Kevin Barry refused to acknowledge from the outset.

---

455 Under Reg. 69 (5) of R.O.I.R / Gov. file 31707 on Kevin Barry, in MS 8043 (8).
456 RO/ 2509 MS 8043 (8).

Photo of a letter from the Kevin Barry memorial Committee, 1958. Tombeagh house.

Photo © Liosa McNamara

Kevin Barry Junior
Photo © Liosa McNamara

The hiding place for IRA during War of Independence.

Photo © Liosa McNamara

Kevin Barry Junior in the Parlour in Tombeagh, beside a portrait of Kevin Barry.

Photo © Liosa McNamara

Kevin Barry junior and the author, Síofra O'Donovan

Photo © Líosa McNamara

Kevin Barry Jr. in the front entrance to Tombeagh house.

Photo © Liosa McNamara

Michael Barry, son of Kevin and Evelyn Barry, with his niece.

Photo © Liosa McNamara

Evelyn and Kevin Barry, at Tombeagh.

Photo © Liosa McNamara

The Barry family at Tombeagh: LEFT TO RIGHT- Ryan, Jenny, Mikey, Mike, Aoibinn, Abigeal, Sadhbh, Neal, Christopher, Niamh, Evelyn, Kevin, Kevin, Liz (Browne).

Photo © Liosa McNamara

Sean Reynolds, prison guard at Mountjoy, in the gallows where Kevin Barry was hanged by John Ellis on the morning of 1st November, 1920

Photo © Liosa McNamara

The chain for the gallows at Mountjoy jail.

Photo © Liosa McNamara

The gallows at Mountjoy jail
Photo © Liosa McNamara

Memorial plaque for the ten executed men over the period 1920-1 at Mountjoy, all hanged by John Ellis. Kevin Barry, Frank Flood, Thomas Bryan, Patrick Ryan, Patrick Maher, Patrick Doyle, Edmund Foley, Thomas Traynor and Patrick Moran. Most of these were young men, tried in courts martial for their part in the War of Independence.

Photo © Liosa McNamara

Chapter Eleven

THE TRIAL

John Joe Carroll felt that the only hope to save Kevin, at this point, was to attack the escort with an armoured car on the way to the court martial, since the IRA had already worked out the route. According to Sean O'Neill, a plan had been sanctioned by GHQ to seize the armoured car during the court martial. It was parked near a bank at Doyle's corner, Phibsboro, for a payroll collection, manned by a one-armed soldier. The Volunteers of the D Company, along with Dick McKee and Peadar Clancy, carried out the attack but it failed, and Willie O'Connell was killed in the operation.[457] This chance to save Kevin was gone. Years later, in retrospect, Carroll felt that the Big Shots 'behind the scenes had the last word. Kevin Barry was more valuable dead than alive.'[458]

What happened to the armoured car that was taking Kevin to the court martial at Marlborough Barracks was another matter that made him twenty-five minutes late for the proceedings.

Marlborough Barracks

The morning of Wednesday, 20 October saw the rain pour. Kitby, Mrs Barry, Seán Ó hUadhaigh, Uncle Pat Dowling , along with Fr Augustine of Church Street and Joe O'Farrell (who was a member of 5th battalion who had once dumped a bag of arms at 8 Fleet Street), arrived at the court martial in a cab. Gerry McAleer was also with the family, along with Eileen O'Neill. They had to wait at the gates to be searched before they went into the court. Although Kevin was late, they went on in before the members of the court martial, who arrived promptly at 10 o'clock, and sat down at the long table.

---

457 Sean O'Neill, WS 1,154, BMH, pp. 12–13.
458 John Joe Carroll to Jim O'Donovan, 1953.

Kitby noticed 'the amount of brass that was gathered together to try one's brother',[459] referring to what must have been a very serious looking panel of court martial officials. She noticed that the presiding officer was a general, 'and there were ten other officers descending from him on either side through various ranks'.[460] She noticed the general (Onslow) was a 'very tall man with a dark melancholy face and a lot of dark hair'. [461]

It was silent. There was no sign of Kevin. Kitby observed the uneasiness at the long table. At 10.20 there was a 'subdued kind of hysteria at the table. We all felt puzzled, but beautifully detached.'[462]

Meanwhile, Kevin's armoured car had broken down, somewhere on the North Circular Road. They waited twenty minutes for another one. Kitby, to whom Kevin told this during an adjournment, said that that was why Kevin had a look of bemusement when he finally arrived at 10.25, looking 'very cheerful and desperately amused when he saw the table full of British officers'.[463] Seán Ó hUadhaigh asked for a short adjournment of fifteen minutes to give him time to consult with his client, quickly explaining to Kevin how the case had been handed over to him at the last minute and that he had had no time to prepare a defence. 'Kevin scowled but came back beaming after the adjournment.'[464]

Percival Clarke, KC, who was with Major D. R. Osborne opened the case by stating: 'This is the first case of its kind … tried by such a tribunal … unfortunately rendered necessary by the conditions through which the country is now passing.' He gave an account of the 'Church Street Shooting Affray', as the *Evening Herald* called it that day.[465] The Judge Advocate General, according to Kitby, 'had made it clear at the outset that they were not accusing him of the death of any or all of the three men killed, that they had only to prove that he was one of a party who came there armed to attack British soldiers, of whom three had been

459 KBM, WS 731, BMH.
460 Ibid.
461 Ibid.
462 Ibid.
463 Ibid.
464 Ibid.
465 O'Donovan, p. 107.

killed, and that any and every member of the attacking party was technically guilty of murder.'[466] The point was that it was the first time that an IRA member, who had been armed while attacking Crown forces, was being brought before a military court, 'rather than the patently unreliable civil alternative'.[467] As the attack had resulted in the deaths of three young British soldiers, Kevin 'would face a capital charge of murder or at the very least, of having been an accessory to murder'.[468]

Kevin declared: 'As soldier of the Irish Republic, I refuse to recognise the Court.'[469] There was 'consternation' at the long table. General Onslow patiently conveyed the gravity of the situation to Kevin, telling him, 'That is a plea of not guilty'.[470] Kevin did not answer, but took out a copy of the previous day's *Evening Telegraph* and started to read it. Seán Ó hUadhaigh explained that 'Another professional gentleman was instructed in this case, but he had to go away and it was only yesterday that I was instructed. This is the first opportunity I have in consulting the accused. But as he has declined to recognise the court, my functions have come to an end.'[471]

Seán Ó hUadhaigh, just before he stepped down, lodged a complaint which the president ordered should not be published 'from the present'. He declared: 'My reason for doing so is to draw the attention of the court to it before I retire, as I feel sure it will be investigated … the accused, not recognising the court, might not call attention to it by himself. The accused is a minor and I was retained by his family.' The president replied that they were in the court for only one purpose, but that he would attend to the complaint. Ó hUadhaigh added that 'The attitude he [Kevin] takes up is that the act he did was an act of war, and I do not see how I can have any further part in the proceedings.'[472] Ó hUadhaigh said, however, that would remain with the family for the duration of the proceedings.

....

466 Ibid.
467 Ibid.
468 John Ainsworth, 'Kevin Barry, the Incident at the Monk's Bakery and the Making of an Irish Republican Legend', Oxford: Blackwell, 2002, p. 376.
469 This was reported in *The Freeman's Journal*, 21 October 1920.
470 Ibid.
471 Ibid.
472 O'Donovan, p. 108.

The complaint lodged by Ó hUadhaigh was regarding Kevin's experience of being badly treated by the officers while he was in custody at the North Dublin Union. It was the least and the best that Seán Ó hUadhaigh could do, since he could not, according to Kevin's own wishes, present a case for the defence. Kevin's sworn affidavit of ill-treatment was taken by Sean Ó hUadhaigh and a Justice of Peace in the North Dublin Union, and published just days before his execution, on 28 October. Again, this was the best that Ó hUadhaigh could do given that he had no capacity to represent Kevin.

Kevin's refusal to recognise the court is important to understand from the perspective of the IRA. Sean O'Neill makes it very clear in his witness statement that it was expected of an IRA man not to recognise the court. Yet GHQ had sent word to Kevin in Mountjoy and instructed Kitby, too, to have Kevin recognise the court, assuring him that 'Counsel would defend him and recognise the Court',[473] but Kevin had always 'turned down the G.H.Q. instruction and threw everything that was rotten back in their teeth'.[474] He stated that if Kevin had 'only to obey G.H.Q. orders and had Counsel to aid him and recognise the court, no one would have blamed him'.[475] What he says next, is that Kevin 'saw in a flash the import of this, the baseness of those who were supposed to lead us, their deliberate reversing of all the orders to every armed Volunteer and kindred organisation, the spineless individuals … '[476] who would eventually compromise when the Treaty was signed in 1921.[477] He stated that if he had recognised the court, and accepted legal representation, he may not have gotten such a sentence. 'The Irish nation and every I.R.A. man could hand up their gun and tradition and settle down for slavery for ever'.[478] By recognising the court, as far as O'Neill and Kevin were concerned, sovereignty was gambled away. 'This was the second and greatest test for Kevin. The first was that greater love hath no man than he would

473 O'Neill, WS 1,154, BMH, p. 12.
474 Ibid.
475 Ibid.
476 Ibid.
477 Ibid.
478 Ibid.

lay down his life for his friends; 2nd; the whole future of Ireland depended on him.'[479]

O'Neill's loftiness and his awe of Kevin's actions, however, were not quite accurate. The outcome, whether Kevin was represented by counsel or not, would not have been very different. It would, however, have put the spotlight on the bullet that was produced as evidence for the killing of Private Whitehead by Kevin.

After each of the sixteen witnesses had made their statements, General Onslow asked Kevin if he had any questions and Kevin said 'no'. Kevin got impatient, according to Kitby. He put down his newspaper and he said 'Look! I have told you I don't recognise the court. I have no interest in what anybody says here. You are only wasting your time asking me.'[480] Kitby noticed the general was 'flushed a very dark red but he said mildly, 'It is my duty to ask you. I think as a solider you can appreciate that.'[481]

'Righto,' said Kevin, 'if it facilitates you, I have no questions.'

From then on, he answered 'no' politely to every question he was asked.[482]

At least in words, Onslow recognised Kevin as a soldier, however frustrating his behaviour was. Onslow was mild and patient, albeit flushed. Kevin had thrown the workings of the court back at their long table, obstinately keeping his newspaper raised, a gesture of defiance that cannot have seemed anything other than disrespectful to the long table. That it was his last act of defiance, was another matter. Of the sixteen witnesses, none connected Kevin directly with the death of Private Matthew Whitehead in the first hearing in the morning, prior to the lunch break.

The Crown counsel described the magazine in Kevin's automatic gun, according to the evidence produced by Captain Barrett. In it, there were two live cartridges and there was another cartridge in another chamber. The two rounds in the magazine were flat nosed and the one in the chamber was round nosed, in a copper casing.

---

479 Ibid.
480 KBM, WS 731, BMH.
481 Ibid.
482 Ibid.

Private Whitehead, O'Neill noted, 'had three bullets in him, including a parabellum bullet and of course finding a similar gun on Kevin they made the charge stick even though that bullet did not necessarily cause the death'.[483] If this was an ordinary trial, Kevin would have been acquitted, as several of the men had parabellums and Kevin could only have shot this private in the head from his position at the lorry.

The adjournment was at one o'clock. Kevin was taken away, the court martial team filed out, and Mrs Barry, Kitby, Ó hUadhaigh and friends went to the North City Arms, a hotel near the Cattle Market. There would only be another hour of trial after this, and even within that short time there was a short adjournment, during which there was time for Kitby to speak with Kevin – for the first time since she had had dinner with him at 8 Fleet Street on Sunday, 19 September. Kevin discreetly told her his own account of what happened at Monk's Bakery, where he had the job of keeping the lorry covered on the pathway outside the entrance to the bakery. He told her that he had knelt to fire a shot that killed a solider. 'He was amused at the evidence given, and that they were unable to account for the death of this particular soldier.'[484] Kitby's account is a little confused as she states two paragraphs later that 'when he stood up after discarding the third round, he lifted a flap of the lorry, fired and got this man'.[485] It is unclear as to whether this was the same shot or a different shot at another solider. That she may have misheard or misunderstood is certainly a possibility, given the rushed circumstances of their meeting, surrounded as they were by British authorities. It would be important, however, in the trial to clarify whether Kevin had shot one, two or all of the three deceased soldiers and to establish that the gun that Kevin Barry was caught with and the remaining bullets in it matched the bullets that had killed one or more of these soldiers. In the end, he would be sentenced for the death of Private Whitehead, whose body had three bullet wounds. The effort made by the Judge Advocate's office and the Courts Martial Officer to link Kevin's gun and the death of Private Whitehead required the elimination of the charges of murdering

---

483 O'Neill, WS 1,154, P 11 BMH.
484 KBM, WS 731, BMH.
485 Ibid.

the other two privates, Washington and Humphries, who had been killed by bullets of a different calibre from those of Kevin's parabellum.[486]

My father, being a journalist, noted how the newspaper accounts were not extensive and were based on the reporters' judgements, rather than the details given in evidence. Only one reporter from the *Freeman's Journal* 'took his courage in his hands and reported the exchange between President General Onslow and Sean Ó hUadhaigh about Kevin's ill treatment'.[487] What constituted the largest body of evidence in the trial were the documents from what my father calls 'the Barry file, removed from Dublin Castle by Jim O'Donovan in 1921', containing the sixteen sworn statements, mostly from soldiers. Somehow, my grandfather had obtained this file and some time in the 1950s he gave it to the National Library. The brown envelope and twine in which he sent it, remains with the file, now classified as MS 8043.

The bullet that was produced in court, which was supposed to demonstrate that Kevin Barry shot Private Whitehead, has since disappeared. My grandfather wrote in his unpublished book, 'Ireland's Kevin Barry', that 'in circuitous ways, all three bullets, the one that allegedly killed Whitehead, the one that allegedly killed Humphries and the one found at Church Street that is believed to have killed Washington, had found their way into his possession in later years'.[488] Now, my father wrote, 'all that can be found is a misshapen piece of lead in an envelope marked "Washington", forming part of MS 8043 in the National Library.'[489] Whitehead was killed by a copper (gold, according to Colonel Palmer) bullet, not lead. Whitehead's entry wound was in the 'left lumbo [sic] abdominal region', and the bullet was lodged in the body with 'no wounds of exit'. Palmer was certain that the bullet found by his attendant in a pool of blood in the surgery, could only have come from Private Whitehead, swept up unnoticed in a mass of blood clots during the operation. This was when the attendant handed him 'a

486 O'Donovan, p. 110.
487 Ibid.
488 Ibid., p .111.
489 Ibid.

golden coloured bullet … which I now identify, that bore the marks of having been fired'.[490]

Captain Barrett stated that on 28 September Colonel Palmer handed him 'a bullet found in the operating theatre after the operations on the two deceased soldiers. It is copper colored pistol bullet.'[491] Later, at the North Dublin Union, Lieutenant Lonsdale of the Lancashire Fusiliers gave him the revolver and ammunition that had been seized from Kevin. Barrett then sent for the Armourer Sergeant of the Lancashire Fusiliers, who stated that the two bullets were the same, 'that two of the rounds in the packets were flat nosed and one was not'.[492]

The bottom line was that the bullet found in the operating theatre fitted Kevin's pistol, his Mauser automatic, 1915 pattern. Maybe a defence counsel would have picked apart the evidence, but even if there had been some cross-examination, the outcome and the verdict would have been the same.

Colonel Toppin, who had written the first rushed report to General Macready on 20 September, outlining the events of that day, brought in the ordnance officer, Lieutenant Thomas Watters of the Royal Army Ordnance Corps, who gave evidence. He testified that the pistol given to him was 'a '1915 Mausa [sic] pistol', with the barrel having been fired through. He declared that the 'magazine would carry … eight rounds, and the three rounds produced fit the pistol, each of a different mark … the expended round fits the pistol. The grooves on the expended round prove that it has been fired, the bullet has six grooves, there are six grooves in the pistol bullet fired out of a pistol of the same calibre and pattern as the one produced.'[493]

Colonel Toppin's 'Very Secret' note to General Macready at GHQ Ireland on 5 October, said, 'The pistol in question together with the round found in the operating theatre are now in possession of my Courts Martial Officer.'[494] This was Captain Barrett. The court martial evidence

490 MS 8043 (8) Statement of Lieutenant Colonel Palmer.
491 MS 8043 (3) Statement of Captain Barrett.
492 Ibid.
493 O'Donovan, p. 116.
494 MS 8043 (6), NLI.

on 20 October 'methodically linked Kevin's automatic specifically with the death of Private Matthew Whitehead. The witnesses had an easy time of it. There was no cross examination.'[495]

We only know of Kitby's conversation with Kevin when the court was adjourned for a short period in the proceedings after lunch that day. We don't know how Kevin interacted with his mother, nor with his dear friend Gerry McAleer, nor with Joe O'Farrell, who would later find Kitby a job in the ESB. Gerry McAleer told my father that 'he was a terrific IRA man, a gunman'. He also noted that it was surprising that the authorities even let him into Marlborough Barracks.[496]

Fr Augustine told my grandfather in 1948 about that day of the court martial. He saw Kevin as 'his usual calm self, not at all perturbed. Mrs Barry had also been very calm throughout the proceedings.'[497] He could see Kevin's face clearly, from about ten feet away. 'He sat on the chair before the presiding Judge, leaning back easily against the support of his chair, his head bent in a meditative mood, his chin resting, as it were, on his chest. He seemed quite indifferent to everything that was passing and even now [1948] I remember thinking how extraordinary it was he was so unemotional in such strange circumstances.'[498]

Uncle Pat Dowling, Sean Ó hUadhaigh and Fr Augustine were, at the end of the short talk with Kevin, talking seriously together. Fr Augustine came over to Kitby and said, 'Katty, we want you to take your mother home. Sean Ó hUadhaigh thinks that this is the adjournment for evidence of character. From what Mr Aston told you, this will be prejudicial to Kevin and we are afraid that the sentence might actually be pronounced in Court.'[499]

Kitby took her mother home on this advice. In any case, no sentence was announced when the court resumed. The circumstances were extraordinary, and the court proceedings under the new ROIA novel and

---

495 O'Donovan, p. 117.
496 O'Donovan, p. 106.
497 O'Donovan, p. 118, Information from Fr Augustine, Capuchin, to James O'Donovan 1948.
498 Ibid.
499 KBM, WS 731, BMH.

unorthodox. The members of the court would usually have reached their verdict and announced it by the end of the trial and the accused would have been publicly informed of the charges. By the end of the day, the Judge Advocate was reported by the *Evening Herald* as announcing merely that 'the court is closed and sentence will be promulgated'.

Kevin was taken away, and Pat Dowling followed him to Mountjoy in a cab, arriving there before the armoured car. As the car passed him, Kevin waved to him. For the rest of that day, none of the Barry family knew what would happen to Kevin.

Mark Sturgis, an old Etonian who had been a senior official at Dublin Castle since July 1920, noted in his diary in mid-October 1920, 'Everybody has been shooting everybody while I've been away – quite gay!'[500] and on 21 October, the day after the court martial, he wrote 'The Bakery Gun Boy, Kevin Barry, is sentenced to death.'[501]

---

500 Sir Mark Sturgis's diary, PRO 30/59.
501 Ibid.

Chapter Twelve

THE SENTENCE

'We knew then that he was sentenced, and later in the day he said that the sentence was handed to him on the evening of the 20th by the Court Martial Officer, who burst into tears and left the cell hurriedly.'[502]

On 21 October, Kate Kinsella, the housekeeper at 8 Fleet Street, came back at 8.30 am – earlier than usual – from Mountjoy with Kevin's breakfast, which she had made on his request every morning. The authorities had refused to accept this breakfast for Kevin. She knew what this meant, because she had seen this happen with the Invincibles, many of whom were hanged in Kilmainham Gaol in 1883. Kevin was not an assassin, but he was being treated like one. Unlike the Invincibles, who informed on each other, Kevin had never opened his mouth. But the refusal of the prisoner's breakfast meant the end.

The warders claimed to know nothing about his sentence and were friendly, but were merely acting on orders. Kitby described the sound of Kate Kinsella's 'loud crying' when she got in the door of 8 Fleet Street, with the breakfast still in her hands. The *Irish Independent* of 21 October said 'We learn unofficially that Barry has been lodged in the condemned cell in Mountjoy Jail, and the sentence of the court martial (whether confirmed by the competent Military Authority or not we cannot say) that he is to be hanged has been intimated to him.'[503]

That day, Kitby visited Kevin. He told her how the District Court Martial Officer, Captain Barrett, who visited him frequently about the

502 KBM, WS 731, BMH.
503 O'Donovan, p. 119.

summary of evidence and with whom Kevin was on good terms, 'burst into tears' the previous evening, when he handed Kevin his sentence. He would be hanged on 1 November 1920. '"Mind," he [Kevin] said. "There is to be no appeal." I said, "No, we wouldn't do that." He said, "I know you wouldn't, but I depend on you to see that nobody in this family lets me down."'[504]

Kitby makes it clear that he was not speaking about anyone in his immediate family organising a reprieve. The concern was about 'our uncles who were kind and good and well intentioned but were not convinced Republicans'.[505] Kevin still hoped at this point that his sentence might be changed to shooting. 'I must say I'd rather be shot,'[506] he told Kitby. As far as he was concerned, he was living in luxury, as he put it to Kitby, 'on the fat of the land, that he had been told he had only to ask for any kind of food and drink and it would be supplied'.[507] There were two Auxiliaries with him that morning, and night and day until the end. He was allowed four visits every weekday, two in the morning and two in the afternoon, up to three persons at each.

Convicted prisoners got 8 oz of bread for breakfast, 1½ pints of stirabout with 3 oz of Indian meal and 3 oz oatmeal for dinner, and 8 oz of bread for supper. On 22 October Captain B. J. Hackett, known as Dr. Hackett, the prison doctor who had tended to Kevin's sprained arm, ordered a diet 'recommended for the prisoner Kevin Barry under sentence of death'. My father found in the prison records at Mountjoy[508] (which no longer exist), this diet listed in Kevin Barry's records:

> Breakfast: 1lb. Bread, ½ lb. bacon; 1½ oz. butter; ¼ oz tea; 1 oz sugar. Dinner: 2lbs potatoes; ½ lb bread, ¾ lb beef (¾ lb of fish on Fridays in lieu of meat) and one small bottle of stout. Supper: 1 lb bread; 1½ oz sugar; 1 pint milk.

504 KBM WS 731, BMH.
505 Ibid.
506 Ibid.
507 Ibid.
508 O'Donovan, p. 122.

Dr Hackett also allowed Kevin to be supplied with cigarettes and fruit in season – 'grapes or apples may be supplied to prisoner Kevin Barry under sentence of death'.[509]

The Condemned Cell

Kevin Barry's cell was at the end of the D-Wing of Mountjoy Prison, just yards from the hang house. It was a spacious cell with a fireplace and a lavatory. When Mountjoy was built in 1847, the cells had a lavatory each but they became damaged and were done away with. During the winters, gas lights were used, just above the cell door. Where previously the cells had hammocks (some of these hooks remain), Kevin had a wooden plank bed.

There was a prison chapel that had barred seating by the altar for condemned men, and it was compulsory for prisoners to attend Mass daily, and twice on Sundays. The chapel was originally built with boxes for each convict so that they could not see or talk to each other. Warders were seated in elevated positions to observe prisoners. The boxes were removed in 1859.

The original entrance to Mountjoy is different from today. Cowley Place, named after Lieutenant General Cowley, was built in 1792, and was the main avenue into the prison. Today, the Female Prison, Dóchas, now stands on the site of the first Cowley Place. The four wings of the prison, A, B, C and D, had three tiers each and radiated like a fan from the 'Circle', the centre of the prison. From that Circle, staff could monitor the spaces that separated the 496 cells.[510]

One of Kevin's two chosen guards who would be with him until execution, was Edward Charles Stewart Proctor from Killeshin, County Carlow. His daughter, Mags Leonard, told my father in 1988 that her father did both night and day duty. 'They'd go in at 7am and leave at 5pm.

---

509 O'Donovan, p. 123
510 Taken from observations at Mountjoy, 2019, and information from Sean Reynolds, Mountjoy guard.

Night duty was 5pm to 7am.'[511] The day Kevin was hanged her father was on day duty. She kept the rosary and prayer book given to him by Kevin. She remembered the Prison Avenue on the day of the execution.

'They would always hang a notice, a small white notice on the prison gates. All the people would kneel in prayer. Kevin was astonishing. He wouldn't tell them anything. All the guards had time with Kevin.'[512]

The hang house, at the end of the D Block, where Kevin's cell was second on the left-hand side, was where Kevin's life would end. Today, cells 30 to 28 give an indication of the size of his cell. The beams and chains in the hang house remain. A trapdoor, which used to be padded with horse hair, opens when the pin is taken out, and the lever is pushed forward. This trapdoor could accommodate two simultaneous hangings – Frank Flood was hanged with Thomas Bryan in 1921.

Frantic Appeals

Although Kitby's boss Ernest Aston understood that Kevin was to be hanged, and that the Barry family refused to make appeals to the 'enemy authorities', he still 'held that he was free to do what he considered his duty to prevent an outrage'. On Monday, 25 October, he asked Kitby for a photograph of Kevin, telling her that he intended to cross the water to England that night with Commander John F. McCabe, an Irish Catholic official in the local government board, who had distinguished himself in the British Navy in the Great War and was a friend of Lloyd George's family.[513] Aston believed that Kevin's execution could be stopped at the highest level, and he believed he'd found the man to stop it. Kitby and Mrs Barry were very hesitant, and even refused to give him a photo of Kevin until the IRA gave her permission to do so. When Aston returned, and Kitby saw him in the office on Saturday, 30 October, her boss was 'very gay and said, "It is all right. the reprieve is through."' Kitby said that 'This was so funny that I laughed. He looked a little hurt … I was

---

511 Interview with Mags Leonard by Donal O'Donovan, 1988. Tape cassette. All rights reserved, private estate of Donal O'Donovan.

512 Ibid.

513 KBM, WS 731, BMH.

so sorry that I had been ungracious, but I explained to him my deep instinct that Kevin was to die on Monday morning. He said: "Don't be morbid! Run home now and tell your mother the good news."'[514] She did go home to tell her mother, but before there was time to figure out what Aston was on about, Frank Flood came to see them with two other men about the rescue attempt.

On Thursday 28 October Ned O'Toole, Kevin Barry's teacher in Rathvilly National School, sent a telegram to the House of Commons to Joseph Devlin MP, a prominent politician who was also the grand master of the Ancient Order of Hibernians. O'Toole wanted to do whatever he could to change the decision to have Kevin executed on the morning of 1 November, 1920. Devlin replied to O'Toole by letter, telling him that he had been to see Prime Minister Lloyd George in Downing Street and that Lloyd George promised to bring the matter to the Cabinet the next day. But when Devlin sent a second telegram to Downing Street at 4 pm the next day, having had no news from the Cabinet, he learned that Lloyd George had taken off to the Isle of Wight for the weekend. Devlin then went to see King George, who, he understood, might be more sympathetic. But the king had gone to Sandringham for the weekend.[515] 'Mr Devlin said that the Cabinet was not unsympathetic but he was afraid that some sinister influence was working against them ... Sir Henry Wilson, the Commander in Chief of the British army, had threatened to resign if Kevin were not executed.'[516] Later, Lloyd George wrote of Wilson: 'He was very clever but erratic and possessed of a sustained egoism which was almost a disease.'[517] Devlin also told O'Toole that Lloyd George had tears in his eyes as they spoke about Kevin. Still, there was apparently nothing he could do.

It is not known if Kevin knew about his schoolteacher's desperate attempts to save him from the gallows. A photograph survives of Kevin and his brother Michael working in O'Toole's award-winning garden.

....

514 Ibid.
515 O'Toole, p. 137.
516 Ibid.
517 Ibid., pp. 137–8.

'Apparently some of the villagers who worked at Lisnavagh [house, in Rathvilly] held O'Toole accountable for Barry's militant activities, although their sympathies switched to pro-Barry after his death.'[518]

For the Barrys, at this time, especially for Kitby, who carried everything about Kevin's case and fate on her shoulders, it was a whirlwind of 'dashing round and dealing with all kinds of people',[519] some who wanted to sponsor petitions for a reprieve, others to offer sympathy, and others to enquire why no rescue plan was in the pipeline. The latter Kitby dismissed harshly as people who 'would not know one end of a gun from another'.[520] She and the family were firmly fixed on their attitude to reprieve. 'Kevin's wishes were to be carried out and no word or action of his family could be twisted into letting him down. He had laid this as a charge upon me so that in adding to my own personal inclinations, I felt I had the sanction of his wishes.'[521]

At this busy time, Kitby bumped into Alderman James Moran, 'a very nice man but not a Republican. He looked very distressed and … said, "you are in a great hurry." I said, "Yes I am up to my neck organising the successful execution of my brother … ."'[522] she looked at his shocked face and realised it had been a cruel thing to say to a man who was 'on the opposite side of the great gulf fixed at the time between Republicans and those we called pro Britishers'.[523] This and the incident with the original lawyer the GHQ had chosen to defend Kevin, Tim Healy, who cried hopelessly over Kevin's case, shows just how convinced the Barrys were that tears were of no value. Commitment to the cause was everything.

On Thursday, 28 October, Kitby had been called to Wood Press at 13 Fleet Street where Dick McKee, Brigadier of the Dublin Brigade, was waiting for her. He wanted her, with Sean Ó hUadhaigh and a justice of peace, to take Kevin's sworn affidavit concerning his torture in the North Dublin Union. McKee was convinced there could be no

518 Turtle Bunbury, http://www.turtlebunbury.com/history/history_heroes/hist_hero_
     kevinbarry.html
519 KBM, WS 731, BMH.
520 Ibid.
521 Ibid.
522 Ibid.
523 Ibid.

reprieve unless they had this, and if it were published in the UK press by Saturday, 30 October, it would have a great effect on public opinion there. Desmond FitzGerald, Dáil Director of Propaganda, met her at 5.30 in Arthur Griffith's office on Brunswick Street (now Pearse Street) in Dublin, with Sean Ó hUadhaigh and a justice of peace, Dr Myles Keogh, who went with Kitby to Mountjoy. Keogh, was, according to Kitby, 'very nervous and puzzled', and his nervousness increased when he saw the armed Auxiliaries in the boardroom with Kevin (where all interviews were conducted after the death sentence), but 'they were most friendly and co-operative with him and deeply respectful with us. Kevin was on the best of terms with every Auxie that guarded him.'[524] There was a fire burning in the grate.

After Kevin gave the affidavit, Keogh was 'in a terrible state of mind', and 'kept trying to impress on Sean and myself that something must be done to save this boy who was in such grave danger'.[525] She said that Sean and she were calmer, as they were always living with this kind of danger.

The affidavit did not get printed in Saturday's papers, as it was hoped, but it did appear in the English and Irish papers on Monday, 1 November, the day Kevin was hanged. There were debates about it in the House of Commons on 5 November. Interestingly, Kevin's warder, Patrick Berry, was certain that Kevin had not been maltreated while he was at Mountjoy. 'I was not aware of any attempt to torture him during his time in prison. It is possible that after his arrest the soldiers may have manhandled him before he came to the gaol. But there was no manhandling as far as I am aware by the warden in Mountjoy. The Auxiliaries had no access to him until he was sentenced to death.'[526]

Kevin had also been visited on 28 October by Gerry McAleer. As far as the Barrys knew, this was his last visit to Kevin. In fact, he had taken Kevin's boots to be repaired on this visit, and he would return them, with information about an escape plan, in a couple of days.

524 KBM, WS 731, BMH.
525 Ibid.
526 Patrick Joseph Berry, Prison Guard in Mountjoy 1906–1922. WS 942, BMH p. 11.

Letter from Kevin Barry to his lecturer, Dr. Coffey in UCD. He wrote this on his last evening: '...Tell my fellow students to say a prayer for me and tell them I will miss them but I will remember them in my prayers tonight [the eve of Kevin's executinon] and also say a prayer for Frank Flood [executed in 1921 by the same hangman in Mountjoy], ... Parting is such a sad thing... this is not goodbye. I will go to the gallows as an Irishman... with love in my heart for a free Ireland.'

'Who signed the confirmation?' Gerry asked him.

'I'm blessed if I know,' Kevin replied.

'Was it Macready?'

'For all I know or care it might have been Charlie Chaplin,' said Kevin. Gerry McAleer, interviewed by Donal O'Donovan in 1988 said that he really felt that Kevin did not care. His 'calm unconcern' was typical of his character. 'He did not believe that he was doing anything wonderfully heroic.' Kevin apparently said, to cheer his friend Gerry up, that he would like to leave him something. He saw Gerry looking down at his shoes and joked that he would like to leave him those 'only I couldn't very well walk barefoot to the scaffold'.[527]

My father asked Gerry McAleer if Kevin ever really took anything seriously and Gerry answered:

527 Interview with Gerry McAleer, by Donal O'Donovan, 1988. Private papers.

'He did – his country and his country's cause. Beneath his carefree laughter lay a heart that loved, and a brain that planned for, Ireland.'[528]

His last letter to Gerry McAleer refers to that visit. It was written on Saturday, 30 October, in purple pencil. He begins:

> I'll hardly get a chance of seeing you any more, hence this epistle … Now Gerry I can't indulge in heroics nor can I curse, so this is a very tame letter – not at all like the ones you used to get from me, but you will make allowances. Give my best wishes to any old Belvederians you meet. You know that it is unnecessary to state you have all my best wishes for success in everything – even love … when the 2nd Meds are assembled tell 'em, boys and girls, that I wish them every success and ask them to say a prayer for me when I go over the top on Monday.
>
> P.S. Goodbye now and remember me to all at home. Your pal, Kevin.[529]

The Archbishop's Appeal

On Saturday, 30 October, the Archbishop of Dublin, Dr Walsh, who had sworn to himself he would never have anything to do with Dublin Castle, called on General Macready at the Royal Hospital in Kilmainham, with Lord Mayor Larry O'Neill. Macready sent them here and there until they reached the Viceroy, Lord French, who told him that their view would be considered but in his diary French wrote that they had come to see him and urged 'me to remit the date and sentence – I refused … the Lord Mayor rang up several times up to 10pm … that in the small hours of the morning he applied by wire to the P.M. but with no success.'[530] The diary entry does not give the impression that he gave a damn. That same day Mark Sturgis wrote in his diary, 'There is, I believe, no question of

---

528 Ibid.
529 By kind permission of Evanna Kennedy, daughter of Gerry McAleer.
530 Field Marshal Sir John French' s diary, 31 October 1920, PRO/59.

remitting the sentence. Two grim looking ropes arrived from Pentonville … yesterday. The execution is fixed for a Monday morning. Rather a pity no one noticed it is All Saints Day. Great play will be made about Barry's youth, 18½ … but he is quite as old as large chunk of the British Army and the three soldiers he and his party killed were all under 19 … the Shinns [Sinn Féin] … boast that they are a rebel army attacking a tyrant … yet using every sort of plea for mercy whenever one of their brave soldiers is up against it.'[531] Macready himself had pointed out to the archbishop that 'the victims of the crime were also mere youths, one being younger than Barry, and they too had mothers to mourn their losses. Barry met his fate with fortitude, the victim of those who preached assassination under the guise of patriotic sacrifice.'[532]

As the appeals continued, the inevitable happened. The hangman's ropes arrived at Dublin Castle that Saturday. Even the previous Thursday, as the affidavit was being prepared, Lloyd George held a 'Conference of Ministers' in Bonar Law's room with Sir Hamar Greenwood. They discussed the boy of eighteen years and nine months who had been sentenced to death for his part in a military attack in Ireland. They discussed Devlin's appeal for mercy on the grounds of youth, but they each pointed out that three soldiers had been murdered, who were around the same age as Kevin, and the prisoner had been found with a revolver which he had fired, one bullet in the barrel and two in the magazine. 'It was precisely young and irresponsible men of this type who were the main cause of the present disturbance in Ireland. Therefore, they agree that they could not recommend any commutation of the death penalty.'[533]

A friend of the Barrys, Kathleen Carney, came to 8 Fleet Street on Sunday, 31 October, the day before the execution. She excitedly told them that James McMahon, the Catholic Undersecretary, wanted Mrs Barry to send a telegram to King George V. Mrs Barry was furious at the mere thought of sending a telegram to the king, and dismissed Ms

531 Ibid., PRO 30/59.
532 O'Donovan, p. 137 quoting from *Macready's Annals of an Active Life*, 1924.
533 CAB 23 NLI.

Carney. It was a number of months before the Barrys would even speak to her again. Kitby told my grandfather, in the context of this well-meant but sad appeal, that there was principle at stake, 'the principle for which my brother was glad to die'.[534]

That same Sunday James McMahon, the token Irish Catholic in the British government in Ireland, made a final plea to Lord French for Kevin's reprieve. He pleaded that although none of the people who were anxious for Kevin's reprieve 'find any excuse for his crime, all unite in the belief that his execution, however just it may be, will produce effects in the country as disastrous as those which followed the equally just executions that followed the Rebellion of 1916'.[535] In response, Lord French felt himself compelled to refuse to exercise the prerogative. Already that day at Parkgate, General Macready, Mark Sturgis and Geoffrey Whiskard had been with Lord French, discussing the Kevin Barry case and the letters and telegrams that had just arrived from the Lord Chancellor of Ireland, Sir James Campbell. He had also sent his appeal to Bonar Law and Sir Hamar Greenwood, urging the reprieve of 'Barry on ground of boyhood and that he acted under duress ... and because his is first capital conviction under new procedure [the ROIA]'. Lord French entirely disagreed. Sturgis wrote in his diary that night: 'I hear Barry is quite calm and unrepentant, not at all like a boy driven into a deed by the orders of others. He will be hanged at 8 tomorrow morning.'[536]

There were appeals from former British Army officers at Trinity College, a doctors' appeal organised by Eileen Dixon (who had seen Kevin's death foreshadowed in his palm a month earlier), a frenzied appeal from Madame Charlotte Despard, the Republican sister of Lord French, who begged her brother to call off the execution. On Friday, 29 October, Erskine Childers wrote a public letter, printed in the *Westminster Gazette*:

....

534 KBM to Jim O'Donovan, O'Donovan, p. 136.
535 MS 31658 NLI LOB DOD p. 140.
536 PRO 30/59 Sturgis diaries.

This lad, Barry, was doing precisely what an Englishman would be doing in the same circumstance and with the same bitter and intolerable provocation – the suppression by military force of their country's liberty. To hang him for murder is an insulting outrage … it is an abuse of power: an unworthy act of vengeance, contrasting with the forbearance and humanity invariably shown by the Irish Volunteers towards the prisoners captured by them … To hang Barry is to push to its logical extreme the hypocritical pretense that the national movement in Ireland, unflinchingly supported by the great mass of the Irish people, is the squalid conspiracy of a 'murder gang'. That is false; it is a natural uprising; a collision between two Governments, one resting on consent, the other on force.[537]

Rescue missions

John Joe Carroll, who had been with Kevin on the raid on Monk's Bakery, felt that no serious attempt was ever made to rescue Kevin from Mountjoy. 'True, the Big shots made a bit of a demonstration – they had men from Dublin Brigade waiting around the vicinity of the prison on several occasions but no one received any instructions.'[538]

This was not quite true. There was a plan that almost worked, except that a priest took Mrs Barry's visiting time and toppled the tightly planned event. But there seemed also to be, in those days coming up to the execution, a rumour that swept through Dublin that Kevin had already been reprieved. 'Lloyd George with his half promises and the tears which, as the cynics said, he could turn on as easily as a housewife turns on the kitchen tap, helped to build the uncertainty that sapped the would-be rescuers' determination.'[539]

In any case, there is plenty of evidence that there were concerted attempts to rescue Kevin from Mountjoy. Patrick Berry, the Mountjoy warder who

---

537 O'Donovan, p. 127.
538 Liberty, April 1960, O'Donovan, p. 142.
539 O'Donovan, p. 142

had been with the hunger striker Thomas Ashe until his death in 1917, was happy to give the IRA information from the inside that would facilitate an escape plan for Kevin. After Kevin was imprisoned, Berry found IRA man Tom Cullen writing for him outside the prison gates after his shift. He told Berry Dick McKee wanted to meet him at a hotel to discuss a plan for rescuing Kevin. Berry told him the only way out for Kevin was from Mass at Sunday morning, when the milk cart would arrive.

'All the rescuers had to do was to go up a few steps and then turn to the left. There would be no trouble holding up the man at the gate at 7.30 am. It would mean no loss of life. Kevin would be in the sacristy side of the chapel … with just one Auxie. They would go in with the milk cart, hold up the warder at the gate, go up three steps and turn left to the chapel. They could hold up the Auxie and take Kevin.' [540] What Berry states next is that he learned from Tom Cullen that Mrs Barry disapproved of rescue plans as she thought Kevin would get a reprieve on account of his youth. This could not have been further from the truth.

John Joe Carroll was involved with a plan that would blow a hole in the prison wall on the Glengarrif Parade side with a home-made bomb. The Volunteers would have had to burst a gate covering the entrance to the wing in which Kevin was prisoner. The Dublin Brigade received orders to stand to for that evening in case the plan took off, but it was abandoned because they were informed from the inside that Kevin Barry's guards had orders to shoot him if there was a rescue attempt. [541] 'It's an extraordinary thing that the H.Q., with all its contacts inside Mountjoy and its secret service men inside Dublin Castle, could not plan any move with the remotest chance of success.' [542]

The most elaborate plan was announced to Kitby at 8 Fleet Street, on the morning of Saturday, 30 October, a plan that she kept secret from her mother, presumably because of the distress that it would cause her. Losing three children was not something Kitby wanted her to contemplate, yet she

....

540 Patrick Berry, WS 942, pp. 9–11, BMH.
541 Oscar Traynor, WS 340, p. 47, BMH.
542 Carroll, *Liberty*, April 1960/ DOD, p. 143.

was fully aware of the risks involved. Frank Flood[543] informed her that she was to receive orders regarding her own, and one other family member's vital part in this event. Kitby told them that her mother was not well, so she agreed to meet them discreetly to discuss the plan. 'The job for myself and [Elgin] was to tackle the two Auxiliaries and prevent them from shooting Kevin before entry to the boardroom of the rescue party.'[544]

The whole affair was to be over by 3.50, in time for the military guard being changed at 4 pm. Just before a British military lorry would drive in with the guards who were going on duty, Kevin would have been already whisked away. When Kitby protested, she was told that it was an order from HQ. She told him that they would all be killed, but Captain Byrne retorted: 'It'll be a pleasure; that's what we're in the army for.'[545]

Kitby refused to tell Kevin of the plan, in case it falsely raised his hopes and since Kevin was 'happy at the prospect of death for the Republic'.[546] Kitby knew that Kevin had no hope of a reprieve. She took Elgin with her on this rescue mission, but before she did, she made her will and had it signed by two servants.[547] She asked Kate Kinsella, the housemaid at Fleet Street, to pray hard and tell her mother what had happened, in case Kitby and Elgin were arrested. Elgin was only sixteen years old and she insisted on being the one to do the rescue with Kitby.

At 3.15 they handed in their names at Mountjoy. Some of the Volunteers were milling in the crowd of waiting visitors – one of these was Captain Byrne. When a 'tall priest' drove up at 3.25 the plan was foiled, as he was admitted to see Kevin Barry before they were. At 3.40 Captain Byrne came over to them and muttered that the plan had to be called off. The priest had ruined the whole thing.

Kitby and Elgin went in, in any case. They were searched by the warders and taken through the second set of gates past a line of Black and Tans and into the main hall, which was buzzing with Auxiliaries.

....

543 Sean O'Neill, WS 1,154, p. 13, BMH.
544 KBM, WS 731, BMH.
545 Ibid.
546 Ibid.
547 O'Donovan, p. 145.

In the boardroom, 'one of the Auxies was standing at a window on the east side, to the right as you face the fireplace. The other was near the west wall on the other side of the fireplace. Kevin was at the fire.'[548]

But when the clock struck 4, they knew the rescue plan had been abandoned. When they left Mountjoy, Kitby and Elgin met an H Company member who was crying as they came down the North Circular Road. In the tram, Kitby said that Elgin cried 'silently and hopelessly'. She said, with typical detachment, that tears had 'psychological value after shock'.[549] While they were in the Wood Printing Works, recovering before they returned to Fleet Street, some of the rescue party came into the office, visibly distressed. They assured Kitby and Elgin that there would be another attempt.

The last-ditch attempt to rescue Kevin involved the two most senior officers in the Brigade, Dick McKee and Peadar Clancy, disguising themselves as clergymen to trick their way in to Mountjoy. It was a last-minute plan, hatched on Sunday, 31 October. They were to take the last visit to Kevin, in place of Kitby and her mother. Kitby and Mrs Barry pointed out 'that it would look extremely suspicious if a mother did not arrive to take her last visit and that, in any case, the visit would have to be applied for by a certain time'.[550]

The plan took root in the Dublin Typographical Provident Society on Gardiner's Place, where many of the printers were members of the IRB. Brigadier Dick McKee, Peadar Clancy and Rory O'Connor were present, and Oscar Traynor claims that Michael Collins and Dick Mulcahy were also there. McKee and Clancy were to be disguised as clergymen, enter the prison during the visiting hours and disarm the Black and Tan who was in charge of Kevin Barry in the visiting room. They were to make their way to the front gate where the Volunteers would wait, and when the front gate was opened on a ruse of delivering a parcel the warder was to be held up, leaving the gate ready for the exit of the party from the visiting room. Mrs Barry was to have a visit on

548   KBM, WS 731, BMH.
549   Ibid.
550   Ibid.

that day. But she was again very perturbed about this effort to rescue her son 'unless some kind of guarantee as to its success could be given that no extra lives would be endangered and she feared the extra loss of life'.[551] So the Brigade O/C called this final rescue plan off. In fact, the IRA had never told the Barrys that Willie O'Connor had died in the attempt to seize the armoured car on the way to Marlborough Barracks on 20 October.[552]

Dick McKee had allowed Sean O'Neill and Frank Flood to find the men to do the job. They found two IRB men who were, 'in their own minds, Robert Emmets'.[553] Frank Flood then asked Gerry McAleer to visit Kevin to bring him the information about the rescue plan, written in a note hidden in the pair of boots that he had taken from Kevin on his visit on Thursday, 28 October. However, Kevin said to him after reading the note: 'Tell them no. I am quite happy to die for Ireland and have no regrets.'[554]

That final escape plan caused Kitby and the Barrys a good deal of embarrassment many years later, when on 22 April 1949 an article appeared in the *Irish Press* under the title 'Mr. Traynor on New Republicans', reporting on a lecture by Traynor. This sentence upset Mrs Barry greatly:

'A plan to send in two men disguised as clergymen in an attempt to rescue [Kevin Barry] was not agreed to by his mother, and Kevin Barry was executed.'

Kitby and her mother went to Sean Ó hUadhaigh to straighten the matter out and eventually the *Irish Press* published a statement that it was a false claim.

---

551 KBM, WS 731, BMH.
552 Oscar Traynor, WS 340, BMH, pp. 47–49.
553 Sean O'Neill, WS 1,154, BMH, p. 13.
554 Ibid.

THE GALLOWS TREE

'The usual interval of life between sentence and execution was three Sundays. Kevin Barry did not have this.' [555]

The Executioner

Kevin Barry's executioner was John Ellis, who had hanged Roger Casement in 1916.

The prison chaplain, Canon Waters, met Ellis in Kevin's cell the night before the execution, and mistook him for a doctor. That was, until the tall, elegant man measured Kevin's arms for pinioning.[556] Executioners usually arrived the day before the execution. Ellis's assistant was called Willis. Ellis himself had been an assistant to the famous hangman, Henry Pierrepoint. Once, when Pierrepoint turned up drunk for an execution, he had reignited an old feud with Ellis and called him an 'Irish bastard', punching him in the face. Ellis had complained about Pierrepoint's behaviour and Churchill had him dismissed.[557]

Ellis was born in Lancashire in 1874. When he wrote his memoirs, he never mentioned Kevin Barry. 'Due to the sensitivity of the case, and fearful of repercussions in later life, neither Ellis nor his assistant Willis made mention of this or other subsequent Irish executions.'[558] Most of Ellis's work in 1921 was at Mountjoy. Kevin was the first of ten men executed, and Ellis hanged seven of them. On 14 March 1921, with his

555   Interview with Sean Reynolds, prison guard at Mountjoy, 25 October 2019.
556   Father Lawrence, WS 899, p. 2.
557   Steve Fielding, *The Executioner's Bible, The Story of Every British Hangman of the Twentieth Century*, London: John Blake Publishers, 2008, p. 61.
558   Ibid., p. 79.

assistants Willis and Baxter, he hanged six men in three double executions. He was a busy man, and he was well paid. On 25 April 1921, Thomas Traynor was hanged for the murder of a soldier shot dead in a Dublin ambush on 10 January, after which Ellis wrote to the Irish authorities complaining about his fee.

> As you are aware you have allowed me £15 for single executions of Sinn Feiners. I am sure you will agree it is little enough. The risk I have, the inconvenience I am put to, also the jeers and insulting remarks I have to put up with. In 1911 I received £11.11.0 for an execution in Cork.[559]

He went on to say that he had missed four days' work because of the commissioned execution and that he had been on the Home Office list as executioner for twenty years.

Ellis's first task when he arrived on 31 October with his assistant Willis was to inspect the new ropes brought in from Pentonville. 'Then Ellis used the spyhole in the condemned cell to calculate the drop, which depends on the height, weight and age of the prisoner.'[560] He chose the rope he thought most suitable, 'shackled it to the chain in the roof of the Hang house, let it hang all night with a sandbag'. It was slightly heavier than Kevin Barry.

An All Saints' Day Execution

The unsuitability of hanging Kevin Barry on a Catholic holiday, All Saints' Day, 1 November, was expressed in a letter by F.W. Doheny in Kilkenny to Sir Hamar Greenwood. 'Quite apart from the outcry against hanging a man on a church holiday, the British forgot, or perhaps simply ignored, the effect of executing a young man on a day when every church in the country would be full to the doors several times over … the English made a martyr of Kevin Barry.'[561]

---

559 Ibid., p. 81.
560 O'Donovan, p. 152.
561 Ibid., p. 128.

General Crozier, Commander of the Auxiliary Division of the RIC, supplied a party of Auxiliaries to watch over Kevin in the prison cell to ensure he did not commit suicide – in that case, Ellis would not have been paid. In his memoir, *The Men I Killed*, he wrote about visiting Barry and of how this reminded him of seeing Johnny Crockett in Flanders, just hours before his execution, for having deserted the army and the horrors of a very severe winter campaign.

> Neither of these lads whined. In France I made Crockett drunk to get him out of his misery. In Ireland some of the men who had most to do with Barry's last hours made themselves drunk to get them out of their misery.[562]

On Friday, 29 October, Fr Augustine, a Capuchin monk of Church Street, who had accompanied the family to the court martial on 20 October, had come to see Kevin before travelling on to Cork for Terence MacSwiney's monumental funeral. As he approached the boardroom, he saw Kevin leaning against the jamb of the door, smiling at him. My father had a transcript of an interview with him from 1948:

> I remember it all with strange vividness … and have often thought since that his sweet and charming smile brightened my way and quickened my step. We met and clasped hands as brothers, for there was a wonderful affection in my heart for that gallant boy who was so soon to lay down his life for the glory of God and the freedom of Ireland.[563]

He referred to Kevin as a devout Catholic and to his 'grand child-like faith and piety'. After prayers, Kevin told Fr Augustine how he was thinking of his mother and sisters and of 'the coming sacrifice'. That

---

562 Ibid, p. 152.

563 These were in the rector's archives at Belvedere College, but are no longer there. The interview is in O'Donovan's *Kevin Barry and His Time*, pp. 149–50, originally given as information by Fr Augustine OFM Cap. to Jim O'Donovan, 1948.

same Friday, however, Kitby found Kevin 'in a state of glee. When I went into the boardroom, he rubbed his hands and said "Did you see the papers? My death is going to be a national calamity" … he was particularly amused at the way the *Independent* was swinging in the lead.'[564] There had not been much in the press about his impending execution that week, as the national focus was on Terence MacSwiney, who had died on 25 October after his seventy-three-day hunger strike. Eamon De Valera had made a statement on the death of MacSwiney from New York, for which he received a twelve-minute ovation.

> MacSwiney and his comrades gave up their lives for their country. The English have killed them. Tomorrow a boy, Kevin Barry, they will hang and, he alike, he will not regret that he has but one life to give. O, God!
>
> They shall be remembered forever,
> They shall be alive forever,
> They shall be speaking forever,
> The people shall hear them forever.[565]

Final Visits

Fr Augustine came back to see Kevin on the morning of Saturday, 30 October. He spoke to him of St Francis of Assisi, and received him into the Third Order (of St Francis), the members of which were bound to dress soberly, fast, pray and hear Mass more frequently. They were also to abstain from dances and theatre and not to take up arms unless in defence of the Church or their native land and not to take unnecessary oaths.[566] It would not be difficult to imagine that Kevin might have hesitated to be received into the Third Order if his whole life was ahead of him. Not to dance, not to go to the theatre, not to have a few drinks and

---

564 KBM, WS 731, BMH.

565 A recording of De Valera's statement was made in a New York Studio; O'Donovan, p. 141.

566 O'Donovan, p. 150.

not to take up arms might have deterred him, if that were the case. It would certainly go against his buoyant, gregarious character.

Fr Augustine gave Kevin the scapular and cross. He seemed happy and at peace, but then, 'from out of the heart of our brotherly conversations, he said, looking straight into my eyes: 'Father, I'm praying for courage.' Fr Augustine assured him that he would be welcomed to Heaven and he left him in peace, he believed. He went on to assist at the Solemn Requiem Mass for the repose of the soul of Terence MacSwiney, whom Fr Augustine had married in Bromyard, Hertfordshire, in 1917.[567]

It was Halloween, and Kevin had visitor after visitor. The final visit was from his mother, Kitby and Michael. Outside the prison there were rows of Black and Tans, who were not normally in Dublin. Two of General Crozier's Auxiliaries and some armed warders were in the room with Kevin. Some of them were in tears. Kitby said, 'Auxiliaries were swarming in the hall. Kevin was cheerful and gay. It was difficult to talk because several of the warders were crying. My mother was composed but quiet, and my brother, Mick, was at no time a great chatterer.'[568]

Kitby gave him a message that somebody outside the jail had given her, to tell him that the University would be outside in the morning praying. 'He became serious at once and he said "Tell them that is foolish. They'll be all shot."'[569]

Mr Meehan, the Deputy Governor, came into the room and said, 'I am sorry, Mrs. Barry. I'm afraid you'll have to go.'[570]

The last thing Kevin said to Kitby as he kissed her was 'Give my love to the boys in the Company.' 'We turned at the door for a last look and he was standing at the salute. When the door closed, my mother was battling with her tears. He was wearing his trench coat that day with the collar turned up and he had a white scarf.'[571]

....

567 O'Donovan, p. 151.
568 KBM, WS 731, BMH.
569 Ibid.
570 Ibid.
571 Ibid.

Mrs Barry did not break down, according to Kitby. They met Canon Waters in the corridor, the chaplain who would be with Kevin until the end, and who would anoint him, and would hold the tiny funeral Mass at the front of Mountjoy jail with Kevin's two warders, Proctor and Berry. As they were leaving, Canon Waters expressed some doubt as to whether Kevin actually realised that he was going to die in the morning. 'He could not understand his gaiety. Mother said: "Canon Waters, can't you understand that my son is actually proud to die for the Republic?"[572] Canon Watters apparently became flustered and left the Barrys upset because 'he was the nearest thing to a friend that Kevin would see before his death, and he seemed so alien'.[573]

Fr Albert, another Capuchin monk, who had ministered to the leaders in 1916 before their executions, got permission to see Kevin at the last minute. When he met Kevin that evening they first spoke in Irish. Kevin sat on a chair with his hands in his trench coat pockets, and he was moved when Fr Albert told Kevin of the Masses that had been said for him, of the Rosaries, hymns and prayers that his fellow students were reciting outside the prison. Fr Albert told the family that Kevin said, 'I wonder could I see them once more?'[574] He wanted to send them a letter, but this would have to have been approved by the governor, so instead he sent the message via Fr Albert. 'Tell them outside I want no pity, but prayers.'[575] Yet Kitby maintained that Fr Albert said to her that Kevin said: 'Hold on. Stick to the Republic.'[576] The crowds had spread up and down the North Circular Road and by 7 o'clock it had swelled to such a size that armoured cars were sent out to patrol. It was because of this, the Barrys were later told, that the final rescue plan was called off – they had planned to burst the wall of the Mountjoy and storm the prison. The operation had been timed for 8 pm.[577]

That Halloween evening, the Barrys went to visit Tom Counihan, Kevin's mentor at Belvedere College. Kevin had asked to see him, they

572 Ibid.
573 Ibid.
574 O'Donovan, p. 157.
575 Ibid.
576 KBM, WS 731, BMH.
577 O'Donovan, p. 158.

said. The rector said, 'You cannot refuse the request of one of your pupils in his greatest hours of need.'[578]

Tom Counihan and Fr Michael Quinlan came to see Kevin that evening, nervous at having just seen a lorry full of Auxiliaries arriving. By this time, the whole space between the outer gate of Mountjoy and the gaol gate was filled with people who had been attracted by the crowds of university students. The sight, however, was not welcoming, with barbed wire and machines guns everywhere. They met Kevin in a large room with a small table and chair on either side. Auxiliaries had revolvers pointing at the table. Kevin said to them, laughing: 'I have the laugh on you fellows now. You are going to spend the rest of your long lives hoping for a good death. I am going to have a good death tomorrow morning.'[579]

Kevin showed them a telegram from Fr John Fahy SJ, who had Masses said for him – Fahy had received him into Belvedere in 1916. Counihan said Kevin knew there was going to be no pardon, and that he had 'made up his mind that the sentence of death would be pronounced by the court martial. He never had any thought save to die for God and for Ireland. He was anxious I should be with him in the morning. That was not possible.'[580]

My father also found a report in the rector's archives in Belvedere, concerning the state of Kevin's soul. Kevin is reported to have said:

> … it is hard to die and takes more than love of country to keep one up. I have a clean slate now, and am glad to offer up my life in atonement for my sins. I have seen a good deal of the shady side of life since I came to Dublin, and fully realise how merciful God has shown himself to me, in saving me from all this danger.[581]

While it has never been obvious in the telling of Kevin's story so far that Kevin had strong faith, as his membership of the Sodality of Our Lady while at school in Belvedere could have been something that he felt obliged

---

578 O'Donovan, p. 158, rector's archives, Belvedere College.
579 Ibid. p. 159.
580 Ibid. p. 159.
581 Ibid.

to take, these words, if they are from Kevin Barry, certainly reveal that his attitude was not all 'gung-ho' about dying for Ireland. He had a firm belief in an afterlife, and in the last hours of his life, he saw some folly in his ways. However, I cannot confirm that these are Kevin's words, since the rector's archives at Belvedere have disappeared. But I can say that my father saw those records, which he quoted in his own biography of Kevin Barry.

The end of things

When Michael Collins entered the Vaughan Hotel on Parnell Square, around the corner from Belvedere College, he was apparently 'in a state of the greatest dejection. He remained brooding the whole night, taking no part in the conversation, the only words he uttered being: 'Poor Kevin Barry!'[582]

All attempts at rescue and reprieve failed, the inevitable encroached as 1 November, All Saints Day, arrived. The British authorities would hang 'the bakery boy'. The *Manchester Guardian* covered the execution with as much venom as any moderately nationalist paper in Ireland. 'The boy met his death with cheerfulness and courage'. Other papers pointed out that the three young soldiers who died were also 'mere youths'.[583]

It was on Halloween night that Kevin Barry first met his executioner, Ellis, and his assistant Willis. Fr Lawrence, who was a priest in St Teresa's Church on Clarendon Street in Dublin, where Kevin had been an altar boy, gave an account of this via his friend, Canon Waters, many years after Kevin's execution. Fr Lawrence asked Canon Waters if the prisoners saw the rope before the execution. He said that they did. Canon Waters said to Fr Lawrence, 'I put my hand on Kevin's heart to see was it fluttering. Well, it was as calm and unruffled as that grass, although my own was fluttering violently.'[584]

582 Batt O'Connor, *With Michael Collins in the Fight for Independence*, London: Peter Davies, 1929.
583 Ferriter, *A Nation and Not a Rabble*, p. 202. Quoting from M.A. Doherty, 'Kevin Barry and the Anglo-Irish propaganda war', in *Irish Historical Studies*, vol. 32, no 126 (November 2000), pp. 217–31.
584 Fr Lawrence, WS 899, BMH, pp. 1–3 http://www.militaryarchives.ie/collections/on-line-collections/bureau-of-military-history-1913-1921/reels/bmh/BMH.WS0899.pdf

He was sitting on an old stool in the condemned cell repeating the thanksgiving prayers with Kevin, the night before the execution. Suddenly, a cultured-looking man entered the cell, asking Kevin to stand up and hold out his hand. Canon Waters thought this was the doctor, and that he was taking Kevin's pulse, but then he noticed that the man pinioned Kevin's two hands behind his back saying, 'I won't hurt you!' The canon realised the strange man was Ellis, the executioner.

When the canon described his last evening with Kevin to Mrs Barry in a letter, the morning of the execution, he omitted to mention that he had met Ellis. He described how he heard Kevin's confession and said Mass at the little altar that had been made the night before by Kevin and his warder Proctor, and two Auxiliaries. Warder Berry recalled:

> On the Sunday, that is the day before his execution, I was speaking to him in his cell. The chaplain [Canon Waters] asked me to leave down the vestments in the cell. There was a special Mass offered for him in the Female Prison on the morning of his execution. I served this Mass. Father Fennelly said it, asking the congregation to pray for the soul of Kevin Barry just about the time of his execution.[585]

Kevin had written two letters that night, had a few hours' sleep and was woken at 6 am. The Republican prisoners did not sing their songs that night, to give Kevin some peace.

Canon Waters wrote to Mrs Barry:

> I put him in a chair to rest as he had been kneeling nearly an hour. I stood by him and whispered prayers into his ear, which he repeated with the greatest docility and fortitude. He made acts of Faith, Hope, Contrition, Charity, Resignation, Forgiveness ... .[586]

---

585 Warder Patrick Berry, Mountjoy Prison, WS 942, BMH, p. 11.
586 This letter and others are in Kitby's witness statement, WS 731. See Appendix D2.

The Gallows

That night before the execution, the Barrys went to bed at 11 o'clock and got up on Monday, 1 November at 7 o'clock and filed off to Mass on Clarendon Street in the Carmelite Church, where Fr Lawrence was a priest.

Kitby described that dark November morning, and how she saw Kevin's face in the news vendor's stall on Grafton Street. 'I think it was the *Daily Mail* had a full-page picture of him and, around the lamp post over it, a news vendor had wrapped the *Freeman's Journal* poster, "He Must Die".'[587] After Mass, they saw the University branch of Cumann na mBan file past, marching back up Grafton Street, led by Captain Eileen McGrane. Kitby would join this branch in 1921. As they passed the Barrys they gave the 'Eyes Right' salute.

About 2,000 people had gathered around Mountjoy by the time Canon Waters and Fr Matthew MacMahon arrived. The two priests had to wait at the main gate of the prison until 7 o'clock, when a warder let them in a side door. A hundred Cumann na mBan women had marched up North Circular Road. Maud Gonne McBride was there. The another paper of 1 November described 'women with shawls drawn closely about them, men and boys well-attired and some tattered, feeling the pinch of winter, and the flickering sickly yellow gas lamps; the sizzling great arc-lamps of the main thoroughfares ... '.[588]

According to a warder who came to see the Barrys three weeks after the execution, Kevin was taken, after Fr Albert had said his goodbyes, to the hang house. This was just beside Kevin's cell. Kevin's arms were pinioned with leather straps, but he said he didn't want them. Ellis asked Canon Watters was he done with the prayers. The two priests flanked Kevin, as was the tradition in Ireland at executions, and walked thirty yards or so into the hang house with Kevin, where the prison governor, C.A. Munro, was waiting with officers. Kevin would have felt fresh air on his face briefly as he walked out of his condemned cell through a door in the hang house that is no longer there today.

587 KBM, WS 731, BMH.
588 O'Donovan, p. 162.

He was asked, once again, if he would give the names of his officers and comrades on the Monk's Bakery ambush. If he told them, he would 'receive a free pardon, be sent at the expense of the British government to finish his medical studies in any university in the world he liked to name, and would receive, in addition, a pension of £2,000 a year for life'. The warder said that Kevin grinned and looked up at the beam and said, 'Yes, I think that will bear my weight all right.' This account appears in Kitby's witness statement. 'We have no confirmation of this story but we believe it absolutely because it carries the truth in it. Nobody could have invented the answer that Kevin is supposed to have given. His whole life is expressed in it.'[589]

Ellis and Willis removed the sandbag from the noose, checked the rope and made sure the white cap was ready – 'a fairly capacious white cotton bag used partly for the sake of the official witnesses, since the varying drop, according to Albert Pierrepoint, 'did not always take a man's head below the scaffold floor', and partly as some mercy to the prisoner so the condemned man could not judge the 'exact moment at which the lever was to pulled'.[590]

The hang house is a neat, contained chamber with two hinged trapdoors, level with the floor. The medical officer and Dr Hackett waited under the trapdoors downstairs. The trades officers were also there. The cap was pulled over Kevin's head when he mounted the scaffold. His legs were strapped by Willis. The rope hung from the chain attached to the ceiling beam. Ellis placed the noose, covered with soft washed leather,[591] around Kevin's neck. Ellis or Willis took the safety pin out and pulled the lever, pointed it towards the drop. And that was that. The canon, who had 'accompanied him to the scaffold, said prayers with him. Immediately, when the body dropped, he anointed him.'[592]

Mountjoy prison records recorded that Kevin was anointed by Fr MacMahon, who climbed the steps to the hanged body. Dr Hackett waited

589 KBM, WS 731, BMH.
590 Albert Pierrepoint, *Executioner Pierrepoint: An Autobiography*, London: Eric Dobby Publishing, 1974.
591 O'Donovan, p. 165
592 Fr Lawrence, WS 899, p. 3.

until he examined the body to make his report in the medical officer's book. 'Death was instantaneous and due to fracture of the cervical vertebrae.'[593]

By now, the crowd outside had more than doubled in size, around 5,000 people. Soldiers were stationed, armoured cars monitored the people cautiously. Prayer, muttered in Irish and English, was the most audible thing until the bell pealed for fifteen minutes after the execution and the crowd was silent. A warder pinned the white notice on the prison wall: 'The sentence of the law passed on Kevin Barry, found guilty of murder, was carried into execution at 8 am this morning. By Order.'

The *Evening Telegraph* reported that 'a cordon of police, under the supervision of an inspector, now appeared, and the people were told to disperse. They refused to leave until they had said the Rosary for the repose of the soul of the poor boy … once again they kneeled on the muddy road, while a fellow student of the deceased gave out the Sorrowful Mysteries in Gaelic. And the police stood looking on.'[594] They reported that Canon Waters and Fr MacMahon were present at his last moments, and that 'Kevin Barry died a brave and beautiful death, marked by great humility and resignation to the Will of God, with prayers on his lips for his friends and enemies. In the execution chamber the boy martyr stood erect and unflinching. The Dublin Castle authorities have refused the request that the remains should be handed over to the boy's mother. The city Coroner has been prohibited from holding an inquest.'[595] Kevin was already a martyr.

It was a quiet, solemn little funeral. Warder Berry described how Canon Waters said prayers as they put Kevin's body 'in a nice coffin. I [warder Patrick Berry] got four other warders to carry the coffin from the workshop to the graveside. There was a general gloom and sadness over the prison. Everyone, Auxiliaries and Black & Tans alike, felt it. They were very fond of him.'[596]

Canon Waters wrote to Mrs Barry on 3 November, telling her how the funeral had taken place very quickly, at 1.30 pm on Monday, 1 November. He found the coffin already closed in a workshop near the grave, where Warder Berry was. It was 'a plain deal coffin without breastplate or

593 O'Donovan, p. 165, Mountjoy Prison records.
594 *Evening Telegraph*, 1 November 1920.
595 Ibid.
596 Warder Patrick Berry, WS 942, p. 12, BMH

ornament, but substantial looking, roughly painted'.[597] (This was confirmed by a current prison guard, Sean Reynolds, who oversaw the exhumation of Kevin's body [and the bodies of nine other executed men] in 2001). The requiem service had begun in the workshop and then four warders (Proctor and Berry among them), bore the remains to the graveside. 'The grave was made in a little laurel plantation in the left, by the entrance gates, not far from the gate into the women's prison, a quiet spot, not likely to be desecrated, but near enough to the highway to remind us of him.'[598]

'It was a sad funeral indeed, but I hope to live and see him removed from this to receive from his countrymen honours due to his heroic virtues.'[599] Canon Waters estimated the grave to be three and a half feet deep. When they were lowering Kevin into it, the warders covered the grave with quicklime and all recited *De Profundis*. Half a dozen soldiers and some matrons looked on from a neighbouring window.

'Poor Kevin, your dear boy, is gone,' Canon Waters wrote to Mrs Barry. 'Deep as is my own grief, I know it is nothing to that which must fill your heart and I pray that God, who alone can do it, will comfort and console you ... You are the mother, my dear Mrs Barry, of one of the bravest and best boys I have ever known. His death was one of the most holy, and your dear boy is waiting for you now beyond the reach of sorrow ... the little book and picture which I am sending he used in his last minutes and I told him I would give them to you.'[600]

The picture was, most probably, a small card of the Sacred Heart with an inscription written on the back – in Kevin's own handwriting –

To Mother from Kev, on the eve of his death.[601]

Somewhere, that card still exists.

---

597 Letter from Canon Waters to Mrs Barry, 3 November 1920, Appendix D2 of KBM, WS 731.
598 Ibid.
599 Ibid.
600 KBM, WS 731, BMH. Appendix D2.
601 The card in question still exists, and was in Mealy's catalogue in 2014. The letters from Canon Waters to Mrs Barry were in possession of Triona Maher, Shel Barry and Bapty Maher's daughter. (The letters were published by James O'Donovan in an article in the *Irish Press* on 17 January 1964.)

Chapter Fourteen

THE BITTER END

'When people have to hang young boys like that, their cause is lost, their day is over.'[602]

Joe Doyle of Tuckmill, near Hacketstown, told my father that his mother received a telegram on the morning of 1 November saying, 'Kevin executed this morning.' It had only been two months since the Doyles had last seen Kevin when he had cycled ten miles from Tombeagh with Matt Cullen to see them, just before he made his way back to Dublin for his exams. At 7.30 am, Pierce Butler of Coomanagh, near Hacketstown, saw several people gathered in silence, reciting the Rosary outside the drive at Tombeagh. There were about twenty ponies and traps.[603] Fr Thomas MacMahon, the parish priest of Hacketstown, was conducting a service at 11 am that morning, when Kevin's friend Pat O'Gorman came in and handed him a note to say that Kevin was dead. The priest asked the people to pray for the repose of the soul of Kevin Barry 'whose soul is just departing'. This was told to my father by May Butler, who was there.[604] The next day, All Souls' Day, 2 November, Peg Scully, Pat O'Gorman's relative, was at the Mass and told my father that 'a child of Tom Barry's could only die in a state of grace and go straight to heaven'.[605]

Many people in and around Tombeagh, Rathvilly and Hacketstown have stories to tell about the morning of Kevin's execution. Some believe that Mrs Barry was in Tombeagh and not in Dublin at the time of the execution. Locals still talk about it, saying that when Kevin was executed,

602 Robert Brennan, *Allegiance*, Dublin: Browne & Nolan, 1950 p. 285 (Brennan was a pro-British shopkeeper in Rathgar).

603 Interview with Kevin Barry junior, 11 January 2020.

604 O'Donovan, p. 170.

605 Interview with Peg Scully, Donal O'Donovan, 1988. All rights reserved.

Mrs Barry saw the light in the Sacred Heart lamp go out when he was gone. The tricolor flew over Hacketstown for two days until the military took it down. Joseph Devlin MP, who had done so much to convince Lloyd George to give Kevin a reprieve after being asked to do so by Kevin's teacher Ned O'Toole, wrote a gushing apology to Ned O'Toole on 1 November: 'I did everything humanly possible for Kevin Barry.' He had begged Lloyd George and other members of the Cabinet, he had even drafted a telegram to King George V, who had taken off to Sandringham for the weekend. 'I cannot tell what sinister influence is at work because I was convinced that I had succeeded ... ',[606] Devlin lamented. There were, according to my father, no votes for Devlin in Rathvilly or Hacketstown after that.

Fr Kearney, who had been denied a visit to Kevin in Mountjoy by Kitby in Kevin's last days, wrote in desperation to Michael Barry, who was back at Tombeagh on 4 November: 'Were you ever by yourself of a cool rainy night when outside the leaves are off the trees and inside the fire is out ... and you are alone ... and you think: What in the world is the good of living? ... That's how I feel all because of Kev. And if I feel that way, how must you feel? Poor old Mick ... Kev is infinitely happy and we are infinitely miserable and after all that's a bit of a paradox ... Kev ... is at home now.'[607] He admitted that when he had seen Mick Barry in town that week, he had not known what to say. It was too enormous.

Some of Kevin's possessions were returned to the Barry family at 8 Fleet Street 'on the Tuesday [2 November] or the Wednesday [3 November] after his death.'[608] A parcel 'full of odds and ends' later arrived with a note from the Governor H. C. Munro of HM Mountjoy Prison. The note was dated 11 February 1921, some months after Kevin's demise. Amongst the possessions were a cigarette case, a fountain pen and a copy of *Knocknagow*, a novel by Charles Kickham, a nationalist, whose book was popular because of its criticism of the landlord system in Ireland. It had been published in 1879, the year that Tom Barry and Judith Barry had purchased the dairy yard in Dublin. Along with *Old*

606 By kind permission of the Kevin Barry estate.
607 By kind permission of the Kevin Barry estate.
608 KBM, WS 731, BMH.

Moore's Almanac, it might have been one of the most common books found in Irish households, and it is not difficult to see why Kevin Barry and other republicans would take the book into prison as reading material. Kitby was given the copy of *Knocknagow*. When she opened it she found that Kevin had inscribed his name in Irish and English inside the cover on the title page:

> Kevin Gerard Barry
> Condemned Cell
> Mountjoy Prison
> 30th October, 1920.
> Caoimhghín de Barra
> Comhlacht H.
> Cath a hAon
> Drong Ath Cliath
> Up the Republic

He had also written this satirical piece on the title page:

> K. G. Barry M. S. [Medical Student]. A dangerous criminal. A decided menace to the British Empire. Captured 20th September, 1920. Tried 20th October, 1920. Hanged 1st November, 1920. Up the prisoners of war. Amongst the many crimes put down to this dangerous man is that he did put pepper in the cat's milk and steal a penny from a blind man, besides wilfully, feloniously and of his malice aforethought smiling derisively at a policeman.

These are not the words of a sanctimonious martyr, they are the words of a young man who, perplexed in the face of his inevitable death, was going to try to meet it with amusement, a sort of final defiance in the face of what was inevitable. That he was atoning for his sins in his final days could not be further from the truth.

Kitby was also given Kevin's fountain 'pen' – one that a friend had given him while he was in Mountjoy. The significance of 'inheriting' this from Kevin was great for Kitby. She said that the pen had a 'heartbreakingly amusing significance. Among his characteristics was a queer instinct for giving the right gift at Christmas and birthdays and times like that.'[609] Kitby recounted how she was presented at a committee meeting with Sir Horace Plunkett, (her boss, Ernest Aston was Honorary Secretary) with an 'outsize fountain pen, about 8 inches long and thick, decorated with gold bands, one of them bearing my name. It was a fascinating toy for Kevin, who carried it with him everywhere he went, and it was one of the things that disappeared forever when he was captured.'[610] They had spoken about the pen at his court martial, and Kevin had asked where it was and was most annoyed that it had not been found. So Kitby felt that her receiving Kevin's pen among his belongings had a particular, poignant significance.

Around Dublin, UCD students climbed the steps to the roof of Earlsfort Terrace to raise the tricolour. It is not known if they removed the Union flag before doing so, but they were threatened with expulsion if they did not take it down.[611] Other UCD students, the day after Kevin's execution, were feeling waves of anti-British sentiment, as the first year medicals were lined up in the dining hall and searched. John Mawbray remembered seeing what came out of the pockets of his fellow students coats: 'revolvers, sheaves of paper … [were] handed over' and taken by waitresses who were in fact members of Cumann na mBan, and would return them promptly. Such a yield from a raid in UCD today would set off endless security alarms. Still … , ' a large part of my hereditary attachment to parliament drained away from me that day … and so many others,' said Mawbray.

In Cork, Fr Augustine visited Kevin's aunt Maggie Dowling, now Sister Cecilia, who felt consoled by the Mass he said for Kevin on 1 November at 7.50 am, exactly the time of the execution. Aunt Maggie kept the memorial card for Kevin until the end of her days.

On 1 November the acting president of the Irish Republic, Arthur Griffith, returned to Dublin from Cork, where he had just attended

609 KBM, WS 731, BMH.
610 Ibid.
611 O'Donovan, p. 169.

Terence MacSwiney's funeral. He took up his pen and wrote to Archbishop Walsh about the death of Kevin Barry.

> Dear Lord Archbishop
>
> The most brutal act yet perpetuated was the hanging of this poor boy Barry. It is a great consolation today to his mother and sister to know how humbly and bravely he died.
>
> I am, your Grace, most faithfully yours, Arthur Griffith.[612]

De Valera was busy fundraising for the Irish Republic in America when Kevin was executed. The Republican Warren Harding was elected on 2 November 1920, the day after Kevin Barry was executed, and American sympathies were swept up in a tide along with the death of Terence MacSwiney, the sacking of Balbriggan and later, in December 1920, the Bloody Sunday massacre at Croke Park. This did not translate into any official US policy towards the Irish cause, nor did it yield arms.

Meanwhile, the British administration was fretting over Kevin's affidavit, which was published in the press the day of his execution. It was read by Mr J. H. Thomas who received it from a 'man who was the employer of this boy's sister' (Mr Ernest Aston), and was printed verbatim in some of the English papers and partially in others. The *Daily News* and *Leader* printed the whole document. The *Times* declared: 'We have received, apparently from an official Sinn Féin source, what purports to be a copy of an affidavit sworn by the boy Kevin Barry …'.

Captain Barrett was worried, and wrote to the Lower Castle Yard to GHQ, reminding them that Sean Ó hUadhaigh had, after a fifteen-minute adjournment in the court martial, declared that he would not be representing Kevin, yet he had made the president of the court aware of Kevin being subjected to bad treatment in the North Dublin Union.[613] The authorities were irked with Ó hUadhaigh for this 'slight', yet the president knew about it, and the *Freeman's Journal* had reported it. The

612 O'Donovan, p. 171.
613 MS 8042 R/O 2609.

problem was that the Judge Advocate General in London wanted to know more about how Kevin had been treated. Barrett was determined to cover it up. When Brigadier General Onslow had asked Barrett to tell Ó hUadhaigh that there was 'no foundation' for his allegations, Ó hUadhaigh said that Kevin's affidavit verified the allegations made in Court.[614]

It seemed that the military authorities in Dublin were determined to cover up Kevin's interrogation. Barrett washed over the questions asked, and got away with it. It created a furore in the House of Commons, when, on 4 November 1920, it came to the attention of the House. J. H. Thomas, leader of the Labour Party, stated, 'I condemn him as emphatically as anybody for the murder of that policeman [sic]. Remember, he went to the scaffold not as a coward: he was a studious boy, loved by everyone who knew him, brave and educated.'[615] Thomas had received the affidavit from a 'man who was the employer of this boy's sister [Mr Ernest Aston]'.[616]

Thomas read out the affidavit. The Chief Secretary declared it was 'a question of veracity as to whether that man swore the truth or whether the officers of the regiment, who deny it, told the truth. I accept the word of the officers.'[617] Others, like Jack Jones, the Tipperary MP, accepted Kevin's word. Joe Devlin, the MP who had tried so hard to get Kevin a reprieve, said the government's hands were 'reeking of the blood of policemen and civilians'. Then it was revealed that the officers had not made sworn statements about this incident – and that was the end of that.

Ernest Aston had visited the Barrys on Fleet Street on 1 November. He told Kitby that he discovered that Lloyd George had broken his word on the reprieve, because on Saturday, 30 November, Sir Henry Wilson, Chief of Imperial Staff, had threatened to resign unless Kevin was executed, 'as he said he could not be responsible otherwise for discipline in the British Army.'[618] Aston was so incensed he wrote a letter to the *Irish Independent* slamming Wilson's part in the 1914 Ulster gun-running

....

614 O'Donovan, p. 174.
615 Hansard, no.134 (1–9 November 1920).
616 Ibid.
617 Ibid.
618 KBM, WS 731, BMH.

activities. Aston remained as convinced as he had been on Saturday, 30 October, when he told Kitby to jump with joy, that the reprieve would be approved by Lloyd George, that Sir Hamar Greenwood personally disapproved of the execution and that no single leading official of the Irish government was opposed to the reprieve. He wrote:

> One word from any member of the Caron-Wilson-Bonar Law gun running junta would have stopped the execution. Mr Lloyd George was threatened with the resignation of Sir Henry Wilson if a reprieve was granted. To that end Mr Lloyd George yielded, and replied to the eleventh-hour appeal of the Lord Mayor of Dublin that 'the law must take its course'. The law! What law? I wrote not as a Sinn Féin partisan, far otherwise ... E. A. Aston.[619]

But Wilson was a milder beast than everyone seemed to think. He knew that Kevin's execution would unleash 'a real spate of trouble over there', although he had also said, in a letter to Macready on 23 October, 'The law is the law and terrorists come under the jurisdiction of the law.' On 29 October he wrote again to him, saying, 'I detest sneaking terrorists ... [but] the balanced view ... is to hold our hand in Dublin. It means that we shall have weakened our right there because of one man. But to execute is to invite the pot to boil over and we couldn't control it.'[620] He was right. It was the beginning of the end for the British Empire. We have also seen from his diary entries that he was appalled by the violence of the Black and Tans and their sacking of Balbriggan and other places in Ireland.

Aston's letter is as full of conviction as any Sinn Féin partisan, however. One wonders whether his determination to free Kevin had been anything to do with a crush on his beautiful, proud and very capable young secretary, Kathleen Barry.

Kitby was surprisingly modest about her own military and political activities in the 1920s after Kevin's death. The focus of her invaluable witness statement to the Bureau of Military History is taken up for the most part

619 O'Donovan, p. 177.
620 O'Donovan, p. 178.

with Kevin's military career, and she even apologises at one point that she took up too much of the story in its narration. She unequivocally supported both Kevin's educational and military activities. In 1915, it was Kevin who bought Kitby tickets for the Manchester Martyrs' commemoration event at the Mansion House when he was just thirteen years old, an event that cemented both their decisions to become committed republicans. Immediately afterwards, Kevin was ready to join the Fianna Éireann, but his mother would not allow it. When Kevin's military career was on the upswing, Kitby watched with awe as he began to be noticed by the likes of Peadar Clancy. She would wait up for him at Fleet Street to share supper with him when he came back from parades or drills.

Kitby must have missed Kevin sorely. A refusal to cry after Kevin's death became the Barrys' way of dealing with his loss. Indeed, they rarely spoke of Kevin over the years. It was too enormous a loss. They all knew that Kevin did what he wanted to do with his life as a soldier of the Republic and they supported that clear decision, yet that meant the physical loss of him for ever. Such is the paradoxical nature of martyrdom. Kevin hardly knew what he would become, and had no air of sanctimony. He rushed at it all, grinning when he got a Lewis gun in a raid, jumping in the back window to burn down Aghavannagh Barracks, becoming petulant when his captain told him he had to miss the action at Monk's Bakery because of his exams. Kevin's military moves were neither considered nor plotted with 'malice aforethought', as the authorities had declared. If there was action, he wanted to be in it. His mind was devoted to the sovereignty of his country and he did everything within his power to attain that sovereignty.

What happened to him happened very quickly in the shadow of the newly passed ROIA. General Macready was determined to 'see the revision of the ROIA applied to the fullest extent, which in the case of Kevin Barry meant proceeding with his execution no matter what'.[621] As the

---

621 John Ainsworth, *Kevin Barry, the Incident at Monk's Bakery and the Making of an Irish Republican Legend*. Queensland University of Technology, p. 380. Letters from Macready to CIGS dated 25, 27, 28 September and 29, 31 October 1920, IWM, Wilson Papers, HHW 2/2B, nos. 9, 10, 11, 35, 37.

first to be court-martialled since 1916, the first to be executed (and being the age he was), Kevin Barry, in the wake of MacSwiney's monumental death, provided another huge banner for the IRA GHQ propaganda machine. Macready knew the difficulty 'of initiating a counter propaganda campaign and the consequence of not doing so'.[622] He knew that Kevin's case 'would be publicised throughout the country as the murder of a patriotic boy by the Government and nothing will be said or known about the fact that he murdered two [sic] young soldiers about the same age as himself …'.[623] Macready was constantly calculating the outcomes of military strategies. It was his job, after all. His instinct in the beginning, when he had first received a telephone message about the incident at Monk's Bakery in which one soldier was killed and two wounded on 20 September, and that they had captured one civilian armed with a revolver, was written quickly at the end of the note to Colonel Toppin, Assistant Adjutant-General about the incident: 'Try for murder'.

Cumann na mBan

Kitby did not join Cumann na mBan until late 1920, although she was 'most anxious to join', but up to that she felt her duty was to the family since her father had died. 'We had a business in Fleet Street and a farm in Carlow, both of which required constant attention, not to mention the rearing and educating of my six young brothers and sisters. My mother depended on me for decisions and, up to 1920, when the war became intense, I felt it would be selfish to run the risk of depriving her of my moral support. It was the intensification of the war with England at the time that swept all other considerations aside.'[624]

It may have been frustrating for Kitby, since Kevin, Shel and Michael were all actively involved with the war before she could be. Elgin, as we

---

622 Ibid.

623 Ainsworth, Ibid. Macready to CIGS,1 November 1920, IWM, Wilson Papers, HHW 2/2B, no. 38. For confirmation that the nationalist press in Ireland did use Barry's execution 'to stir up popular feelings against the government', see Doherty, Kevin Barry, 223–5.

624 KBM, WS 731, BMH.

shall see, became very active at a later period. When Kitby joined Cumann na mBan late in 1920 just after Kevin's death, she was surely driven by an urge to compensate for the loss of Kevin as much as she was driven, like thousands of other Irish people, to push all the harder against the British authorities in the shadow of the deaths of MacSwiney and Kevin Barry.

After Kevin's death, the Bloody Sunday massacre on 21 November 1920 saw thirty-two people killed or wounded – thirteen British soldiers and police, sixteen Irish civilians and three IRA prisoners. Michael Collins had attempted to assassinate the British undercover 'Cairo Gang', and in retaliation for these killings, the Auxiliaries and RIC went for a shoot-out at a Gaelic football match at Croke Park, killing sixteen and wounding sixty civilians. The *Freeman's Journal* noted a similarity, in the apparently wanton nature of the retaliation, to the Amritsar Massacre in April 1919. Dick McKee and Peadar Clancy, who had been key figures in Kevin Barry's later life, and who were involved in the planning of the killing of the 'Cairo Gang' on 21 November, were held at Dublin Castle and shot. All of this, along with the deaths of MacSwiney and Kevin Barry – within a month – turned the majority of the Irish public against British authority in Ireland. Collin's plan had in fact worked: the heart of the British intelligence operation was in rags.

Women in the War

Kitby says that by 1920 'I was forced by circumstances to take a prominent part'.[625] Kitby, Elgin and Shel were all involved at one time or another in Cumann na mBan. Elgin Barry's future husband Mac O'Rahilly (she married him in 1935), whose father, Michael Joseph O'Rahilly, had died in action in 1916, had a sister, Aine O'Rahilly, who had been very active in the foundation of Cumann na mBan at Wynn's Hotel in Dublin in 1914.[626]

We have seen how Kate Kinsella, who was not even a member of Cumann na mBan, looked after and distributed funds and, in some cases, munitions during the war. Cumann na mBan members (and non-members like Kate Kinsella) carried clandestine messages to IRA commanders,

625 This is from Kitby's written comments on Jim O'Donovan's 'Ms. No.1', Kevin Barry.
626 http://www.bureauofmilitaryhistory.ie/reels/bmh/BMH.WS0333.pdf#page=1

fed the men in safe houses and manned the mass protests that took place outside Mountjoy Gaol and other prisons when Volunteers were executed.

'It [Cumann na mBan] did not explore new avenues of political theory, being content to stay within the framework of the new nationalism by following the new ethos of the Volunteers, and also by embracing the Irish Ireland ideals espoused by Sinn Féin'.[627]

Military violence towards women did not generally occur in combat during the War of Independence since they were mostly not in combat – but violence of a different sort was endemic. Rape, largely ignored by historians, was frequent; the victims silenced themselves, so it is very difficult to research this phenomenon. What is recorded to some extent, was the 'bobbing' of women by both British soldiers and IRA men who assumed they were too close to RIC officers, or were seen to be, in some way or other, 'turncoats'.

Elizabeth Bloxham, a Protestant Cumann na mBan activist from the west of Ireland recalled when she was a teacher in Wexford, and her branch of Cumann na mBan was raided by British soldiers. 'He [the officer] ordered me to open my handbag and empty all its contents on to the table. [He] read all the letters that were in it ... one contained in it an appointment for holding a meeting of Cumann na mBan in Wexford town ... I was then ordered to take off my coat which I refused to do and the angry soldier ordered his subordinate to "search this woman". These were the days when girls were roughly searched and had their hair cut off by British soldiers.'[628] Another prominent Cumann na mBan woman, Peg Broderick-Nicholson, Section Commander for the Galway branch,[629] was involved in intelligence work from 1920 involving dispatches and delivery. She also ran revolvers and ammunition. Like Elizabeth Bloxham, she encountered forced haircuts and described how she had her hair cut ' ... to the scalp with very blunt scissors'.[630]

627 Ferriter, *A Nation and Not a Rabble*, p. 211, quoting Aideen Sheehan, 'Cumann na mBan: policies and activities', in David Fitzpatrick (ed.), *Revolution? Ireland, 1917–1923*, Dublin: Trinity History Workshop,1990, pp. 88–97.

628 Elizabeth Bloxham, WS 632, BMH, p. 30.

629 Peg Broderick-Nicholson, Section Commander for the Galway branch of Cumann na mBan, from Galway, WS 1682, BMH, p. 5.

630 Ibid.

The Civil War

According to Ernie O'Malley, it was not until the Civil War that female Republicans were considered on a par with male ones. 'During the Tan war the girls had always helped but they had never had sufficient status. Now [in the Civil War] they were our comrades, loyal, willing and incorruptible comrades.'[631] Todd Andrews admitted that he had not seen before that women had a role outside the home, until the Civil War, when he saw that women 'could operate successfully as administrators or political advisors or that they could develop a consuming interest in politics which would dominate their lives. I had listened far too long to my mother's derisive comments on suffragettes'.[632]

During the Treaty Debates in 1921, Cumann na mBan had split – 419 members voted against, with sixty-three voting in favour. In the Civil War, the moderates drifted away and only the most radical members of Cumann na mBan remained active in supporting the anti-Treaty side. Cumann na mBan was banned in 1923 and over 500 of its members were imprisoned during the Civil War.

After Kitby joined Cumann na mBan in late 1920, her life, 'like that of every other Republican … centred around the activities of the IRA. I did anything I was asked to do for our army and was in close touch all the time with every battalion in Dublin because I had friends in them all.'[633] Kitby was active until about 1925. In 1921 Kitby was involved in an incident when she was a fully committed member of Cumann na mBan University Branch under Captain Eileen McGrane and 1st Lieutenant Kathleen Murphy. There was a message for Tessie Power that her sister had been arrested. Tessie's house had to be cleared of all traces of IRA occupation. 'A number of 4th Battalion officers lived there. The Power girls had their brother, an IRA man, stay there. It was only a matter of days until Tessie's sister's connection with that house would be revealed, and they had to get the house cleared.'[634]

631 Ernie O'Malley, *The Singing Flame*, Dublin: Anvil Books, 1978, p. 148.
632 Andrews, p. 263
633 KBM, WS 731, BMH.
634 KBM, WS 731, BMH.

The IRA men did most of the clearing, but Tessie Power did the last of it – she wrapped two rifles in paper, draped them in her navy cape and took them away to give to a tram conductor she knew who kept them safely until the tram got to Fleet Street, where Tessie dumped them in the basement of the Barry home. Mary McCarthy and Kitby collected these from the basement. They missed the last tram. Curfew was at 10 pm. 'We walked down Leinster Road and it was 9.50 when we reached Rathmines. 10 o'clock struck when we were at Stephens Green and by God's grace we reached our destination. We burst into hysterical tears.'[635] It isn't typical of Kitby to describe bursting into tears – she frequently describes in her witness account how other people burst into tears, especially men like Kevin's first defence lawyer, Tim Healy.

Kitby's revolutionary activism reached a peak during the Civil War, which had begun on 28 June 1922, when the Four Courts, GHQ of the Republicans, was shelled by the pro-Treaty forces. Meanwhile, the anti treaty Dublin Brigade, occupied hotels on O'Connell Street in Dublin. The last of these to be evacuated was the Hammam Hotel, after a full week of a siege. Cathal Brugha (who would be shot by the Free State pro-Treaty forces when he eventually left the building), was in the building with about ten men and five Cumann na mBan women, among them Kitby. She and the other Cumann na mBan women defied Brugha's order to leave the building for three days while the hotel was under siege. Finally, when the hotel was about to go up in flames, Frank Henderson gave Kitby £800 of the Dublin Brigade funds, which she carried under her clothes as she was marched down Amiens Street. She was released after an hour without having been searched. When she got home she gave the money to Kate Kinsella who kept it in her bosom until 26 November 1922.[636] 'By the time I came up on 26th November to take charge of the Prisoner's Dependent Fund, it was all used up and she [Kate] had receipts for every pound of it. All during the Civil War Kate was a centre for despatches and she never made a mistake about them. She had many GHQ and Brigade despatches at the same time

635 Ibid.
636 O'Donovan, p. 24.

and never confused them, although she kept them all in her bosom wrapped in separate pieces of newspaperr.'[637]

Meanwhile, the hotel went up in flames after being shelled and levelled to the ground. Kitby had been very proud of her refusal to leave the building, scoffing at the men who ordered her to leave. "You may disapprove of me all you like for refusing to go when I was told but you mustn't disapprove of the men. And you can ask Jack O'Meara or Ned Reilly or Dan Keeffe if we hindered the fight or kept them from holding out as long as they would otherwise have done. They were great – they were sports and let me do heaps of things.'[638]

Between June and October 1922, Kitby had been responsible for communications[639] between the Director of Communications, General Liam Lynch, in Cork, and the Dublin IRA. Kitby worked closely with Lynch during the Civil War along with Oscar Traynor and De Valera. In Cork, she met her future husband Jim Moloney, who worked under General Liam Lynch. She thrived on this kind of work. 'Kitby was a very dominant figure. Jim Moloney [her husband] was a kindly soul in the sugar company, while she worked in the ESB. When she retired she took to her bed, summoning people to her room – it was like the Royal Command.'[640]

One of Kitby's letters to Jim Moloney reveals more of her frustrations about being a woman during a war.

> My dear,
>
> I'll take your ring anytime you want me to and I'll wear it if you want me to and I'll do anything you want me to. All the horrid things you said that night, you told me I wasn't a woman at all so I decided if I ever got a chance when the war was over I'd vamp you and so you'd see whether I was or not. [641]

637 KBM, WS 731, BMH.

638 Eve Morrison, 'One Woman's Civil War in Ireland', *Irish Times*, 23 May 2013, https://www.irishtimes.com/culture/heritage/one-woman-s-civil-war-in-ireland-1.1391600

639 Florence O'Donoghue, *No Other Law*, Dublin: Anvil Books, 1986, p. 277.

640 Interview with Michael O'Rahilly, 2019.

641 Eve Morrison, 'One Woman's Civil War', https://www.irishtimes.com/culture/heritage/one-woman-s-civil-war-in-ireland-1.1391600

Whatever they had argued over seems to have touched a nerve in Kitby. Behind her glamour and beauty, there was a woman who was capable of almost anything that a man was in the realm of household management and war. When Todd Andrews, who was by that time Adjutant under Liam Lynch, in Cork, met her in the wilds of West Cork he was struck by this elegant woman in the middle of the road, applying lipstick.

> In the wilderness of West Cork to be faced with such an exotic figure was as if we were seeing an apparition ... lipstick was not commonly used even in the cities, certainly not by the women of the Republican movement. This was an exceptional young woman ... a sister of Kevin Barry, a woman very prominent in Republican circles, working close to De Valera. It was as an emissary from him that she had come down from Dublin to discuss details of the coming meeting of the Executive.[642]

Before the Civil War, in early 1922, De Valera asked Kitby to join Countess Markiewicz in a provisional government delegation, to seek support for the new Republic. Austin Stack, J. J. Kelly (Sceilg) and Fr Michael O'Flanagan were also in the delegation. De Valera was concerned about the countess and instructed Kitby to keep 'Madame [Countess Markiewicz] on the rails. Make her act every inch the countess.'[643] Apparently the countess was a bit wild, like Grace O'Malley. They needed her reined in for the American tour.

They sailed on the *Aquitaine* on 1 April 1922 and when they were met in New York, a reporter from the *New York Evening World* reported the countess to be 'not a martial looking person – frail, and almost deprecatory except when she is talking about the Irish Republic'.[644] Kitby, however, was described as 'slow and sweet; her accent captivating'. In Philadelphia Kitby and the countess went to church on Easter Sunday, escorted by 500 Irish Volunteers and a brass band.

642 Andrews, p. 160.
643 Elizabeth Coxhead, *Daughters of Erin*, London: Secker & Warburg, 1965 p. 114.
644 O'Donovan, p. 198.

My great Aunt Kitby Barry (Kathleen Moloney). She took to her bed in the late 1960s. Photo by Basil Hannah

Kitby did some fund-raising on her own, arriving in Butte, Montana, in May to considerable fanfare amongst the Irish Catholic community there. Kitby here was noted to be a 'winsome Irish lassie, with dark blue eyes, the matchless skin of her soft climate, white teeth well set behind a mobile mouth and a wealth of brown hair that her black sailor hat did not half conceal'. [645]

The Civil War erupted on their return from America. It was not until 1924 that Kitby did any fundraising again. She sailed for Australia to fundraise for the Irish Republican Prisoners' Dependants' Fund (IRPDF). The fact that they were women – she was with Linda Kearns – raising money for the IRPDF, and not 'men espousing an Irish political cause, meant they were able to pitch successfully their appeals to audiences who held differing views on Irish politics'. [646] That the two women could 'shape their public appeals in Australia fit in with the prevailing ideologies of non-violent Irish nationalist woman roles, enhance any images of women as grieving mothers, sisters and widows who cared for Irish male soldiers'. [647] It is an academ-

645 Ibid.
646 Ibid.
647 Dianne Hall, Victoria University, 'Irish Republican women in Australia: Kathleen Barry and Linda Kearns' tour in 1924–5', in *Irish Historical Studies 2019*, 43 (163), p. 74

ic argument that does not exactly fit with what we have seen so far of Kitby Barry, who was so unyielding in principle. But perhaps it suited Kitby by that time to be just what she was after Kevin's death: a grieving sister. And perhaps it suited her to keep her mouth shut on the Australian tour, as she would have known that any form of extremism would have defeated the purpose of the fundraising tour.

Shel Barry

Kitby tends to dominate the story of the Barry family. It is a great pity that no other members of the family gave their witness statements to the Bureau of Military History. Shel Barry, if she had done so, would have given a fascinating account. She was in the local branch of Cumann na mBan in the Carlow Brigade during the War of Independence, active in 'procuring and carrying messages from Dublin to our home. She was up to her neck in any Volunteer activity that took place there'.[648] Again, this account is given by Kitby, who admits that while Shel was very active, but she herself, since she lived in Dublin, had 'nothing more dramatic happen than finding myself on a couple of occasions in a carriage carrying a gun when a Black and Tan got in at Baltinglass to travel to Dublin, or vice versa'.[649] It is even possible that there was some envy of her younger sister's activities.

Shel went on to marry Bapty Maher from Athy, County Kildare, and they had three children – Kevin, Triona and Johnny. Bapty had a successful business as a publican and an undertaker. The funeral home was run at the back of his bar, 'Bapty's'. According to Kevin Barry junior, 'Bapty looked like someone from the Abbey with a fine big broad hat and a black suit. He was famous as far as America. He had a nerve, and didn't always act as if he was married. He was in the pub most of the time.'[650]

Triona Maher was a vital source of information for my father when he was researching his book. She told him that while Michael Barry was in Lincoln Prison from 1921 to 1922, Shel ran the farm. It must have been

---

648 KBM, WS 731, BMH.
649 Ibid.
650 Interview with Kevin Barry junior, 2018.

very challenging. Sadly, the farm at Tombeagh was badly hit financially. In more recent years, Kevin Barry found little bottles of Powers whiskey in the garden under the bush. It is possible that these belonged to Shel, which would indicate that she was under considerable stress over those years at Tombeagh, more than she would have been able to admit.

Shel moved into the flat on Molesworth Street in Dublin with her mother during the 1940s. Her marriage to Bapty Maher had been a challenging one, and they had separated, hence her decision to live at Molesworth Street. 'Shel had been dealt bad cards in life. Bapty had been a great friend of Kevin and Mick [Barry], and he had played rugby up until his 40s. He was larger than life, a wild man. He had inherited half the family farm and he had entrusted his son to support Shel from the farm when the marriage broke down.'[651]

When Michael Barry was imprisoned during 1921, Shel wrote to him frequently, as all the Barrys did. Like all of them except the younger Monty and Peggy, she mixed news of the farm with political news. In September 1921 she wrote from Fleet Street:

> Perhaps you heard of the four men being arrested in Hacketstown on Saturday last – there was a general round up, great excitement and they took Matt Cullen, [Nick] O'Toole, Joe Byrne, the rate collector and Donohue. I'm thinking they are somewhere in the Curragh … we got the threshing done on Monday, they were done by dinner time, Kelly's engine. The black cow calved this morning. They're feeding up the Grey one that worked the bog all last year to sell her in the April fair … they have the potato ground harrowed and Joe has the lea nearly ploughed. They spent a day, yesterday, fencing from the river up to the bank of the garden, along the Boss's ditch … I am making a cake to send you tomorrow and Mother is putting in some lump sugar. I suppose Kathy will send you something from town also.[652]

---

651 Interview with Michael O'Rahilly, 2019.
652 By kind permission of the Kevin Barry estate.

Michael Barry

Michael Barry was Battalion O/C Of the Carlow Brigade. He had never lived in Dublin, as he was the eldest, and held full responsibility for the management of the farm at Tombeagh, which is why it was vital for the Barry women to write to him about the state of things at Tombeagh, to put his mind at rest. Not long after Kevin's execution, Michael was arrested in Tombeagh in December 1920. He was hiding in the small attic room that De Valera was too tall to fit into. 'He heard soldiers downstairs and heard them say that he must be in the house because his clean shirt is out and ready for Mass.'[653]

Michael was charged with possession of two bullets found on the farm, one of which had been cut down 'so as to make a more serious wound'. In February 1921 the *Nationalist and Leinster Times* reported that he had been sentenced to eighteen months' imprisonment for being in possession of arms, being in possession of uniform – Kevin and Michael's Celtic caps that they wore as children – and a 'lock of hair', which had been found in the house. There had been a 'hair cutting outrage' fifteen miles away, but the likelihood of Michael's involvement in this were slim, although this was never investigated at his court martial on 24 January 1921. He was held at Beresford Barracks, Curragh Camp, before being transported to Lincoln Prison.

The authorities had presumed that the 'lock of hair', which they found at Tombeagh, was 'bobbed' from a woman as an IRA punishment attack, but the family maintained that it came from Kevin's Aunt Maggie who had cut it off when she took her final vows as a nun and had sent it home. She became Sister Cecilia, the matron of the Bons

---

653 https://www.irishlifeandlore.com/product/kevin-barry-b-1941/ Interview with Kevin Barry by Maurice O'Keefe, Irish Life and Lore.

Secours Hospital in Cork. The question of the provenance of the pony-tail (it is far more than 'a lock of hair') remains unanswered. It is now on loan to the Irish Wars exhibition in Collins Barracks in Dublin, displayed as an example of a 'bobbing' punishment. Aunt Maggie's descendant Dorothy Dowling maintains that Mrs Barry, in her grief for Kevin, would have done anything to protect her other son Michael, given the danger he was now in, being the brother of a famous IRA Volunteer who had been executed. Aunt Maggie's ponytail could have been given to her mother, Ellen Dowling (Nana Dowling), after her vows were taken when she joined the order, and kept in the house at Tombeagh. She suggests that Michael Barry had this ponytail in his possession when he was arrested because his mother had given it to him as a talisman. It is not hard to imagine that Mrs Barry would have resorted to any kind of bargaining with God, or resorted to the use of such 'talismans' to protect her only remaining son in the weeks after Kevin's death. The Dowlings were very religious, and this is a plausible explanation. Whether it is correct or not, it does not take away from the fact that the *Nationalist and Leinster Times* reported that it had been found in the house at Tombeagh, and not actually 'in his possession'.[654]

On 11 March, 1921, the Staff Captain in the Curragh Camp wrote to Mrs Barry at Tombeagh:

> Herewith envelope containing one pigtail of girl's hair taken when Michael Barry was arrested on 31 December 1920. Please acknowledge receipt.
>
> Staff Captain
>
> 14 Infantry Brigade
>
> The Curragh[655]

---

654 Information from Dorothy Dowling, 2020.
655 By kind permission of the Kevin Barry estate.

On 12 June 1921, Kitby wrote about Monty and Peggy and Shel being at home at Tombeagh. Bapty was in 'Ballykinnler [sic] for the duration of the war. The regulations printed on your notepaper forbid the transmission of any news relating to public events so I can say nothing. I'm afraid if your censor is a purist he will think some things stand out … we belong irrevocably to the criminal classes … I hope that if ever I personally enjoy the hospitality of his Brittanic Majesty, I shall not have to wear anything as woolly as your little coat looked. I shouldn't like to be a criminal but what I should like less is to get shot. The most harmless people are getting shot on the streets now in ambushes. Every time I see a military lorry my bones shake for fear that somebody would throw a bomb at it and I might get hit by a bullet from one of the rifles, I should hate to die.'[656]

With Michael imprisoned until the general release of prisoners after the signing of the Treaty, the family had to hire a labourer to manage the farm. Shel, as we have seen, was struggling. When Gerry McAleer and Charlie O'Neill went to help the Barrys at Tombeagh with the 'hay help' in the summer of 1921 while Michael was in prison, they were both arrested and interned. McAleer's daughter, Evanna Kennedy, described to me what happened as recounted by her father:

> Daddy had come down with some other UCD students [Charlie O'Neill] to help the Barry family do the 'hay-help' the year after Kevin died, in 1921. There had been bad weather, and Mrs. Barry needed help to save the hay that year. There had been a swoop 'arrest' by RIC men. Anyone associated with the Barrys was suspicious, so Daddy was arrested and spent a day or two in Carlow prison. He was in the Curragh for 6 weeks after that. Daddy had binoculars, and could watch the races at the Curragh from his 'camp'.[657]

Gerry McAleer was not in the IRA, but was arrested on suspicion of being so because he was seen to be associating with the Barry family. He remained friends with the Barrys for the rest of his life. Gerry wrote a

656 By kind permission of the Kevin Barry estate.
657 Interview with Evanna Kennedy, 2019.

sarcastic note to Honoria Aughney, with whom Kevin and he had studied in UCD. She lived in Tullow, County Carlow: 'Thanks for the hospitality we're getting in Co. Carlow. We came down to help Mrs. Barry with the hay and this is what we get.' [658]

Gerry McAleer's career with the RAF took him to Hong Kong, Singapore and the United Kingdom, and it certainly would not have helped if he had had any known IRA associations.

Kitby wrote to Michael Barry from Fleet Street on 21 February 1921, describing how they went to Kildare and had lunch and a walk in the convent. 'By the way, I believe Kildare is to be the Black and Tan head-quarters. They must be properly scared when they have to have military protection. The name Black and Tan has got so mixed lately that I can't know whether it is the RIC or … nice for the castle to have discovered the mysterious H.Q. of the IRA. The next thing they will get is the "Commander in Chief". Then they can rest on their oars for a while. We shall have been wiped out for the nth time …'.[659]

Mrs Barry's letter to Michael sent from Tombeagh on 18 August 1921 contained descriptions of people coming up to help with cutting the oats, the turnips and the hay. 'The colt is lovely, he grew very big and fat. Kathy will give you all the political news. Gerry and Charlie got out; Paddy Foley and others arrested the same day were let home last week. I suppose no others will be let out. Joe Farrell is in Mountjoy and allowed letters. As I came by train last evening, Mamie Doyle was here. She came with Rita [Michael Barry's fiancée] to meet me but maybe E. is able to drive now. The foal is very good; the pony is in great form too. It was a dry season for oats. Matt is in Mountjoy, has a good time [Matt Cullen] … Mother.'[660] Her attention to the pastoral life weaves seamlessly with the political news, which she deferred to Kitby to convey.

Michael was released from Lincoln prison in February 1922, fourteen months after his arrest. He quickly returned to his role as adjutant of the 3rd battalion, Carlow Brigade. The farm at Tombeagh had to be

658 Information from Honoria Aughney to Donal O'Donovan, 1988, DOD, p. 184.
659 By kind permission of the Kevin Barry estate.
660 By kind permission of the Kevin Barry estate.

his priority once he came out of prison. The farm, however, took a long time to recover financially. Michael's son Kevin lives at Tombeagh with his wife Evelyn, and their children live close by or in Dublin. Kevin, interviewed by Maurice O'Keefe in *Irish Life and Lore*,[661] recalled that after the Second World War, Americans came to the house 'talking guns, drinking whiskey up the lane. Hard men that couldn't settle down after the war, trigger happy.' He remembered his father talking and drinking with them.

Elgin

Elgin O'Rahilly (Madame O'Rahilly, née Barry) was just a year younger than Kevin, so it was not until the Civil War that she became a member of Cumann na mBan. She had, however, been involved in Republican activities before that. Her son Michael O'Rahilly describes an incident she recounted to him that involved a bag of arms during the War of Independence that had to be brought from the Barry's home and hidden elsewhere.

> There was a bag of ammunition in No. 8 Fleet Street, the Barry family home, and they needed to get it out of the house for fear of a raid by the Black and Tans. She [Elgin] took off with it on horse and trap towards Rathmines. There were runners advising on the military checkpoints all along. They were heading for the Terenure area but there were checkpoints on all the exits from St Stephens Green. Having gone around the Green twice, Elgin, who had been at school in Loreto Convent on the Green, remembered 'The Lane', a side entrance by the gate at street level. The lane had been roofed and had lockers along the wall and this provided a useful hiding place, which Elgin set about straight away, and stuffed the arms into a locker.[662]

---

661 https://www.irishlifeandlore.com/product/kevin-barry-b-1941/ Interview with Kevin Barry by Maurice O'Keefe, Irish Life and Lore.
662 Dr Michael O'Rahilly interview, February 2019.

In August 1923, a detention order signed by Richard Mulcahy led to Elgin's imprisonment in the North Dublin Union, where Kevin had first been detained after his arrest. Elgin, along with some veterans including Maud Gonne, Mary MacSwiney, Lily O'Brennan, Máire Comerford and Eithne Coyle, went on hunger strike.[663] Again, Kitby's support was uncompromising, and the whole family were very concerned as the conditions in the North Dublin Union were atrocious – overcrowded with very poor facilities. Finally, on 23 November the strike was called off, and the remaining female prisoners in the North Dublin Union, including Elgin, were released in December 1923. Kitby, in a letter dated 26 November 1923, conveys the relief felt by the Barry family. In it she expresses her joy that the two people she loved best, Elgin and her own future husband Jim Moloney (who was also on hunger strike), were not going to die.[664]

Kevin's younger sisters

Not all of the women in Kevin Barry's family were engaged in military activism. Peggy Barry relished her memories of Kevin, of how he used to take her and Monty to Mass, his indulgence of them when they were at Tombeagh, leaving sweets under their pillows to find when they woke up.[665] Monty and Peggy were so young that events between 1920 and 1923 passed them by. Monty wrote regularly to her older brother Michael during 1921, when he was in prison. In early 1921, Monty wrote to him when he was in Beresford Barracks in the Curragh. 'I am sure you are glad to get out of Baltinglass [prison] even though you can't see Ma and Shel every second day, you have company all day. I am going to school pretty regularly now and I've made an act for Lent to go in at nine. I've to do dry-up now so tooraloo!' Signed from 'Moy' – Monty Barry.' [666]

My grandmother married Jim O'Donovan, who had been the Director of Chemical Warfare during the War of Independence. He had a great interest in her brother Kevin, and somehow acquired the civilian file on

663 O'Donovan, p. 199.
664 By kind permission of the Kevin Barry estate.
665 Information from Peggy Barry to Jim O'Donovan, 1958.
666 By kind permission of the Kevin Barry estate.

Kevin Barry ('MS 8043') from Dublin Castle. It informed much of my grandfather's research for his book about Kevin Barry. Kitby refers in her statement to 'some serious writing … about my brother, written by a sympathetic Republican with a long military record'. She was not happy with the manuscript and it was never published. She sent my grandfather notes which picked apart many of the claims he made. In these, she made it very clear that Fr Albert had indeed conveyed to her, after he saw Kevin before his execution, that his message was 'Hold on and Stick to the Republic!' and not what the newspapers had reported. 'I heard the exact words spoken by Fr. Albert',[667] she wrote.

MS 8043 formed the basis of Jim's biography of Kevin Barry, along with his interviews with relatives of Kevin Barry and IRA companions like Matt Cullen in the C Company in Carlow, with whom Kevin Barry attempted to burn down Aghavannagh Barracks on GHQ orders. Matt Cullen lived a long life, but he never made a witness statement to the Bureau of Military History, so those interviews with Cullen are the only direct account we have of Kevin's military activities during his last summer in Carlow in 1920.

As if she wasn't steeped enough in Republicanism, her marriage to Jim put my grandmother even closer to it. My grandfather became heavily involved in the IRA in the 1930s, putting his family at considerable risk. As I have said at the beginning, my father felt neglected by his father, who was married to an ideology, obsessed with a united Ireland and also perhaps with the rising power of Germany in the late 1930s, when he traveled to Hamburg for meetings with the Abwehr, German intelligence. When the Abwehr spy Herman Goertz, came to Ireland, he stayed in my father's family home in Shankill, County Dublin. My father described his arrival: 'After supper, a stranger arrived by car. The first place of safety was my vacant room. Thereafter, Goertz stayed in the garage by night.'[668] Monty brought meals to Goertz, who hid his code in the eaves of the stable. He stayed until he met the new IRA Chief of Staff, Stephen Hayes.

'In September 1941, just as my brother and I were setting off for school, eight Garda cars arrived at Florenceville [the family home]. They

---

667 By kind permission of the Kevin Barry estate.
668 Donal O'Donovan, *Little Old Man Cut Short*, Ashford: Kestrel Books, 1992, p. 34.

were under the command of Superintendent W. P. Quinn, who headed the Bray Police district, and Sergeant Michael Wayne.'[669] That was that, and my grandfather was taken away to be interned in the Curragh for two years. My father was sent to boarding school in Blackrock College, where the dorms were full of rats, while my grandmother resourcefully took in lodgers, and made cheese to survive those barren years. It cannot have been easy for her. She, the maid Mary Conroy, my father and his brother Gerry had been questioned as the guards searched the house.

My grandfather regretted his actions in the very end. When he was in Our Lady's Manor, Dalkey, where we used to visit him, (and saw the stubs of his fingers). He said that it was 'foolish for me, personally'. He had to fight to get his position back at the ESB, after being interned in the Curragh for two years.

Mary Barry (nee Dowling)

Behind all these forthright members of the Barry family so entwined in the cause of a free Ireland, was Mrs Barry. Born Mary Dowling, she had been widowed since 1908 when Tom Barry died, leaving her to rear seven children alone. My father saw her as a woman of 'great dignity' who managed gracefully on her own over her forty-five years as a widow. After 8 Fleet Street was sold she moved into a cold-water flat in Molesworth Street. Elgin Barry's daughter Ruth Sweetman remembers her in Molesworth Street , where 'She lived on the fourth floor where it was dark, at the top of the building. There were three landing windows. I remember her wrapped in a black shawl, like all old women in those days. She came out to mind us when my mother was sick, by bus. I went to meet her at the bus stop. She was a very kind woman, a big bundle of love. I remember her embraces in Molesworth Street.'[670]

One of the most extraordinary documents that I came across while researching this book, was the collection of telegrams written by Mrs Barry to the mothers of the other executed men. I sat at the table in the kitchen at Tombeagh, with my sister Kristin. Kevin Barry junior took out

669 Ibid.
670 Interview with Ruth Sweetman, 2019.

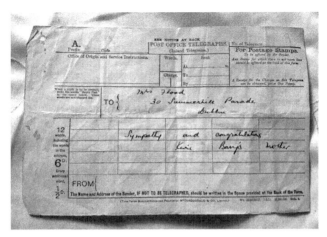

The telegram sent by Mrs Barry to Mrs Flood. By kind permission of the Kevin Barry estate. Photo by Síofra O'Donovan.

a shoe box, and showed us the collection of telegrams, each with the same message: 'Sympathy and Congratulations'.

This message appears in the short telegrams she sent to the mothers of each of the other nine men who were executed after Kevin Barry.[671] It was only when I saw these that I really understood the complicated nature of the loss experienced by each of these mothers. Sympathy for the loss of their sons, and congratulations that they had given their lives for Ireland. This is encapsulated in another note to my grandfather in the margins of his biography of Kevin Barry. Kitby writes that in the wake of Kevin's death, 'we were literally mad (insane) but we were not miserable – it was not acceptance of pain – it was loyalty to the Republic'.[672]

When the Barry sisters gathered around the bed of Mrs Barry as she was dying in a nursing home in Dublin, there was rancour between Peggy and Kitby, the oldest and the youngest of the clan. Kitby had a rosary wrapped around her mother's hand and Peg said, *sotto voce*, 'Of course you know what she [Kitby] will have wrapped around her hand when she is dying.' She was referring to a telephone, implying that Kitby's love of talking on the telephone came above prayer. But for the most part, the

671 By kind permission of the Kevin Barry estate.
672 By kind permission of the Kevin Barry estate

sisters were very close. Elgin was 'not gregarious, not a mixer', but she was very close to my grandmother Monty. The sisters – Shel, Monty, Elgin and Peggy – would all meet on Fridays in Bewleys.[673]

Mrs Barry died on 10 August 1953. The *Irish Press* ran an obituary on 11 August.

> Mrs Mary Barry, 3 Molesworth Street, Dublin, mother of Kevin Barry, who was executed in Mountjoy Prison on November 1, 1920, died yesterday in a Dublin nursing home at 82. During the War of Independence and the Civil War her homes in Dublin and Carlow were constantly used by Republican leaders on the run ... Mr. De Valera and the late General Liam Lynch, a link in the chain of 'safe houses' between Dublin and the South ... the remains will be removed from the Bon Secours Hospital, Glasnevin, at 6 o'clock this evening to St Teresa's Church, Clarendon Street, Dublin ... the funeral takes place tomorrow after 9 o'clock Mass to the family burial ground at Tinneclash.

Mrs Barry's death was 'the greatest event of 1953' for my father. He noted that 'principal among the overflowing congregation was Eamon De Valera, who after Mass took position against the outside wall of the church to greet the mourners. The Taoiseach [Eamon De Valera] was accompanied by his aide de camp, Colonel Sean Brennan. Heads held high and full of contempt for their Prime Minister, the Barry clan marched past the man they would have died for in the Civil War.'[674]

My father was not proud of this. He regarded De Valera's presence at his grandmother's funeral as a courageous act, especially since he knew well that the Barrys had no time for him after 1936. De Valera, as we have seen, was a frequent enough visitor to the Barrys in the War of Independence, and used their house in Tombeagh as a safe house on at least two occasions. An attic room was assigned to those in need of being hidden during troubled times, but De Valera, 'Long Fellow', as he was known, was too tall to

....

673 Dr Michael O'Rahilly, February 2019.
674 Donal O'Donovan, private papers, 1991 talk given to Carlow Historical Society, 1989.

fit into it. Elgin Barry recalled that he stayed in the new room at Tombeagh instead. Pat Gorman told my father[675] that De Valera often stayed in the house, and that his father, James O'Gorman, the hackney car owner in Hacketstown, drove him, as he drove Todd Andrews. He also referred to Michael Barry 'going over the mountains with De Valera, to the Barton house in Glendalough House, Annamoe'.[676] These recollections are confirmed by pencilled notes in Michael Barry's handwriting.[677] These notes also refer to 'convoy through Battalion and Brigade area and Safe conduct of President de Valera, General Aiken, Comdt. Dowling, Austin Stack', the latter of whom had been a Commandant during the 1916 Rising, and a founder member of the Irish Volunteers in 1913.

It was, in any case, a fairly familiar relationship that he had with the Barrys. While De Valera stayed at Tombeagh, a local man Tom Molloy was the watchman on the driveway, jumping in and out of the ditch and 'crawling down the muddy drive if he had anything to report'.[678] However, even then, Michael Barry did not see De Valera as a friend. 'His arrival was signalled ahead; his bodyguards came first; the family was shepherded into the kitchen, and the Presidential visitor, keeping himself to himself, said neither hello nor goodbye to anybody.'[679]

Since he was in fact on the same side as them during the Civil War, the pro-Treaty side, it is difficult to understand why they were all so set against him, until we look at what happened when De Valera came to power with Fianna Fáil in 1932 and 'an olive branch was thrown to IRA men imprisoned under the previous administration, and they were released'.[680] My father knew that his father Jim voted for De Valera in 1932. It was when the military courts were reinstated in 1936 to deal with the IRA, that Jim O'Donovan and the Barrys started turning against De Valera – because they felt that he had betrayed them, and all foreseeable hope of a United Ireland.

675 Pat O'Gorman to Donal O'Donovan, 1988, O'Donovan, p. 186.
676 Ibid.
677 By kind permission of the Kevin Barry estate.
678 Interview with Kevin Barry junior, 2018.
679 O'Donovan, p. 189.
680 O'Donoghue, *The Devil's Deal*, p. 73.

The Assassination of George Plant in Portlaoise Prison

George Plant, a Church of Ireland Tipperary man, turned to the IRA after being harassed by the RIC for speaking to two Republicans in 1916, one of whom was Dan Breen. After being beaten in custody by the RIC, George served with the IRA during the War of Independence and was on the anti-Treaty side in the Civil War. According to Kevin Barry junior, in 1929 Plant and his brother were called back from America, where they had been for a number of years, to Tipperary, to help fill the depleting coffers of the Fianna Fáil Party by means of a bank raid.[681]

They were arrested and given a seven-year sentence, but when De Valera came to power with Fianna Fáil in 1932, an amnesty for IRA prisoners gave them the chance for release. He banned the IRA in 1936. Although he abolished the Oath of Allegiance to the British monarch in 1937, and introduced the presidency of Ireland, along with a claim to Northern Ireland, the IRA still maintained that they were the legitimate army of Ireland.

By 1939, hurtling into the Second World War, Ireland, under De Valera's direction, was in what was termed the 'Emergency'. In a neutral Ireland, De Valera was determined that IRA links with Germany, which were spearheaded by Jim O'Donovan, had to be stopped, as they threatened Irish neutrality and Anglo-Irish relations. Most of the IRA men who were interned in the Curragh at that time were pro-German.[682] Emergency legislation was brought in, and if found guilty in court, 'you got the bullet. Plant knew too much and was shot in Portlaoise prison, and not allowed to even see his wife and daughter the week before the execution.'[683]

There were just two possible verdicts under the new legislation: death or acquittal. Just one week after Plant's sentence was passed in 1941, he

681 https://www.irishlifeandlore.com/product/kevin-barry-b-1941/ Interview with Kevin Barry junior by Maurice O'Keefe, Irish Life and Lore.
682 O'Donoghue, p. 203.
683 https://www.irishlifeandlore.com/product/kevin-barry-b-1941/ Interview with Kevin Barry junior by Maurice O'Keefe, Irish Life and Lore.

was executed by a six-man firing squad from the Irish army for the murder of John Devereux, an IRA man who had turned informer.

'The pro-treaty camp could be very cruel, but Fianna Fáil could be just as cruel,' said Kevin Barry junior.[684] But it was the assassination of Plant that may have been at the heart of the Barrys' unyielding dislike for Eamon De Valera. In fact, De Valera came down to Hacketstown in the early 1970s and stopped in his chauffeured car to ask if Tombeagh was nearby. 'But he didn't call into the Barrys.'[685]

Making Peace

My father carried the burden of healing this bitterness towards De Valera generated by the Barrys and by his own father, Jim. At least, he felt he did. He tried to make his own amends with De Valera. In 1973, he went to meet De Valera when he was president, at Áras an Úachtaráin. De Valera turned to my father as he was leaving and said: 'Would you say something to your father from me? Tell him I hope there is not bitterness in his heart towards me as there certainly is no bitterness in my heart towards him.' When my father conveyed this to his father, he would not speak to him for four days.[686]

My grandfather perhaps harboured more bitterness towards De Valera than the Barrys did. Sadly, he may never have resolved it. In the early 1970s both my grandparents were residents in a nursing home. Monty was tragically rendered immobile by strokes, so incapacitated that I cannot imagine how hard it was for her children, who knew her spark and wit, to see her like that. My grandfather, on the other hand, although in a wheelchair because of MS, was sharp as a pin and full of rage. One historian who visited my grandfather regularly said that he was 'enraged and caged' and said that he felt bitter about his condition, and embittered that the IRA were 'so inefficient'.[687] For my father, visiting Jim was painful. 'It was always a struggle for me because I was jarred or half jarred … bringing him a bottle of

684 Ibid.
685 Ibid.
686 Private papers of Donal O'Donovan.
687 O'Donoghue, *The Devil's Deal*, p. 241, Interview with John Duggan, a retired Lieutenant Colonel from Limerick.

whiskey as a kind of compensation.' It was always a relief to me to discover that my grandfather had not become a Nazi supporter, despite his early admiration. His 'confessions' in later but mobile years with his dentist Joe Briscoe, a Dublin Jew, revealed that Jim 'was one of those … who realised their mistake [in supporting Nazi Germany] … I think everybody knew then that the IRA ideology was 'England's enemy was Ireland's friend'.[688] My grandfather spent many hours with the chaplain of his nursing home towards the end of his life, and I feel he was trying to prepare himself for his next journey, a little less burdened by his past.

On a happier note, when De Valera attended the fiftieth anniversary commemoration in Rathvilly on 1 November 1970, he met members of the Barry family. Dr Michael O'Rahilly recalled De Valera driving up with his aide-de-camp in a Rolls Royce. This time, the Barrys – at least some of them – spoke to him. Elgin O'Rahilly went up to De Valera and welcomed him.[689]

My father felt that 'Kathy and Shel, Michael and Elgin – all the older Barrys – played their part in passing on the torch lit by Kevin. But the mainstream of Irish politics moved on and left them lying in the bitter backwaters of uncompromising Republicanism. Kathy at least, with her style, leadership and experience, could have gone on to add lustre and weight to any Cabinet; panache and persuasion to any embassy.'[690]

What Kitby left behind, a testimony to Kevin's life and to the Barry family, was invaluable. It was as valuable to my father as it is to me. However, at the time he was researching, only family were allowed to access the document, as it had still not been released to public access. Kitby had already given Jim extracts from her statement, but 'she withheld the essential fact – told to her by Kevin Barry during a recess in the court martial – that he had shot a specific soldier with the fourth round fired with his .38 Mauser automatic. This was Private Matthew Whitehead of the 2nd Battalion of the Duke of Wellington's Regiment.'[691] He wrote then, that 'under the guidelines for the Bureau of Military History testimony, I could

688 Ibid., p. 243.
689 Interview with Michael O'Rahilly, 2019.
690 O'Donovan, p. 200.
691 O'Donovan, *Little Old Man Cut Short*, p. 206.

not directly give my source ... My father, even though he presented three spent bullets to the National Library, didn't know, though he must have suspected, that Kevin Barry had used one of them to kill Whitehead. And his son is not allowed to reveal his source in print. It is high time that the Bureau's buried treasure was opened to the public.'[692]

She was an extraordinary woman, as Todd Andrews noted when he met her in the wilds of West Cork, putting on her lipstick. She was extraordinary when she was trying to fix the sandbags in the Hammam Hotel, against De Valera's orders, or fundraising in America with Countess Markiewicz, or so admirably managing her whole family after her father's death. Whether she withheld evidence about Kevin's actions at Monk's Bakery, I will leave to the discretion of the reader.

I feel that she may not have gone on to 'add lustre and weight to any Cabinet', because there is a burden that a family carries when somebody dies young, and who becomes so enormous in their afterlife. We all felt it, and we feel it, even the great-nieces and -nephews of Kevin Barry. My father wrote this poem to him, in 1989:

> Are you the nephew of?
> Who tried to inveigle the elegant tart
> In the train from Rathvilly
> Who murdered a gallon of Smithwick's
> Lying on a bed with a Belgian bird
> In the Glendalough Inn by the lake beyond Laragh.
> Are you the nephew of?
> Robbed a Lewis gun laughing
> From the King's Inns showing
> Dinny Holmes his new toy
> Are you the nephew of?
> Was caught under a soldier's lorry
> Was tortured, tried and fed apples and grapes
> Till he hang-dangled dead from an alien rope.[693]

---

692 Ibid.
693 Private papers of Donal O'Donovan, 1989.

Chapter Fifteen

YOURS 'TIL HELL FREEZES

I
n 1920–21, the author of the Kevin Barry ballad came to the door of 8 Fleet Street. Kitby said that he was 'an Irish worker on the Clydeside, home on holiday. I do not remember his name. He showed us the verses. We were polite.'[694] The Barrys did not allow this famous ballad to be sung in their homes. It was maudlin, my grandmother said. It was sentimental, my father said. It was never sung in our family home. But in my college years, I was known to stand up in Dublin pubs and sing Kevin Barry at the top of my voice, although I hardly knew the lyrics. It was not out of a sense of patriotism, just something that always seemed to be beneath the surface after a drink or two. I have a suspicion that if the Barrys allowed themselves to sing it, it might have unleashed a grief that they could not have stopped. Or my father, for that matter.

A letter to the *Irish Times* on 5 August 1951 by Séamus de Búrca (who is related to the Barrys on the Dowling side) protested that the 'The melody, like the words, belongs to the man who wrote it, who gave both to the Irish Nation without any reward. Let us preserve this song about a gallant soldier inviolate.'[695] The melody may not have been original but the ballad was sung 'by the oppressed everywhere'. Paul Robeson issued a 12" record of the original ballad in 1957. My father related how Robeson came upon the ballad, when Peadar O'Donnell and a friend were travelling across America in a car, and the tyre burst and out stepped Paul Robeson from a limousine to offer his help. One thing led to another, and when he expressed interest in recording an Irish song, O'Donnell

694 Kitby Barry's written comments on James O'Donovan's Manuscript 1, GOD. Also in O'Donovan, p. 190. These notes are still extant, but the manuscript is not.
695 O'Donovan, p. 190.

suggested 'Kevin Barry'. Robeson wrote down the words while Peadar sang the melody. The recording was made on the TOPIC label in the UK as a 78 record first released in the 1950s.[696]

In July 2018, Boy George (George O'Dowd) sang 'Kevin Barry' on air during the episode of the BBC's 'Who do you think you are?' in which his ancestry was revealed. O'Dowd had long thought that he was related to Kevin Barry, because the ballad was sung so often in his home. But on the show it was revealed that Thomas Bryan was his great uncle. In 2018 he made a pilgrimage to the gallows in Mountjoy where Thomas Bryan was executed on 14 March 1921.[697]

There are about twenty-six poems and ballads about Kevin Barry in the appendices of my father's book. This verse, by Terry Ward, the London Editor of the *Irish Press*, was written around 1934.

> I Cannot Forget
> The sight of that straight young neck
> In the clasp of the hempen rope
> That day in November. [698]

Some lines from a loftier poem by Thomas Furlong show a more traditional representation of Kevin as a tortured prisoner who loved his country and died for it. This was published in the *Evening Herald* on 1 November 1920.[699]

> What were his crimes? Come let his torturers tell;
> The first – he loved his native land too well'
> The next – the darkest, blackest, let us see –
> He longed – he hoped – he tried to make her free.

Almost all baby boys baptised in Roman Catholic churches on the Tuesday and Wednesday after the execution were christened Kevin,

696 O'Donovan, p. 191.

697 Information from Sean Reynolds, guard at Mountjoy Jail, 2019.

698 O'Donovan, p. 224. Published in *An Phoblacht* under the pen name 'F.Mac A.', 4 November 1933, and again in *Goodbye, Twilight: Songs of the Struggle in Ireland*, London: Lawrence and Wishart, 1936.

699 Thomas Furlong, *The Evening Herald*, 1 November 1920, O'Donovan, p. 217.

according to the *Irish Independent* of Thursday, 4 November 1920. Some, even up to recent years, were given the name Kevin Barry, before their surname. Luka Bloom, the brother of Christy Moore, was christened Kevin Barry Moore.

Memorials

The old UCD Council Chamber at Earlsfort Terrace has been repurposed as the Kevin Barry Recital Room, and it was here that my father's book, *Kevin Barry and his Time*, was launched by Charles J. Haughey, a hero of my father's until, as he said, Fianna Fáil sent Ireland to ruin. Elgin Barry, the last surviving member of the Barry siblings, was there, a striking and elegant woman. The stained-glass window of Kevin Barry was still there in 1989 but was removed to the medical building on UCD's Belfield Campus in 2010. The O'Rahilly (Mac O'Rahilly as he was known) was chairman of the Kevin Barry Memorial Committee while he was at UCD from 1923 to 1924. He and the Kevin Barry Memorial Fund lobbied and fundraised for fourteen years for the stained-glass window of Kevin Barry that was to be placed in the UCD Council Chamber. It was originally to be a memorial to both Kevin Barry and Frank Flood. £100 was collected in the college in 1921 but they needed another £400. He described the two students as 'murdered in Mountjoy Gaol by the British Army of the Occupation'.[700]

In 1931 The O'Rahilly was elected to the governing body of the UCD and by 1934 a site had been decided on for the memorial window. The window was made by Richard King in the Harry Clarke Studios and was unveiled in 1934 by The O'Rahilly. The final design of the window consisted of eight panels depicting scenes from Irish history from the death of Cú Chulainn, Red Hugh O'Neill, Robert Emmett … right up to the execution of Kevin Barry in Volunteer uniform. Sadly, Frank Flood was eclipsed from the final design for the window. Mac O'Rahilly had very much wanted Flood to be there alongside Kevin.

....

700 Information from a notebook in possession of Dr Michael O'Rahilly.

The unveiling of the memorial to Kevin Barry in Rathvilly, Co. Carlow, 1958.

Kevin Barry, in this glass incarnation, is surrounded by violet-coloured flames, suggesting martyrdom and something more saintly than the political hero that he is. His ghostly face looks ten years younger and more innocent than it did in 1920, but overall the work is, as is any stained glass from the Harry Clarke Studios, minutely detailed and beautifully coloured in a style that combines Gothic and Art Nouveau.

It may be no coincidence that the sculptor of the image of St Kevin of Glendalough in St Catherine's Church on Meath Street in Dublin used Kevin Barry's image to represent the saint. Fr John Costello (the curate who had been in the Hammam Hotel in July 1922), oversaw the redecoration of the church, funded by a large donation from a Mr Wall of Thomas Street.[701] Leo Broe was commissioned to cast the heads of Irish saints and somehow among this (perhaps by some clandestine canonisation process of the Republican Father Costello), a head of Kevin Barry, which was supposed to be St. Kevin of Glendalough, was placed among the saints. The image was taken from that of Kevin Barry, perhaps because the artist could find no recorded image of what the seventh-century St Kevin looked like. It suggests that Kevin had become something of a martyr-saint.

Broe's son Desmond was then commissioned to make the statue of Kevin that was to be erected at Rathvilly in 1958. It became a memorial site where the fiftieth anniversary of Kevin's death was commemorated.[702] In 2020, there are designs and plans under way for a new statue of Kevin Barry, to commemorate the centenary of his death.

De Valera unveiled a plaque to Kevin Barry and the Church Street Ambush in 1938. It isn't known if the Barrys attended this unveiling, or whether, by this time, rancour had already set in. In any case it no longer exists, as most of Church Street has been demolished. There was a plaque to Kevin Barry on the exterior wall of 8 Fleet Street until the 1990s, when the street was refashioned into a parade of pubs, clubs and bars in Temple Bar, now one of the most popular locations in Europe for wild stag parties. Kevin

701 O'Donovan, p. 194.
702 O'Donovan, p. 197.

Barry has disappeared from the history books of the Junior and Leaving Certificate curricula – overshadowed by Michael Collins, no doubt in part due to the feature film by Neil Jordan, but also perhaps because Kevin Barry is wrongly perceived to be the mascot of the current IRA and Sinn Féin.

The Forgotten Ten

In the weeks after Kevin's execution, one of the most significant visits for Kitby and Mrs Barry was that, on a Monday afternoon, of Canon Waters. 'He was full of kindness and sympathy and appreciation of Kevin's brav-ery. Any bad impression of himself that he might have left on [Mrs Barry] was completely wiped out.'[703] In a postscript to the letter he had written to Mrs Barry, he wrote that he did not see the remains but 'the Governor of the prison told me that his face was in no way changed except for a very slight discoloration and that beyond this there was no sign of violence.'[704]

About three weeks after 1 November 1920, Kitby and her mother were invited by the governor of Mountjoy, Colonel Munro, to visit Kevin's grave. The next time Kitby would see the grave was in 1948 when she visited it alone. She was pleased to hear that the British soldiers on guard had in fact planted flowers on Kevin's grave and 'kept it in spotless order'.

The push to have the ten bodies reinterred took decades. In 1989, when my father wrote *Kevin Barry and his Time*, the bodies were still bur-ied in Mountjoy. 'In 1922, 1932 and again in 1948, native Governments suggested that re-interment would be appropriate.'[705] The families had been told that the bodies could not be released for family funerals be-cause it would be in violation of Section 6 of the Capital Punishment Act. Even so, some families, like the Barrys, were invited by the governor on a few occasions to visit the graves, but the tradition of visiting the gravesides was largely impossible. Following the War of Independence, Mountjoy Prison was transferred to the Irish Free State. In the 1920s, some of the families of the dead men requested that their remains be returned to them for proper burial. In 1922 Michael Collins had wanted

---

703 Appendix D2, KBM, WS 731, BMH.
704 Ibid.
705 O'Donovan, p. 194.

The unveiling of the memorial to Kevin Barry in Rathvilly, Co. Carlow, 1958.
Left of monument: Mrs. Thomas Clarke. Right of monument: my grandmother
Monty O'Donovan in white beret behind Kitby Moloney (Barry) in glasses and
black coat. Far right Michael Barry with his son Kevin Barry (junior). Behind
Kitby is Madame O'Rahilly (Elgin Barry) and Mrs. Cronin (Peggy Barry). To the
immediate right of the monument is Mrs J.B. Maher (Shel Barry).

the bodies to be exhumed, but the Civil War put a spanner in the works. The Free State government at that time said the men were too long buried for anything to be done about them. The effort for reburial was joined in the later 1920s by the National Graves Association, through whose efforts the men's graves were identified in 1934, and in 1996 a Celtic cross was erected in Glasnevin Cemetery in their memory.

Kevin Barry, having been the first to be executed since Roger Casement in 1916, was not the 'last straw' in the war against British rule. He was the first of ten, known as the 'Forgotten Ten'. Kevin's friend Frank Flood was hanged on 14 March 1921 with Bernard Ryan. On the same day Thomas Whelan and Patrick Moran were hanged, and Patrick Doyle was hanged with Thomas Bryan. Thomas Traynor was hanged on 25 April 1921 and Edmund Foley and Patrick Maher on 7 June 1921.

Thomas Whelan's mother, Brigid Whelan, had her photograph taken outside Mountjoy as her son was being executed on 14 March 1921. She was wearing a shawl, and had the look of the 'sean bhean bhocht' about her. Just to her right in the crowd, Maude Gonne – mother of Sean McBride – is looking downwards. The photograph appeared in a newspaper after the execution and is now exhibited in the Irish Wars exhibition in the Collins Barracks. Whelan was hanged at 6 am on 14 March 1921, the first of the six to be hanged that day. They were executed in pairs, to save time, giving new meaning to the saying 'killing two birds with one stone'. Outside, a crowd of 40,000 had gathered to pray. His mother held a candle as he was executed and was said to have told a reporter that she had left her son 'happy and cheerful, you would imagine he was going to see a football match'.

By 1994, Tess Kearney, Secretary of the National Graves Association, had obtained consent from nine of the families for the bodies of the ten executed men to be exhumed. Patrick Moran's family did not want him removed due to their concerns that there would be no remains. Some relatives had been reluctant to support the re-interments, perhaps because they felt that, just as Robert Emmet wanted no epitaph until 'my nation takes its place upon the nations of the earth', so the executed should remain where they were until an all-island republic was achieved. Kitby had said that 'Kevin died for the Republic and should stay where he lay until the Republic is established.'[706]

The Archaeology

By 2000, after the Good Friday Agreement of 1998 that certainly helped to move things along, there was agreement from the families of the ten men that the exhumations should go ahead. Tess Kearney, who had worked so hard to see this happen, passed away that year. On 1 November 2000, a ceremony was held for the Ten at Mountjoy, attended by the families, a government committee, the Ancient Order of Hibernians and the National Graves Association representatives. For whatever reasons, this Fianna Fáil government, with Bertie Ahern as Taoiseach, was the one that was going to oversee a state burial for the Forgotten Ten. At

706 Information from Kitby Barry to Jim O'Donovan, GOD, O'Donovan, p. 184.

this smaller ceremony in 2000, the relatives of the men were brought to the hang house. On 28 June 2001, the exhumation order was signed and State Pathologist Dr John Harbison was called in to do the forensic analyses, along with an archaeologist and a team.

Dr Harbison began the procedure with little hope. As the exhumations began in August, he struck a cautious note: the Volunteers had been buried as criminals in quicklime,[707] so there might not be much of them left. Rumours that the graves had not been accurately mapped, and that there was a danger that they might inadvertently dig up the remains of William Mitchell, the only Black and Tan executed for murder during the War of Independence. (He and a comrade who then committed suicide had shot a well-to-do Protestant farmer while burgling his home in Wicklow, the quietest of all the counties, in February 1921.)

An NCO in the British Army had drawn a map of the collective gravesite, on which he marked the position of each body. When the British left in January 1922, they handed over the map to the Free State. Ten complete skeletons were revealed to archaeological excavation. The British sketch, as it turned out, had been extremely accurate. Kevin's was number one, on the left-hand side of the plot. Exhumation yielded a few bone parts and a pen that had probably been in his jacket pocket. Everything recovered was sealed in his coffin together with the surrounding earth.

When the ground had been cleared the grave-cuts were revealed. Present at the whole procedure was Sean Reynolds, a guard at Mountjoy who is now retired. He described how 'once you cut the soil, the grave cuts were revealed. The archaeologist opened a hole the size of a biscuit tin over each grave cut. The soil was removed and the bodies' remains were then revealed.'[708]

Among the remains of the bodies were items that the executed men were buried with – their own possessions – cufflinks, rosary beads and pens. In Kevin Barry's grave, they found that he was wearing a dark-coloured waistcoat. 'It was dark navy blue, and you could still see its shape

---

707 Information from Sean Reynolds, guard at Mountjoy Jail, 2020.
708 Sean Reynolds, Interview with Síofra O'Donovan, 25 January 2020.

and the earth around it was stained from the dye. There was a pen and rosary beads with him.'[709] The bodies were given new coffins in a workshop in Mountjoy that had been converted into a temporary mortuary.

'The most remarkable thing was that their boots were intact. Black leather ankle length boots that were of such quality that they had survived eighty years in the earth.'[710]

The State Funeral

On Monday, 15 October 2001, *The Guardian* reported how, 'on a cold November day in 1920, a handful of warders watched as 18-year-old Kevin Barry was buried ignominiously in the unconsecrated grounds of Mountjoy Prison in Dublin, after being hanged for his part in killing three British soldiers.'

It was reported that over 7,000 spectators 'braved the drizzle to clap and cheer the coffins ... driven with pomp ... around 650 relatives of the dead gathered for a private ceremony at Mountjoy, and helped to carry the coffins, draped in Irish tricolours, to waiting hearses.'[711]

Among the relatives interviewed by *The Guardian* was Kevin Barry junior. He was asked for his response to the media racket about the commemorative reinterment being hijacked by Fianna Fáil and the then Taoiseach Bertie Ahern for political gain in the run-up to the general election. Others, too, felt it was insensitive to pay tribute to the tradition of violent republicanism in the wake of 9/11, especially since the Northern Ireland peace process was at such a delicate stage. Kevin, with typical clarity and pathos, felt that the implications were unjustified and responded to this and to the media at large with: 'People are looking at it as if he was a criminal. That is the last thing in the world he was,' he said. 'You can't view his death in present-day terms.'[712]

At the ceremony in Mountjoy on 14 October 2001, the bodies, now in their new coffins, were laid on trestles over the original graves that

709 Ibid.
710 Ibid.
711 *The Guardian*, 15 October 2001, Rosie Cowan, Ireland correspondent for the Guardian.
712 Ibid.

were now covered by grass. Plastic sheeting covered with pea gravel was placed over the graves when they were taken out. There were readings and a Mass at 12 noon, conducted by the head chaplain. A harpist played with a soloist. Family pall-bearers carried the bodies in their new coffins, draped with tricolours, to the hearses. One of these pall-bearers was my father, and his brother Gerry.

For Kevin Barry junior, as for many relatives of the interred men, the most poignant part of the ceremony was at Mountjoy. He understood for the first time in his life, what these men's' deaths had meant to people when he saw them touch the glass on the hearses. 'droves of people, rubbing their hands along the glass of the hearse and blessing themselves. I never realised until then that Kevin was as well liked as he was, until that day.'[713]

There was a prison officer guard of honour lining the route from Mountjoy to the North Circular Road. Army officers proceeded to the GPO in a guard of honour as the funeral cortège passed to applause. A lament was played on the pipes at the Pro-Cathedral, where the coffins were brought in.

In the *Irish Times* on 15 October Frank McNally reported that 'Sometimes it had a determined, almost rehearsed look about it … although attendance along the route included many well-known republicans, among them the leaders of the 32 County Sovereignty Committee, there were few overtly political displays'.[714] He also reported that when the Sinn Féin leaders arrived at the gates of Glasnevin cemetery, where nine of the bodies were to be buried, 'there was raucous cheering from their supporters'.[715]

In the Pro-Cathedral, Cardinal Cahal Daly told the congregation that force was no longer a means to achieving peace, in the wake of the Good Friday agreement. Taoiseach Bertie Ahern 'stuck to the theme of the just-ness of the War of Independence, and the right of succeeding generations to honour it'. He cited the statement by Erskine Childers that Kevin Barry

....

713 https://www.irishlifeandlore.com/product/kevin-barry-b-1941/ Interview with Kevin Barry junior by Maurice O'Keefe, Irish Life and Lore.
714 Frank McNally, *The Irish Times, 15 October 2001*.
715 Ibid.

was 'doing precisely what any Englishman would be doing under the same circumstances and under the same provocation'. Nine of the ten bodies were buried at the cemetery in a plot beside Roger Casement. The body of Patrick Maher was to be buried with his family in County Limerick.

Kevin Barry junior observed that the funeral 'would bring tears to a stone'. However, at Glasnevin, some people with northern accents jeered the Garda and defence forces with 'you're not a real army', to which Kevin Barry junior responded when he was asked about it in the *Irish Times* on 15 October, that 'It would not bother me. There's nothing you can do to stop that.' In the same report by Joe Humphreys and Eithne Donlon, Ms Pat Traynor-Sheridan, grand-niece of Thomas Traynor, was reported to have said, 'we were nervous of disruptions, of people coming out in bala-clavas. That was going to be a risk no matter how the ceremonies would be done.' She, like Kevin Barry junior, was hurt by the media commen-taries about the Ten. 'We wouldn't be where we are today if it weren't for these men.' A niece of Bernard Ryan, Eileen O'Sullivan, was particularly irked by the comments of *Irish Times* columnist Fintan O'Toole. 'He should go back and learn his history. These guys laid the foundations of the State and we were very much hurt by his comments.' O'Toole had denounced the state funeral as 'A Grotesque Denial of Bloodshed'. [716] He wrote that nobody could deny the Irish tradition of political funerals and martyrs, such as that of MacSwiney and O'Donovan Rossa, but called the planned event 'funerary propaganda', and that this was why Fianna Fáil 'imagined that this would be a good time to claim the grave of Kevin Barry'. He wrote that it was 'an act of denial, deliberately designed to sanitise the ambiguities of people like Kevin Barry whose idealistic cer-tainties makes them reckless of other people's lives'. As a response to the media's anticipatory condemnation of the state funeral, Tom McGurk responded in the *Sunday Business Post* with an article called 'A War Worth Remembering', with the subtitle, 'Those who condemn Kevin Barry and others for their violence ignore the fact that colonisation is in itself an act of violence.'[717]

716 Fintan O'Toole, *The Irish Times*, 2 October 2001.
717 *The Sunday Business Post*, 7 October 2001.

Sinn Féin leader Gerry Adams, who attended the funeral Mass and was at Glasnevin along with Martin McGuinness and Joe Cahill, said the state funerals were 'a fitting tribute'.

Maurice Manning, a lecturer in politics at UCD, was a Fine Gael senator who believed the state funeral would make few waves 'in the current international climate ... because the world is too preoccupied with other matters and Unionists already have plenty of other things to latch on to anyway'.[718] The unearthing of old bones brings with it the wounds that put them in the grave.

Reactions of the Public to the Re-interment

Letters in the *Irish Times* in the week following the state funeral poured in, varying wildly in sentiment. One letter from M. M. Ireland in Blackrock, County Dublin, praised the 'wonderful occasion and the fine music faultlessly performed at the Pro Cathedral ... They did the Volunteers proud.' Another letter from John Ballantine in Ballinteer, voiced a more cynical perspective – that the re-burial of the Volunteers was 'first and foremost timed to coincide with the Fianna Fáil calendar'. And it was 'embarrassing to see the shame of our "Defence Forces" on display. Most soldiers were marching out of time! At one stage, the lead man was nearly hit on the back of the head with a coffin, as the pall bearers sped up!' He went on to dismiss the Defence Forces as 'ill equipped and poorly motivated'. Another letter from Niall Ginty called the whole ceremony a 'cringe-inducing display of military corpulence and general shoddiness'. A letter to the editor in the *Irish Times* on 16 October 2001 from Edward Dwyer in Glasnevin showed a certain bitterness about the lack of remembrance for several hundred other executed who were buried in unmarked graves in prison walls in Ireland. 'In a country which has abolished the death penalty it is barbarous that the remains of any executed persons should lie within our prison walls.'

From D. Gallagher in County Mayo came a forceful letter:

....

718 Interview with Willie Dillon, *The Irish Independent*, 29 September 2001.

Sir, with reference to Kevin Barry and his comrades, some of your readers and writers seem to overlook a number of important points:

1. The British were an occupation force, their soldiers conscripted and paid. They killed Irishmen and Irishwoman in Ireland.

2. The Volunteers were unpaid and fighting on their own land to free it.

3. When they surrendered to the British they should have been treated humanely, as were prisoners taken in the Great War. Execution was a crime, indeed murder.

On Wednesday, 17 October, a letter from the son of Kevin Barry junior, Michael Barry in Hacketstown, County Carlow, thanked – on behalf of the relatives of Kevin Barry – the Army, the Air Corps, the Navy, the Garda and the prison staff at Mountjoy for their professionalism. 'They are a tribute to the nation.'

Controversies in Commemoration

The historian Tim Carey[719] was quoted by Willie Dillon in his article in the *Irish Independent* on Saturday, 29 September 2001 with the headline 'Kevin Barry: patriot or terrorist?' 'It was wrong to view our history through the prism of Northern Ireland. They were part of an Independence movement which laid the foundations of the State. They fought and died for what they believed in. They were convicted of attacking or killing military, not civilians. For people to equate Kevin Barry with the Taliban is absolutely scandalous.' Maurice Manning also felt it was not fair to equate the acts of Kevin Barry and other men as terrorists. He was quoted in the *Irish Independent*: 'One of the great mistakes is to take people and historical events out of their context. When you say terrorism today, you immediately think of the Twin Towers and some of the terrible atrocities of the North.'[720] However, Manning did believe that

719 Tim Carey, *Hanged for Ireland: The Forgotten Ten, Executed 1920–21: A Documentary History*, Dublin: Blackwater Press, 2001.

720 'Kevin Barry: Patriot or Terrorist?' *The Irish Independent*, 29 September 2001.

the timing of the burials and the sheer scale and volume of the event did little to prevent the stirring up of old wounds and much to promote a power-hungry Fianna Fáil, who were facing into an election. 'Fianna Fáil and Sinn Féin are locked in a battle for the nationalist vote. There was huge pressure put on RTÉ for maximum coverage.'[721]

The Twin Towers had, of course, just collapsed and the demonisation of the Muslim world had begun to rise to levels that may have been precedented only by the Crusades of the Middle Ages. In 2001 the media narrative struck out with the 'Taliban' and 'Bin Laden' as the new dirty words. Some criticised the state funeral with its exhumations as appallingly timed, just weeks after this terrorist attack that had rocked the world. It was inevitable that there would be interpretations of the state funeral as divisive. However, in Ireland, things had tentatively begun to improve since the Good Friday Agreement in 1998. For the first time since 'The Troubles' in Northern Ireland, there was a semblance of peace.

Partition had, as it had in India in the wake of their newly found independence, caused war. When Michael Collins had signed what was offered by Lloyd George in 1921, he said himself that he knew that he was 'signing [his] own death warrant'. There are obvious parallels with the Indo-Pakistan war in 1947–48, fought over the princely state of Jammu and Kashmir, the first of four Indo-Pakistan wars fought between the two newly independent nations. British colonialists had a habit of leaving wars in their wake.

Why Kevin?

One of the many people who had petitioned the Viceroy for the reprieve of Kevin Barry was Fr Frank Browne of the Society of Jesus. He wrote in the *Belvederian in 1921*:

> It was to be expected that within the calm harbour of our College walls some ripple would be raised by the great storm that is surging around and over our land, but we little thought that through

---

721 Ibid.

our boyish lives would come so great a wave as that which swept across the land when Kevin Barry died.[722]

Despite the intensity of the lobbying on Kevin's behalf for reprieve, none of the attempts were successful. What the international attention did do was everything the Crown did not want – it raised Kevin up to the status of a martyr. In refusing to relent, the British authorities had made him into one. Kevin had no lofty ideas of blood sacrifice like Pearse, though he certainly had piety at the end of his life, and was well counselled by religious mentors. In his affidavit he appeared to downplay the torture to which he was subjected by the Lancashire Fusiliers in the North Dublin Union. But in the course of the events leading from arrest to execution, he held to principles that would cost him his life. He could never divulge the names and addresses of his companions, he could not allow himself to be granted a reprieve, and similarly he could not deign to have legal counsel in court. All of this was submission to the 'an alien authority', as Kitby put it. Death itself would yield better boons from the afterlife, evoking as it did an unstoppable wave of public sympathy.

A question that remains is, why Kevin? Why Kevin, and not Thomas Bryan, not Frank Flood, not Patrick Moran, not Patrick Maher? Not Bernard Ryan, Patrick Doyle, Thomas Whelan, Edmund Foley or Thomas Traynor? Five of these executed men were in their twenties and Frank Flood was only nineteen. Three were in their thirties. All of them, like Kevin, had mothers and fathers. Some of them had wives and children. Why not, as an outraged letter writer to the *Irish Times* pointed out, all of the hundreds of other Volunteers who lost their lives in the War of Independence? Why not the heroic hunger-strikers – most especially Terence MacSwiney, whose writings in *The Principles of Freedom* inspired Gandhi and Nehru for the next wave of great resistance to British rule, in India? Why does nobody sing about MacSwiney?

Todd Andrews wrote in his memoir *Dublin Made Me* about the intense national and international campaign to save Kevin's life, and that it helped 'more than any single incident since 1916 to stoke the

722 *The Belvederian*, 1921

fires of hatred of the British. Not since they hanged Casement in 1916 had anyone been executed. I doubt whether MacSwiney's death aroused such bitter anti-British feelings.'[723] MacSwiney was not somebody that the 'rank and file IRA' could identify with, as he was Lord Mayor of Cork and, for the younger Volunteers, was somewhat unreachable. 'But it was easy to imagine ourselves in the plight of Kevin Barry.'[724]

Frank was just a year older than Kevin. They had been to the O'Connell Schools together, were part of the same Company, and had taken part in the same ambushes in the King's Inns and at Monk's Bakery. 'But as Kevin Barry passed into the nation's mythology, Frank Flood's name is scarcely remembered.'[725]

It seems inexplicable that Kevin was remembered and Flood was forgotten, that he was so quickly brushed aside in the designs for the memorial stained-glass window, despite Mac O'Rahilly wanting him to be included. In 1921, at Mattasa's Ice-cream and Coffee House, Frank Flood would have his last cup of tea after a large ambush at Clonturk Park. He was 'the gay, exotic and lovable Francis, hardly out of his teens at the time when he threw everything to the winds and joined the A.S.U. … he was every inch a boy and showed a natural boyishness and found outlets for his boyish flights of fancy and good humour.'[726] His execution on 14 March 1921 'came as a staggering blow to us all'.[727]

The Big Fellow

Michael Collins felt acutely the frustration with trying to devise an escape plan for Kevin from Mountjoy. In the 1970 RTÉ documentary *Kevin Barry*, my grandfather made his first and last television appearance, despite being, as the interviewer Cathal O'Shannon said, 'confined to a wheelchair … his recollections of events were clear and lucid'. My grandfather explained why none of the escape plans had worked. He described how Michael Collins

723 P. 180.
724 Ibid.
725 Ibid.
726 Sean Prendergast, WS 755, BMH, p. 477.
727 Ibid.

Photo of Kevin Barry's memorial grave at Mountjoy Prison, prior to exhumation, 2001.

Rathvilly 1958 unveiling of memorial statue.

spent the night before the execution 'practically in tears and frustration, the fact that he could do nothing, and that he realised he could do nothing'.[728] Collins had a 'painful ability to enter into the victim's mind',[729] and the night before Kevin's execution, in his headquarters (not far from Belvedere College on Parnell Square), he was 'in a state of the greatest dejection. He remained brooding the whole night, taking no part in the conversation, the only words being uttered: "Poor Kevin Barry!"'[730]

Collins had vowed that there would be 'no more lonely scaffolds', that the men who were fighting for independence would not languish and die in prison, unsupported by those who were the directors of the national movement.[731] This statement about 'no more lonely scaffolds' had a great impact on my father – so much so that he subtitled his book *Kevin Barry and his Time* with *No More Lonely Scaffolds*. It might have also been due to the fact that Kitby Barry, his aunt, had such a great fondness for Michael Collins that even the brutality of the Civil War did not smother it. When she left her employment with Ernest Aston and went to join Cumann na mBan, she was 'up to her neck' in fund-raising, even fighting at the Hammam Hotel, resisting Cathal Brugha's orders. When she heard that Collins had been shot, she 'wept buckets, so far from loathing his memory, I have often since his death called on his spirit to fulfil the promise he made me that last time I saw him …'.[732] We don't know what that last promise was, but we do know of her last visit to her brother, Kevin Barry. During this last visit to Kevin with Mrs Barry and with Michael Barry, Kitby realised at some point that the Cumann na mBan, who were praying outside, would march away in the morning from Mountjoy, and Kevin would be dead. For a moment or two, she could think of nothing to say. Some of the warders were crying. Kevin was whistling 'Steady Boys and Step Together', swinging his leg to the tune under the table. He

728 O'Donoghue, p. 241, RTÉ documentary, Kevin Barry, Cathal O'Shannon, October 1970.

729 Margery Forester, *Michael Collins, The Lost Leader*, Dublin: Gill & Macmillan, 2004.

730 Batt O'Connor.

731 Forester.

732 Kitby Barry's written comments. Jim O'Donovan's Manuscript 1 of Kevin Barry biography.

gave her a sideways smile. The deputy governor, Mr Meehan, told them that time was up. It was 5 pm on 31 October 1920.

'So we said goodbye and the last thing he said to me as he kissed me was "Give my love to the boys in the Company." We turned at the door for a last look and he was standing at the salute. When the door closed, my mother was battling with her tears.'[733]

It was the last time they would ever see Kevin Barry. One hundred years later, he is still fulfilling his promise to be here 'until hell freezes.

733 KBM, WS 731, BMH.

BIBLIOGRAPHY

A

Ainsworth, John, *Kevin Barry, The Incident at the Monk's Bakery and the Making of an Irish Republican Legend*, Queensland University of Technology. The Historical Association, Oxford, July 2002. Vol. 87, No. 287 pp. 372–87.

Anand, Anita, *The Patient Assassin, A True Tale of Massacre, Revenge and the Raj*, New York: Simon and Schuster, 2019. Andrews, C. S., *Dublin Made Me,* Cork: Mercier Press, 1979.

B

Barry, Tom, *Guerrilla Days in Ireland*, Cork: Mercier Press, 2013.

Bew, Paul, *Churchill and Ireland*, Oxford: Oxford University Press, 2016.

Breen, Dan, *My Fight for Irish Freedom*, Dublin: Anvil Press, 1964.

Brennan, Robert, *Allegiance*, Dublin: Browne & Nolan, 1950.

C

Callwell, Major General Sir C. E., *Field-Marshal Sir Henry Wilson – His Life and Diaries*, Vol. II, London: Cassell and Company, 1927.

Carey, Tim, *Hanged for Ireland: The Forgotten Ten, Executed 1920–21: A Documentary History*, Dublin: Blackwater Press, 2001.

Chisholm, Hugh, 'Forster, William Edward', in Chisholm, Hugh (ed.), *Encyclopædia Britannica*. 20 (11th ed.), Cambridge: Cambridge University Press, 1911.

Clayton, Anthony, 'Deceptive Might: Imperial Defence and Security, 1900–1968', in Judith M. Brown and Wm. Roger Louis (eds.), in *The Oxford History of the British Empire*, Volume 4: The *Twentieth Century*, Oxford: Oxford University Press, 1999.

Collins, Michael, *The Path to Freedom, Articles and Speeches of Michael Collins*, Cork: Mercier Press, 2018.

Coogan, Tim Pat, *The Twelve Apostles*, London: Head of Zeus, 2017.

Conlon, L., *Cumann na mBan and the Women of Ireland 1913–1925*, Kilkenny, 1969.

Connell, K. H., *Irish Peasant Society*, Dublin: The Irish Academic Press, 1996.

Courtney, Shay (Chapters on the Military), *Tom Kehoe and Mick McDonnell in Cnoc an Eanagh, The Hill of the Marsh, Stories of Knockananna from Yesteryear*, Government of Ireland, 2006.

Coxhead, Elizabeth, *Daughters of Erin*, London: New English Library, 1965.

Cronin, Sean, *Kevin Barry*, Cork: National Publications Committee, 1965.

Crowley, John, William Smith, Mike Murphy (eds), *Atlas of the Great Irish Famine*, Cork: Cork University Press, 2012

Crozier, F. P., *The Men I Killed*, London: Michael Joseph, 1937.

Curran, Joseph M., *The Birth of the Irish Free State 1921–23*, Tuscaloosa: University of Alabama Press, 1980.

D

Dangerfield, George, *The Damnable Question*, London: Constable, 1937.

de Vere White, Terence, *Kevin O'Higgins*, London: Methuen, 1948.

Doherty, M. A.,'Kevin Barry and the Anglo-Irish propaganda war', in *Irish Historical Studies*, xxxii (126) (November, 2000), pp. 217–31.

Durnin, David, *The Irish Medical Profession and the First World War*, Basel: Springer Nature Switzerland AG, 2019.

F

Fanning, Ronan, *Eamon De Valera, A Will to Power*, London: Faber & Faber, 2016.

Ferriter, Diarmaid, *Dublin's Fighting Story 1916–21, Told by the Men Who Made It*, Cork, Mercier Press, 2009.

— *A Nation and not a Rabble: The Irish Revolution 1913–23*, London: Profile Books, 2015.

Fielding, Steve, *The Executioner's Bible, The Story of Every British Hangman of the Twentieth Century*, London: John Blake Publishers, 2008

Forester, Margery, *Michael Collins, The Lost Leader*, Dublin: Gill & Macmillan, 2004.

Foster, Roy, *Modern Ireland 1600–1972*, London: Penguin, 1990.

— *Charles Stewart Parnell – The Man and his Family*. London: Harvester, 1979.

G

Gillespie, Elgy (ed.). *The Liberties of Dublin*. Dublin: E.&T. O'Brien, 1973.

Gillis, Liz, *Women of the Irish Revolution 1913–1923*, Cork: Mercier Press, 2016.

H

Hall, Dianne, Victoria University, 'Irish Republican women in Australia: Kathleen Barry and Linda Kearns' tour in 1924–5', in *Irish Historical Studies* 2019, 43 (163).

Hickey, D. J., and Doherty, J. E., *A Dictionary of Irish History 1800–1980*, Dublin: Gill & Macmillan, 1980.

Holmes, Denis, *Dublin's Fighting Story 1913–21, Told by the Men who Made it*, Tralee: *The Kerryman*, 1948.

Hopkinson, Michael, *The Irish War of Independence*, Dublin: Gill & Macmillan, 2004.

J

Jeffrey, Keith, 'Macready Sir (Cecil Frederick Nevil, first baronet (1862–1946)', in *Oxford Dictionary of National Biography* (online ed.), Oxford: Oxford University Press

Johnston, Máirín, *Around the Banks of Pimlico*, Dublin: Attic Press, 1985.

K

Keenan, Desmond, *Ireland, 1850–1920*, Bloomington: Xlibris Corporation, 2005.

Kiberd, Declan, *Inventing Ireland: The Literature of a Modern Nation*, London: Vintage, 1996.

L

Lee, Joseph, *The Modernisation of Irish Society 1848–1918*, Dublin: Gill & Macmillan, 2008.

Leeson, D. M., *The Black and Tans : British Police and Auxiliaries in the Irish War of Independence, 1920–1921*, Oxford: Oxford University Press, 2012.

M

Mac Eoin, Uinseann, *Survivors*, Dublin: Argenta, 1980.

MacCaffrey, James, 'Giraldus Cambrensis', in *The Catholic Encyclopedia*, Vol. 6 , New York: Robert Appleton Company, 1909.

MacManus, Seumas, *Old Folk Tales* (publisher unknown).

Macready, Nevil, *Annals of an Active Life*, London: Hutchinson and Co.,1924.

Matthews, Ann, *Renegades: Irish Republican Women 1900–1922*, Cork: Mercier Press, 2011.

Morley, John, 'New Phases of the Irish Revolution, 1880–1882', from *The Life of Gladstone*, London: Macmillan and Co., 1907.

Moynihan, Maurice, *Speeches and Statements of Eamon De Valera 1917–1973*, Dubin: Gill & Macmillan, 1980.

Murphy, Father Brian P., OSB, *The Origins & Organisation of British Propaganda in Ireland 1920*, Cork: Aubane Historical Society, 2006.

N

Noonan, Gerard, *The IRA in Britain, 1919–1923: 'In the Heart of Enemy Lines'*, Liverpool: Liverpool University Press, 2014.

O

O'Brien, R. Barry, *Life of Charles Stewart Parnell*, London: Smith, Elder & Co., 1898.

Ó Broin, Leon, *In Great Haste*, Dublin: Gill & Macmillan, 1983.

O'Connor, Batt, *With Michael Collins in the Fight for Independence*, London: Peter Davies, 1929.

O'Connor, Frank, *The Big Fellow*, London: Corgi, 1969.

O'Connor, Ulick, *A Terrible Beauty is Born*, London: Panther, 1985

O'Donoghue, David, *The Devil's Deal, The IRA, Nazi Germany and the Double Life of Jim O'Donovan*, Dublin: New Island Books, 2010.

O'Donoghue, Florence, *No Other Law,* Dublin: Anvil Press, 1986.

O'Donovan, Donal, *Kevin Barry and His Time*, Dublin: Glendale Press, 1989.

— *Little Old Man Cut Short*, Ashford: Kestrel Books, 1992.

O'Mahoney, Ross, 'The Sack of Balbriggan and Tit for Tat Terror', in David Fitzpatrick (ed.) *Terror in Ireland*, Dublin: The Lilliput Press, 2012.

O'Malley, Ernie, *The Singing Flame*, Cork: Mercier Press, new edition, 2012.

— *On Another Man's Wound*, Cork: Mercier Press, new edition, 2013.

O'Sullivan, Donal, *The Irish Free State and Its Senate*, London: Faber & Faber, 1940.

O'Toole, Edward, *Whisht for Your Life, That's Treason – Recollections of a Long Life*, Dublin: Ashfield Press, 2003.

P

Pierrepoint, Albert, *Executioner Pierrepoint: An Autobiography*, London: Eric Dobby Publishing, 1974.

R

Ring, Jim, 'Childers, (Robert) Erskine (1870–1922)', in *Oxford Dictionary of National Biography*. Oxford: Oxford University Press, 2004.

Roberts, Andrew, *Churchill: Walking with Destiny*, London: Penguin, 2019.

Ryan, Dr. Mark F., *Fenian Memories*, edited by T. F. O'Sullivan, Dublin: M. H. Gill & Son Ltd, 1945.

T

Tharoor, Shashi, *Inglorious Empire*, Minneapolis: Scribe US, 2018.

Tripp, Charles. *A History of Iraq*. Cambridge: Cambridge University Press, 2007.

Townshend, Charles, *The Republic: The Fight for Irish Independence*, London: Penguin, 2014.

— *The British Campaign in Ireland*, Oxford: Oxford University Press, 1975.

W

Wade, Stephen, *Britain's Most Notorious Hangmen*, Barnsley: Wharncliffe Books, 2009.

Woodham-Smith Cecil, *The Great Hunger: Ireland 1845–1849*, London: Penguin, 1962.

INTERVIEWS

Interview with Kevin Barry junior at Tombeagh, Carlow, June 2018.

Interview with Dorothy Dowling, niece of Kevin Barry, 2020

Interview by Donal O'Donovan with Pat Gorman and Peggy Scully, 1988

Interview by James O'Donovan with Matt Cullen, Carlow, 1953

Interview by Donal O'Donovan with Triona Maher, 1988

Interview with Dr. Michael O'Rahilly, Wicklow, 2019

Interview by Siofra O'Donovan with Ruth Sweetman, Dublin, 2019

Interview by Siofra O'Donovan with Evanna Kennedy, Dublin 2019

Interview by James O'Donovan of Fr. Tom Counihan, 1953

Interview by Donal O'Donovan of Jerry McAleer, 1988

Interview by James O'Donovan with Bob O'Flanagan, 1953

Interview by Siofra O'Donovan with John Maher, 2019

Interview with Michael Moriarty, Carlow, 2019

Interview with Tom Kehoe, Knockananna, Wicklow, 2019

Interview by Donal O'Donovan with Sheila Hannah, 1996

Interview by Siofra O'Donovan with Alice Cullen, Carlow, 2019

Interview with Con Foley, Knockananna, Wicklow, 2019

Interview by James O'Donovan with Peggy Barry, year unknown

Interview by Donal O'Donovan with Mags Leonard, 1988

Interview by Jim O'Donovan with John Joe Carroll, 1953

Information from Honoria Aughney to Donal O'Donovan, 1988

Interview by Siofra O'Donovan with Sean Reynolds, prison guard at Mountjoy, 25 October 2019.

https://www.irishlifeandlore.com/product/kevin-barry-b-1941/ Interview with Kevin Barry by Maurice O'Keefe, *Irish Life and Lore.*

BUREAU OF MILITARY HISTORY

http://www.militaryarchives.ie/collections/online-col-lections/bureau-of-military-history-1913-1921/reels/bmh/BMH.WS0899.pdf

WITNESS STATEMENTS

Kathleen Barry Moloney, WS 731

Patrick Berry, WS 942 BMH

Elizabeth Bloxham, WS 632

Peg Broderick-Nicholson, Section Commander for the Galway branch of Cumann na mBan, WS 1682

Vincent Byrne, WS 423, BMH

Seamus Kavanagh WS 493, BMH

Michael Knightly, WS 835, BMH

Father Lawrence, WS 899

Pádraig Ó Catháin, Adjutant of the Carlow Brigade, WS 1,572 BMH

James L. O'Donovan, WS 1713, BMH

Sean O'Neill, WS 1,154, BMH

Sean Prendergast, WS 755, BMH

James Slattery, BMH WS 445

James Sullivan, WS 518, BMH

Oscar Traynor, WS 340,

PAPERS AND MANUSCRIPTS

Kevin Barry private papers

Diary of Sir Mark Sturgis, Public Record Office, London

War Officer Papers, Public Record Office, London

Dowling and Moriarty private papers

Donal O'Donovan papers, National Library of Ireland

Donal O'Donovan private papers

James O'Donovan papers, National Library of Ireland

MS 8043 NLI R/O 2609, CAB 23 NLI, MS 31658 NLI,MS8042 R/O 2609

The National Archives, (UK) Cabinet Papers.

Field Marshal Sir John French' s diary, 31 October 1920, PRO/59.

Rector's Archives, Belvedere College, Dublin (As in Donal O'Donovan's *Kevin Barry and his Time*, Dublin: Glendale, 1989).

Prison Records, Mountjoy Prison (As in Donal O'Donovan's *Kevin Barry and his Time*, Dublin: Glendale, 1989).

Wilson Papers, 26 July 1920, quoted in Paul Bew, Peter Gibbon and Heaney Patterson, *Northern Ireland 1921–96: Political Forces and Social Classes* (Manchester, 1995; original in Martin Gilbert, *Winston S. Churchill: Companion*, Vol V, Part 2, *Documents in the Wilderness Years, 1929–1935* (London, 1981).

The Belvederian 1917, 1919, 1920, 1921, 1935, 1945, 1970.

An Phoblacht, November 1929.

ONLINE RESOURCES

Teenage Tommies, BBC Two, first broadcast 11 November 2014.

http://news.bbc.co.uk/2/hi/uk_news/northern_ireland/1596618.stm

http://www.turtlebunbury.com/history/history_heroes/hist_hero_kevinbarry.html

Bruen of Oakpark Papers, see also No. 23 MSS 48,331-48,341 NLI, Collections 170 and 23.

Vince Hearne, Interview http://www.from-ireland.net/song/michael-dwyer-1/

http://www.irishcultureandcustoms.com/Poetry/FLedwidge.html

https://www.irishtimes.com/culture/heritage/one-woman-s-civil-war-in-ireland-1.1391600

The Project Gutenberg EBook of Ireland under the Tudors, Volume I (of II), *Ireland under the Tudors*, by Richard Bagwell.

UCD DIGITAL ARCHIVES

Kevin Barry papers

Elgin Barry papers

Kathleen Barry Moloney papers

James O'Donovan papers

http://digital.ucd.ie/view-media/ucdlib:39126/canvas/ucdlib:39627 also in MS
8043 NLI .

ACKNOWLEDGMENTS

First thanks go to my father, Donal O'Donovan, for instilling in me an unending love for my great martyr uncle Kevin Barry, and for writing a book about him, claiming that I gave him the inspiration at eleven years old to do so. I could not have written this book without my father's work behind me, and his father's work behind him. Thanks to my grandfather Jim O'Donovan, who left me with the mystery of the missing manuscript of his book about Kevin Barry. (Maybe Kitby Barry burned it.) Thanks to David O'Donoghue for his support and advice, to Joyce Birmingham for her patient reading of my chapters, and for her encouragement. Thanks to my dearest sister Kristin, who passed away before she could see this book come into the world, to Michael Ryan for his huge support in the turbulent journey this book had me undertake. Thanks to Louise Hogan for helping me research in Carlow and Wicklow, to Líosa McNamara for her exquisite photographs, to Kevin Barry for his patience and generosity in the times I spent in Tombeagh, to Evelyn Barry for her warmth, hospitality and encouragement, to Michael Moriarty for his support and guidance, to Dorothy Dowling for her invaluable information, to Con Foley and to Tom Kehoe in Knockananna for their time and their generosity, to the Cullens for their help, to the Rathvilly Committee for the Commemoration of Kevin Barry, to Liam Kelly and Belvedere College for their help with my research, to Ruth Sweetman for her candid memories of Mrs Barry, to Evanna Kennedy for her generosity and her memories, to Dr Michael O'Rahilly for his kindness, to all the Barrys for their generous moral support, thanks to Patricia O'Beirne for her unending support in the journey of writing this book. And to my son Sherab for listening to my rambles about our ancestors. To John and Laurie Maher for their support and to Sean Reynolds for his patient revelation of all that happened in Mountjoy. Thanks to Declan Kiberd, Maurice Manning and Deaglán de Bréadún for their time and support. Thanks to the Museum of Independence, Kilmurray, County Cork, for their wonderful tours and support in my research into Terence MacSwiney and the Manchester Martyrs. To Michael Patwell for showing me Collins's house in Clonakility and encouraging me to keep going. To Cill Rialaig Arts Centre in Ballinskelligs, County Kerry, and to the Tyrone Guthrie Centre in Annaghmakerrig, County Monaghan, for an inspiring retreat in the depths of the winter. Thanks to Gearóid O Lúing, librarian in the National Library of Ireland. Thanks to the staff of Bray and Greystones Libraries, Brenda Malone in Collins Barracks. To Wicklow County Council Arts Office and Louth County Council Arts Office for their kind support. With huge thanks to Garry O'Sullivan, Alba Esteban, Fiona Biggs and Maria Soto for their care and attention to every detail of this book.

INDEX OF NAMES

W